A PICTORIAL HISTORY OF THE

DODGERS:

FROM BROOKLYN TO LOS ANGELES

DEDICATION

To Al Campanis

- Who helped prepare Jackie Robinson for major league baseball at Montreal in 1946 and has been a Dodger ever since as a player, scout, coach, manager and now executive director of player personnel.

- Who was a classmate at New York University, and a student, scholar and captain.

- Whose marvelous cooperation made this work possible.

A publication of
Leisure Press
597 Fifth Avenue: New York, N.Y. 10017

Copyright © 1984 Leisure Press
All rights reserved. Printed in the U.S.A.

Library of Congress Catalog Card Number 84-7825

ISBN 0-88011-045-7

A PICTORIAL HISTORY OF THE
DODGERS:
FROM BROOKLYN TO LOS ANGELES

Gene Schoor

LEISURE PRESS

NEW YORK

ACKNOWLEDGMENTS

It would be impossible to list all those marvelous friends and colleagues who have loaned me their heads and hearts and their works in this gigantic undertaking. However there are some very special people I must acknowledge.

Paul Zimmerman—Former sports editor of the *Los Angeles Times* for some 35 years (now retired).

Ross Newhan—Feature columnist of the *Los Angeles Times*.

Al Campanis—Vice President of Personnel for the Los Angeles Dodgers.

Danny Goodman—The late director of advertising for the Los Angeles Dodgers.

Bob Farrell—Former feature columnist for the *Brooklyn Eagle* (now extinct).

Tommy Holmes—Author of *Dodger Daze and Knights* (McKay Co., 1953). Covered the Dodgers for 40 years.

Howard Liss—For his help throughout this project.

Mr. Milt Gross—*New York Post*.

Al Buck—*New York Post*.

Irving Rudd—Former publicity director for the Brooklyn Dodgers.

The Public Relations Department, L.A. Dodgers.

Photos: L.A. Dodgers, *Brooklyn Eagle*, *Daily News*, Wide World Photos, Tom Holmes, *Dodger Blue Book*.

A very special note of thanks to my wife, Fran Schoor, for her invaluable good taste in selections after finding her way through 150,000 Dodger photos.

CONTENTS

"The story—in words and pictures—of the
DODGERS, in Brooklyn and Los Angeles, is not only
the story of a marvelous baseball organization. It
is the story of the men, their dreams and their
aspirations that made this America, this greatest
country of ours, the greatest nation in the world.
For where else would a group of men who come
from every type of family background go on to
become legends—the stuff that heroes are made
of."

—Tom Lasorda

"The *DODGERS* are a team with a history that boggles the imagination...Down through the years have tumbled some of the most colorful, outrageous characters to ever put on a pair of spikes. Heroes galore replete with deeds of ninth inning derring do, tragedians to outrival Pagliacci and enough near misses and frustrations to drive a saint to drink."

—Vin Scully

BIG
BLUE
WRECKING
CREW
ALWAYS

PART I

THE DODGERS—
A HISTORY OF GREATNESS

George Taylor (1884)

G	W	L	FINISHED
109	40	64	3

Charlie Hackett (1885 partial)

G	W	L
40	15	25

Joe Doyle (1885 partial)

G	W	L
33	13	20

Charlie Byrne (1885-1887)

Year	G	W	L	FINISHED
1885	39	25	14	5
1886	141	76	61	3
1887	138	60	74	6

Brooklyn Managers
American Association
(1884-1889)

1

IN THE BEGINNING

1883-1913

It was not until 1883 that George Taylor, city editor of the New York Herald, suggested to three of his friends that they might make a dollar or two with a ball club in Brooklyn. The three were Charles H. Byrne and Joseph J. Doyle, New York businessmen, and Ferdinand A. Abell, who maintained a gaudy gambling house at Narragansett Pier, R.I. Liking the idea, they bought a franchise in the Interstate League and built a park on a plot lying between Fourth and Fifth Aves. and extending from Third to Fifth Sts. Since that was roughly where George Washington had led his troops in the Battle of Long Island, they called it Washington Park. One of the small staff they hired was Charles Ebbets, who had been a draftsman, an architect, a state assemblyman, a small-time publisher and a door-to-door salesman of his own books. Now he sold tickets or took them, busied himself about the office and hustled score cards in the grandstand. He loved baseball and there was no task—no job— too difficult for him. He worked around the clock, and the owner loved him.

Byrne managed the team, which not only did a walloping business from the start, but won the pennant, whereupon the partners sold their franchise in the Interstate League and bought one in the American Association, which they held for six years. It was in that time the team was first called the Dodgers, or Trolley Dodgers, a name applied generally to all inhabitants of Brooklyn. In 1889,

Byrne appointed one Bill McGunnigle as manager in his stead.

That was the year the name of the team was changed to Bridegrooms, since six of the players married during the season. McGunnigle won the pennant and, the six honeymoons apparently having ended, the team was called the Dodgers again. In 1890, they moved into the National League and won another flag. Right after that, McGunnigle was fired. Another partner, George Chauncey, a financier, had been taken in, and he persuaded the others to replace McGunnigle with John Montgomery Ward and shift the scene of their operations to the old Brotherhood Park in East New York, which he owned.

Events moved swiftly through the next nine years. Chauncey, first to recognize Ebbets' genius as a baseball man, sold him half of his stocks in the club and, when Byrne and Doyle died, which they did within a year or so of each other, he engineered the election of Ebbets as president. Meanwhile, Ward had flopped as manager, the team staggered under Dave Foutz, Bille Barnie and Mike Griffin. Business fell off in East New York and Ebbets pulled the club out of there.

Washington Park had been sold and the stands razed, so Ebbets leased the ground between First and Third sts. and Third and Fourth aves., built anew and called his creation Washington Park. This was in 1898 and, near the end of the season, when

Bill McGunnigle (1888-1990)
And The Bridegrooms

Year	G	W	L	FINISHED
1888	143	88	52	2
1889	140	93	44	1
1890	129	86	43	1

In 1889 the Brooklyn team of the American Association were known as the Trolley Dodgers. But when six of the players married during the season, the name of the team was changed to the "Bridegrooms" and William McGunnigle became the manager. McGunnigle won the championship that year. Then, when Brooklyn entered the National League in 1890, McGunnigle again won the pennant for the Dodgers.

Monte Ward (1891-1892)

Year	G	W	L	FINISHED
1891	137	61	76	6
1892	158	95	59	3

In 1891 Monte Ward, one of early baseball's most popular figures, was named to manage the Brooklyn Trolley Dodgers. Ward succeeded Bill McGunnigle, who had won pennants in the two years he managed the team. Ward was a fascinating character. He began his career in baseball as a talented pitcher, then switched to shortstop. Meanwhile he became a successful and respected lawyer and an outstanding golfer. He was not, however, exactly a ball of fire as a manager. Attendance dropped and the team slipped far down in league play. In 1893, he resigned to become manager of the Giants.

Dave Foutz (1893-1896)

Year	G	W	L	FINISHED
1893	130	65	63	6
1894	134	70	61	5
1895	133	71	60	5
1896	133	58	73	9

Monte Ward resigned as the manager of the Dodgers in 1893 after the team had dropped to the bottom of the league. His place was taken by Dave Foutz, a pitcher and a very popular figure in Brooklyn. But Foutz was ill during much of his four unsuccessful years as Dodgers' manager. In 1896 after the Dodgers finished in tenth place (there were twelve clubs in the league then), Foutz returned to Baltimore where he died within a few months.

Griffin failed, Ebbets himself took over. But he belonged in the office not in the dugout. In 1899, there was a new manager, Edward Hanlon, who had molded the great Orioles and developed the likes of John McGraw, Hughie Jennings, Willie Keeler and Wilbert Robinson.

Hanlon's presence in Brooklyn was brought about when Harry B. Von Der Horst, who owned the Baltimore club, bought stock in the Dodgers and, to strengthen them, stripped the Orioles of most of their best players and sent them, with their manager, to Washington Park. Such a maneuver would not be countenanced today, of course. McGraw and Robinson were slated for the Brooklyn draft, but insisted on remaining in Baltimore. Even without them, Hanlon had a team he thought good enough to win the pennant that year: Bill Kennedy, Jack Dunn, Doc McJames and Jimmy Hughes were the pitchers, and Duke Farrell and Jim McGuire the catchers. He had three men capable of playing first base—Jennings, Dan McGann and John Anderson. Tom Daly was at second base, Bill Dahlen at shortstop and Jimmy Casey at third. On the picket line were Keeler, Joe Kelly and Fielder Jones. They won, too—and now the team was called the Superbas, after a celebrated vaudeville act of the time, "Hanlon's Superbas."

They won again in 1900, with Iron Man Joe McGinnity added to their pitching staff and Jimmy Sheckard to their outfield string but, in 1901 and again in 1902, their ranks were depleted in raids by the "outlaw" American League. Although they were third in 1901 and second in 1902, the attendance had dropped and Abell and Von Der Horst tired of the venture, so Ebbets borrowed from his friend Medicus to buy their stock. Now, save for 750 shares he gave Medicus in gratitude, he was the sole owner of the club.

The Superbas wound up fifth in 1903, but picked up a hard-hitting first baseman named Tim Jordan, who was to become a great favorite in Brooklyn. The next year, Ebbets bought Doc Scanlon, a first-rate pitcher from Pittsburgh, and picked up Billy Bergen, a catcher, and Harry Lumley, an outfielder. Still the team reeled and spun and when it hit bottom in 1905, Hanlon was dismissed and Patrick J. (Patsy) Donovan, who had managed the Cardinals and the Senators, was engaged as manager.

Meanwhile, although the Superbas couldn't win, there was many a lively afternoon at Washington Park, especially when the Giants were there. The Giants, who had won the pennant in 1904, were winning it again in 1905 and delighted in not only beating the Superbas but humiliating them and, led by McGraw, in taunting Ebbets, conspicuous in his box seat at every game. One day, when Ebbets

Ned Hanlon (1899-1905)

Year	G	W	L	FINISHED
1899	150	101	47	1
1900	142	82	54	1
1901	137	79	57	3
1902	141	75	63	2
1903	139	70	66	5
1904	154	56	97	6
1905	155	48	104	8

Ned Hanlon, a brilliant manager with Baltimore in the 1890's, moved to Brooklyn and was named manager in 1899. During that period there was a popular vaudeville group known as Hanlon's Superbas. Subsequently, some alert newspaperman promptly dubbed the Brooklyn team, the Superbas. The name caught on and all during Hanlon's regime in Brooklyn, the team was known as the "Superbas". Under Hanlon, they won the championship in both 1899 and 1900.

called out in protest as McGraw stormed at an umpire, the Giant manager whirled on him and blasted him with epithets. Ebbets wasn't quite sure he had heard right. Fuming, he said:

"Did you say I was ----?"

"No," McGraw said, loudly enough to be heard by those seated near Ebbets. "I said you were a ----."

Ebbets was almost frantic.

"I'll attend to you!" he shouted at McGraw. "I'll have your case up before the league!"

McGraw, unabashed, laughed at him. Ebbets demanded that Harry Pulliam, president of the league, discipline McGraw for his conduct, but nothing happened—nothing save that a feud began between the Giants and the Superbas that hasn't ever really died out and that Ebbets and McGraw never spoke to each other again except in purple insults.

In 1906, the Superbas became the Dodgers once more and finished fifth. In 1907, they were joined by Nap Rucker, a wild left-hander in the beginning but a great pitcher before he got through, whom Ebbets had bought from the Augusta club in the Sally League and who was to take his place among the all-time heroes in Brooklyn. They were fifth again that year and when they plunged to seventh in 1908, Ebbets released Donovan and appointed Lumley, the best all-around player on the team, to succeed him.

It was in 1908 that Ebbets dreamed of a site for a new ball park—and found it in Flatbush. His friends told him he was crazy. It was on the edge of a disreputable settlement called Pigtown. Bounded by Bedford Ave., Sullivan St., Franklin Ave. and Montgomery St., it was a garbage dump surrounded by squatters' shanties. It was pinned down by deeds and squatters' rights from which it could be freed only by a lot of money that, although he had prospered reasonably by Washington Park, he didn't have. Maybe he was crazy. But he didn't think so. Improved transportation facilities had brought a boom to Flatbush. Crazy or no, he would go ahead with his plans. Four years, during which he sweated, scraped, saved, borrowed and mortgaged every tangible asset he had, passed before, on March 4, 1912, ground was broken for the new park.

"What are you going to call the joint?" Abe Yager, sports editor of the *Brooklyn Eagle,* asked.

"I don't know," Ebbets said. "Washington Park, maybe."

"That wouldn't mean anything out here," Abe said. "Why don't you call it Ebbets Field?"

And so it was called and, little more than a year later, it was a reality. The first game was played there on April 5, 1913, with a capacity crowd of 25,000 looking on, and Rucker beat the hated Giants, 3 to 2.

Now to cut back for a moment. It also was in 1908 that Ebbets hired a man who was to make marked development in the progress, slow as it was, of the Dodgers. He was Larry Sutton. A frustrated ball player himself in his home town of Oswego, N.Y., he was a minor league umpire and Ebbets, meeting him during a National League conclave at the old Waldorf in December, had been deeply impressed by Sutton's observations on ball players he had seen and signed him as a scout.

Through the years, Sutton, roaming the sticks, would come back with players that would win pennants—or almost die trying—and would make the Dodgers one of the most exciting and often the most bewildering club in baseball. The first was Zach Wheat, a raw-boned young man of 21 off a farm near Hamilton, Missouri. Another early find was Casey Stengel, whom Larry turned up in Aurora, Illinois, although Casey was out of Kansas City.

"How did you know about him?" Ebbets asked Sutton. "I had never heard of him—and I don't even know where Aurora is."

"Well," Larry said, "I was like you. I was in Chicago, not knowing where to go from there, and I wandered into a railroad station and saw a sign, 'Chicago and Aurora,' so thought I'd go to Aurora. I figured they might have a ball player there. Seems they did."

Larry, prowling in the high grass leagues, was bringing in the players, and there would be a day when there would be enough. Meanwhile, Ebbets was having a rough time of it in more ways than one. Lumley, a fine ball player, didn't exactly pan out as a manager, although he hardly had a fair test since his material was mostly on the shoddy side. He lasted one year, and Ebbets brought in Bill Dahlen...and the team still staggered.

The cost of buying the land for the new park exceeded the yield of Ebbets' saving, scraping and borrowing. He had to have a lot of money—and he had to get it in a hurry. So he bought the 750 shares of stock he had given to Medicus and then sold 50 percent of the club to the McKeevers, wealthy contractors and enthusiastic baseball fans.

Now it was the season of 1913, with the Dodgers in their new park, drawing good crowds, making it plain than Ebbets wasn't crazy when he decided to move to Flatbush—but still unable to win. In November, Dahlen resigned after a talk with Ebbets and, a few days later, Charlie announced that the new manager was Wilbert Robinson. Robbie, having quit baseball once in 1902, had returned as a coach with Jack Dunn in Baltimore in 1908 and, the following year, had been brought to New York by his old pal McGraw to coach the Giants pitchers. By now the old pals weren't pals any more. Robbie was footloose—and Ebbets grabbed him. An astonishing era in Brooklyn baseball was dawning.

Manager Patsy Donovan (1906-1908) and the 1907 Brooklyn team.

Year	G	W	L	FINISHED
1906	153	66	86	5
1907	153	65	83	5
1908	154	53	101	7

Harry Lumley (1909)

G	W	L	FINISHED
155	55	98	6

Manager Bill Dahlen (1910-1913)

Year	G	W	L	FINISHED
1910	156	64	90	6
1911	154	64	86	7
1912	153	58	95	7
1913	152	65	84	6

Following Hanlon's dismissal in 1905, Patsy Donovan was hired as the Brooklyn manager until 1909, when player Harry Lumley was named for that year. In 1910 Bill Dahlen was named to succeed Lumley and served as manager until he resigned at the end of the 1913 season.

Charlie Ebbets in 1913

George Chauncey, a Brooklyn financier, had backed the Brooklyn Baseball team back in the 1880's and joined a faction that controlled a team called "The Bridegrooms." It was Chauncey who first hired thirty-two year old Charlie Ebbets to help him organize and promote the team. No task was too difficult for the ambitious Ebbets . . . no day too long. He sold tickets, hawked score cards, attended to all the office duties, and made friends for the club. Ebbets soon became indispensable. He got a financial toehold on the team in 1890 when he bought a few shares of the stock. By 1898, Charles Ebbets was elected president of the Brooklyn team. Ebbets kept solidifying his stock interest in the Trolley Dodgers Using borrowed money, he finally bought out the remaining owners. By late 1904, he owned practically all of the stock of the Brooklyn Trolley Dodgers. But Charlie Ebbets had a dream . . . a dream of a modern new ball park to house his Dodgers. And he never wavered in that dream. He began to beat a path to various Brooklyn banks and other financial institutions. Finally, after relinquishing 50% of his stock to the McKeever Brothers, he was able to get the finances to build his dream park. And finally, on April 9, 1913, the most modern, magnificent ball park in baseball opened. Appropriately, it was called "Ebbets Field."

Year	G	W	L	FINISHED
1914	154	75	79	5
1915	154	80	72	3
1916	156	94	60	1
1917	156	70	81	7
1918	126	57	69	5
1919	141	69	71	5
1920	155	93	61	1
1921	152	77	75	5
1922	155	76	78	6
1923	155	76	78	6
1924	154	92	62	2
1925	153	68	85	6
1926	155	71	82	6
1927	154	65	88	6
1928	155	77	76	6
1929	153	70	83	6
1930	154	86	68	4
1931	153	79	73	4

Uncle Wilbert Robinson (1914-1931) (as a Baltimore player)

2

THE UNCLE
WILBERT ROBINSON ERA

1914-1931

The inscription in the Baseball Hall of Fame at Cooperstown, New York reads like this on a certain plaque:

WILBERT ROBINSON
"Uncle Robbie"

Star catcher for the Famous Baltimore Orioles on pennant clubs of 1894, 1895 and 1896. He later won fame as manager of the Brooklyn Dodgers from 1914 through 1931. Set a record of 7 hits in 7 times at bat in single game.

Fifty-one long years have passed since they asked Wilbert Robinson for his resignation as manager of the Dodgers. It has been 46 years since he died. Several new generations of baseball fans have grown up since his stylist stout figure last waddled across the flamboyant Brooklyn scene.

Present day fans know vaguely that he was a ballplayer. They do not know that he was a very good one. He must have been. He was the Captain of the Baltimore Orioles, most famous team in the land prior to the turn of the century. It was back in 1892 that he got six singles and a double in seven times at bat and, after 89 years, that still stands as a major league record for a nine-inning game.

The present day fan knows that he was a manager and here the picture is distorted because it is all tangled up with the whacky state of Brooklyn baseball in the twenties. This was the era of the fabulous Daffy Dodgers, when according to popular legend, no afternoon in the old Ebbets Field orchard was complete unless three Brooklyn baserunners piled up at the same base at least once. The fact of the matter is that Wilbert Robinson was a shrewd operator of a baseball team. In his book, "The Dodgers", Tommy Holmes, the former baseball expert for the old Brooklyn Eagle, points out that Robinson, twice—in 1916 and in 1920—actually sneaked the Dodgers through to pennants with teams that manifestly were inferior.

Later on Robbie faltered. He found himself up to his armpits in a situation no one could solve. The type of mind that might solve our current international conflicts might have had some luck, back in those halycon days, whipsawed between two hostile groups of stockholders each of which controlled a 50% voting block of Dodger stock.

Uncle Robbie, as he was always called, was a colorful, earthy character with a Falstaffian naturalness that endeared him with many. He had a genuine love for life and living.

Robbie was born on June 2, 1864. In another Massachusetts town, a few miles from Hudson, where Robbie was born, a two year old toddler named Cornelius McGillicuddy was still in his mothers' arms. Six year old John L. Sullivan had just started his early schooling.

Little Wilbert was the son of the leading village butcher and was soon doing errands for the store. He worked in the shop and later in the slaughter yard and in-between times he was playing baseball. He started in his backyard and soon became the catcher and captain of the neighborhood team. He learned to catch by lowering the clothes line, standing behind it and having his brother throw balls that tipped the rope as they came into his hands.

At 16 years of age, Wilbert was playing town ball for the Hudson Semi-pro team with his brother Fred. He was broad shouldered and strong as a bull and could easily hold his own with the grown men who played with him. When he was 19, in 1883, which incidentally is the year that Brooklyn had its first professional baseball team, Wilbert hooked up with Haverhill of the old New England League.

For that period, Haverhill must have had a fine team. Its manager was Frank Selee, who later went on to manage The Boston Nationals. The teams' star pitcher was John Tener, who later became governor of Pennsylvania and still later became president of the National League. As a matter of fact, Tener was the National League president when Robbie led the Dodgers to the pennant in 1916 and his telegram of congratulations to Robbie was about the old Haverhill battery making good.

The very next season, Robbie played for the Athletics. He was then a lithe, well-built young man, fast on his feet with a strong arm and a good batting eye. One season with the A's he stole 48 bases, which is outstanding base running in today's game.

Romance caught up with Robbie in Philadelphia and he married a sweet young Irish lass, here on a visit with relatives. She never returned to Ireland after meeting Robbie. She was Robbie's lifelong companion and was known to everyone as "Ma" Robinson. The couple had one son—a brilliant student in Baltimore, who tragically died of a brain hemorrhage in 1918.

In 1890 Robbie was traded to the Orioles and by 1892 manager Ned Hanlon proceeded to develop the swaggering, slugging Gashouse Gang of that era. Each member of the Orioles was a tough, no-nonsense competitor. There was John J. McGraw, Willie Keeler, Hughie Jennings, Joe Kelly, Joe Corbett (brother of Jim Corbett), Dan Brouthers, Steve Brodie and the famed pitcher, Iron Man Joe McGinnity.

"I was the soft soap artist of that crew," said Robbie in later years. "The umpire would call a close one against us at the plate and usually McGraw would come storming in. McGraw would climb up and down the umpire's family tree. John knew all the cuss words and some new ones and used them all very well. He would scream and yell and then I would have to come in and make some excuses to the umpires."

The greatest day of Robbie's career was June 10, 1892. The Orioles played St. Louis in Baltimore and the Oriole hitters were having a field day. They

John McGraw

Wilbert Robinson

pounded out 25 hits and 25 runs. In seven times at bat, Robbie drove out six singles and a slashing double, a major league record that still stands. He also batted in 11 runs for another record that lasted for 32 years.

Robbie was a fine hitter. He was among the leading hitters in 1893 when he slugged for a .338 average and in 1894 he was better with a .348 average. During the next 3 years he hit .264 in 1895 and then way up to .354 in '96 and for the next three years, hit for a .313 average. Good enough to get him a $1 million per year contract in today's market.

Meanwhile a close association developed between John McGraw and Robbie, possibly because they were so opposite in their temperament that they got along well. And they made successful business partners. Their enterprise was the Blue Diamond, a cafe that swiftly became a rendezvous for the leading sportsmen in Baltimore. The Blue Diamond exerted a tremendous influence on both men. The Orioles did not win in 1897 and 1898, and the city of Baltimore, perhaps accustomed to too much of the best, failed to support the club.

H.B. Von der Horst, the owner of the Orioles, did not appreciate the city's failure to support the team, and did something about it. He bought an interest in the Brooklyn team in the winter of 1898 and started to move some of his greatest Oriole stars into Brooklyn.

There were immediate repercussions. McGraw and Robbie would not leave Baltimore, one of the reasons being that they would have to give up the Blue Diamond. Von der Horst stormed and raged but finally had to give in to Robbie and McGraw. And they remained in Baltimore, while such great stars as Willie Keeler, Hughie Jennings, Kelly and Hanlon went on to Brooklyn.

That was in 1899 and it was not a successful nor a happy season for Robbie and McGraw. The Orioles had named McGraw as manager and Robbie his team captain and assistant. It didn't help matters meanwhile, when Hanlon's Brooklyn team won the pennant.

A second Major League operation under Ban Johnson was ready to operate and so the National League in order to fight the new league and to survive, dropped Baltimore and three other teams.

McGraw and Robbie's contracts were sold to St. Louis and they did not like it at all. There was, of course, The Blue Diamond. Finally they went to St. Louis until 1901, when the American League opened for business and again there was a Baltimore team. And once again it was managed by John McGraw and his chief assistant was Uncle Robbie.

Along about this time, Andrew Friedman, President of the New York Giants was having a difficult time with his managers. He couldn't get a winner. In desperation he named McGraw as the manager of the New York Giants and John jumped back to the National League.

Robbie stayed on with the Orioles until 1903, and when the Orioles dropped to the Eastern League, Robbie decided to retire. He was now 40 years old.

Robbie decided to open a meat market and did so in Baltimore for several seasons, until a hurried call from McGraw. Would Robbie take an important trip with the Giants? The team was in a torrid pennant race with the Pirates and there was a need for someone to ease the nervous Giants...and keep the players loose and easy. And Robbie did just that. He arrived in New York and in short order had half of the team in stitches with his jokes and stories. The other half of the team were in bars drinking their favorite booze...getting drunk one night and winning ball games the next day.

Within 24 hours the Giants were like a bunch of happy school boys. They forgot their troubles and won the final game from the Cubs. Robbie's wonderful personality helped win the World Series. The players were so appreciative, they gave Robbie a good chunk of World Series money.

Robbie became a Giant and stayed on with McGraw for a couple of years. He was credited with the development of Rube Marquard, who was purchased from Indianapolis for the then record sum of $11,000. Robbie worked with other pitchers and catchers and had them working together—and smoothly.

Suddenly a coolness developed between McGraw and Robbie. It happened one night after the Giants had dropped a close ball game to the Athletics in the World Series. McGraw said that Robbie had "fouled up and had blown a couple of signals."

Soon the two pals were not talking very much and word of this got to Charlie Ebbets, who had just built a new ball park in Brooklyn in 1913. Ebbets suggested to his partners that Robinson would be a dandy choice as the new manager of the Brooklyn team.

Now in the winter of 1913 with a new ball park and fan interest increasing, Ebbets suggested to his partners that Wilbert Robinson replace Bill Dahlen as manager of the Brooklyn team. His partners, by then the McKeever Brothers, were wealthy bankers and contractors and they agreed to go along with Ebbets' choice.

There were a number of reasons why Ebbets' choice was a shrewd one. One was Robbie's tremendous popularity with the New York sportswriters. Damon Runyon had already nicknamed him "Your Uncle Wilbert" and there were stories and columns all over the sports pages about Robbie and his antics. The Brooklyn club at the time needed all the popularity it could get, having been caught squarely in the middle of the baseball war with the old Federal League.

It was obvious that Robbie didn't have enough of anything when he first took over as manager of the Dodgers in 1914. He did have a few good ball players in Jake Daubert at first base, George Cutshaw at second, but the left side of the infield was like a sieve. A Flatbush hero—Zach Wheat—was in full bloom in left field. He had Casey Stengel, who was a good hitter and full of color—and a couple of good pitchers in Jeff Pfeffer, Nap Rucker and Ed Reulbach.

Robbie also liked his catcher, Otto Miller, from the very first moment he saw him in spring training. Miller was a team player, never complained, always hard at work.

"You can help me a lot, Otto," Robbie said. "You're my kind of catcher, and we can develop some of these pitchers."

Robbie also had Ollie O'Mara at shortstop, Gus Getz at third base and Kid Elberfeld, a real old-timer to fill in at short.

Few of the players had more than a nodding acquaintance with Robbie before he took over the club; they knew of him as a coach of the Giant pitchers. The pitchers soon discovered that Robbie knew most of the answers. As a former catcher, he knew a good deal about how to handle pitchers. He gave them more leeway than most managers, and he could kid the players and dress them down in a way that was not offensive.

One day Casey Stengel had a hard time catching a fly ball in right field for the final out in a close game. Robbie stamped into the clubhouse and growled at Stengel.

"What's the matter with you?" Casey asked.

"What's the matter? What the hell were you staggering around under that fly ball for?"

"Well, I got it, didn't I?"

"Yes, you got it. But Jesus Christ, you give me heart disease every time you go after a ball."

They glared at each other. Stengel turned toward his locker to hang up his pants, and Robbie looking at his retreating figure said:

"Oh, well, with an ass and legs like that, you shouldn't be a ball player. You should be a -----"

Stengel spun around, he was angry.

"What the hell should I be?" he demanded.

"I was just trying to think," Robbie said. "But I give up. You're too old."

He shook his head sadly, and walked into his cubby hole of an office. Everybody roared with laughter, including Stengel.

Brooklyn finished in fourth place in 1914, but the following season, Robbie lifted them to their highest position in years, third place.

Ebbets was so pleased with Robbie's work that he called him into his office, tore up his contract and gave him a new three year deal with an increase in salary.

And then—in 1916 it happened. The Robins, (named now after Robbie) won the National League pennant while nobody was looking—literally and figuratively. Everybody that year was watching the amazing antics of John McGraw's Giants.

The Giants had finished absolutely last in 1915. In 1916 McGraw made several trades and hurriedly whipped together a team that won 17 straight games. Then the team sagged. McGraw made additional trades and suddenly his born-again club started off on a winning streak that amazed all of baseball. They ran off 26 in a row that to this day is a record.

And all it got them was fourth place.

There was an air of confidence at Daytona Beach, Florida in 1916, where the Robins trained in the spring. It was a feeling they had not known or felt previously.

"Give me three fellows who can pitch and four who can hit and I'll win the pennant this year," Robbie said.

He had the hitters. Now he had the pitchers, or thought he had. With the exception of Pfeffer, most of them were shop-worn, but they all knew how to pitch and they were big: Pfeffer, Jack Combs, Larry Cheney, Rube Marquarrd, Nap Rucker.

Robbie didn't say anything to his players, but he just had a good feeling about his year. And so he was in high spirits all the time he was there; so were the players and they worked some of those spirits off pulling practical jokes on each other. They pulled one on Robbie.

One spring day in Daytona, Ruth Law, a pioneer aviatrix, gave flying demonstrations while the Dodgers were training. Somehow, Robbie got involved in an argument as to whether a baseball dropped from an airplane could be caught.

"I bet I could catch a baseball if somebody threw one out of the plane," Robbie said.

The players didn't believe him.

"Oh, not from 4,000 feet, but I bet that I can from about 400 feet."

And so one afternoon Miss Law agreed to take a player with her and he would drop a ball. There was a big crowd at the beach the next day—to watch the big catch and the plane flight—for in those days even a short flight over the beach was a hazardous undertaking to most of the people.

Frank Kelly, the Dodger's trainer, volunteered to drop the ball. When Kelly climbed into the plane, he carried...not a baseball...but a large juicy grapefruit. The plane took off, circled around, and then swooped down to about 400 feet as Robbie set himself for the catch. He saw a speck drop from the plane and come hurtling down, twisting, curving. In its last, plummet-like dive he was directly under it. Then, as he tried to catch it, it whistled through his hands, struck him on the chest and burst, knocking him down and drenching his face and upper part of his body with its juice.

"I'm killed, I'm blind," Robbie screamed sitting on the sand, his eyes closed, his hands tightly clenched. "It's broke open my chest! Help! I'm bleeding. Somebody please help me!"

All the while Robbie was rolling around, his players and the big crowd were roaring with laughter.

Robbie, of course, knew he had been set up. He never knew who framed him, but he looked sideways at Casey Stengel all season long and then at the end of the season, traded him to Pittsburgh for Burleigh Grimes. And under Robbie, Grimes became a top-notch spitball pitcher.

In 1916 the Dodgers played consistent ball all year with an odd collection of cast-offs. Pfeffer was the pitching ace with Marquard, Combs, Smith and Cheney winning big games. Robbie got Fred Merkle from the Giants and put him on first base.

The Robins couldn't shake the Phillies or the Braves through the long month of September, and then the Giants with their 26 in a row made it a 4-team race. With the crowds at Ebbets Field larger and larger, and noisier, the Robins moved in front as the Braves knocked the Giants out of the race and the Phils and Braves knocked each other out.

The World Series was, however, another story. Boston's Red Sox won it, four games out of five. It was a series distinguished chiefly by the second game in which a young Boston left hander Babe Ruth outpitched the Robins' Sherry Smith in one of the great pitching duels of all time, as the Red Sox pulled the game out by a 2-1 score in fourteen innings. Ruth pitched thirteen scoreless innings and allowed six hits, while Smith gave up but seven.

The 1916 Robins weren't built to last and for the next three years they finished seventh once and fifth twice. But the 1916 championship and the attendant publicity had served to focus attention on the Dodgers and from then on they were the most colorful team in baseball.

Meanwhile, World War I came and went and Robbie won his second pennant in 1920. This was just as surprising as the events of 1916 and again Robbie won with a patchwork club of cast-offs. Ed Konetchy, a veteran of a dozen seasons was at first base. Pete Kilduff, a Giant and Cub discard, was the second baseman. Jimmy Johnston had been shifted to third, while Olson was the shortstop. Zach Wheat, Hi Meyers and Tommy Griffith were the Dodger outfielders, while Grimes, Al Mamaux, Clarence Mitchell, Leon Cadore, Pfeffer, Marquard and Sherry Smith were the pitchers.

Once the season got underway, the Robins with Grimes, Pfeffer and Cadore pitching well got off to a great start. The Giants were crippled with the loss of Frank Frisch, while the Cubs and Pirates beat each other. On May 1, in Boston, the Robins and Braves played one of the most remarkable games ever—a 26 inning, 1-1 tie. Two pitchers, Leon Cadore for the Robins and Joe Oeschger for the

1916 DODGERS

Top Row - (from left to right) Casey Stengel, George Cutshaw, Duster Mails, Rube Marquard, Sherry Smith, Artie Dede, Wheezer Dell. Middle Row - Ed Appleton, Chief Meyers, Jeff Pfeffer, Larry Cheney, Nap Rucker, Ivy Olson, Gus Getz, Zack Wheat. Sitting - Jack Coombs, Ollie O'Mara, manager Wilbert Robinson, Jake Daubert, Jimmy Johnston, Hack Miller, Mike Mowrey.

Braves, started and finished the game. At the end of the 26th inning, with darkness closing in around the park, Umpire Barry McCormick called the game. It was played off on June 25 and the Braves won, 2-1.

By September 1, the Robins had beaten off challenges by the Giants, Reds and Pirates and were never headed after that. On September 27, the Robins clinched the championship.

The Dodgers again had little luck against Tris Speaker and the Cleveland Indians. Grimes and Smith beat the Indians in two out of three games at Ebbets Field; then the teams moved to Cleveland, where the Dodgers lost four straight and the Series.

The fifth game was the crusher. Cleveland won it 8-1. Clarence Mitchell, the Dodgers pitcher, was at bat in the fifth inning and smashed a drive on a line to the right of second base. Bill Wambsganss, the Indians' second baseman, speared the ball with one hand, then stepped on second base to double up Kilduff, who had headed for third base; then Wamby completed the unbelievable triple play by tagging Otto Miller, who had got underway as the ball was hit.

It was the only triple play in World Series history—and the only un-assisted triple play.

Adding insult to that injury, Elmer Smith, the Indians' right fielder, hit a grand slam home run, the first in World Series history, as the Indians romped to win the Series.

It was at this time, too, that a great new interest appeared in Robbie's life. Dover Hall, a huge tract of land a few miles outside of Brunswick, Georgia, had been a rice plantation and the woods were full of deer, possum, coon and birds. There were marshes that teemed with water fowl and a stream for fishing. Other baseball men were in on the deal, but the two chief owners were Robbie and Tillinghast L'hommedieu Huston. Cap Huston had become a very wealthy man and, at this time, was half owner of the Yankees with Col. Jake Ruppert. Cap wanted to take Robbie out of Brooklyn and make him the manager of the Yankees, but Ruppert was sold on Miller Huggins. Meanwhile the Dover Hall club had become a sort of national sports institution. And baseball men flocked in for the activities during the off-season.

As it happened, this was Robbie and his Robins at their peak years. For the 1920 club, like the 1916 team, was not built to last, and in 1921 the Dodgers finished fifth; in 1922 they were sixth, and sixth again in 1923. They were lean years, yet Ebbets and Robbie would somehow manage to come up with a couple of players who glittered with color.

A great character walked into Robbie's training camp at Jacksonville in the spring of 1922. He would be a great pitcher in the near future, but he was already a great character in his own way a great man. His name was Dazzy Vance.

"I will bet a hundred bucks," he once said, "that if I dropped in on every minor league club in the country, I would know at least three men on every one of them."

Ebbets didn't want any part of Vance, a towering, broad-shouldered funster, who had failed with the Yankees and Pirates even though he could throw a baseball through a brick wall. But Charlie did want Hank DeBerry, a catcher who had been Vance's battery mate at New Orleans. New Orleans made up a package deal with Vance and DeBerry and $5,000. So Dazzy came to the dodgers and in a couple of years developed into the National League's best pitcher.

Vance won 18 games that year with a listless ball club and repeated with 18 more wins in 1923, and in 1924 Dazzy was the best pitcher in the National League as he won 28 games and lost but 6. And all around the league they were talking about his fireball. They were also talking of him as a very quaint guy, which he was. In his many years of roaming the baseball trail, he had fashioned his own ideas as to how a man should live, and he was going to stick to them.

Robbie was smart enough to let Dazzy go his own way—and satisfied to let him pitch his own way, too. He pitched the way he lived, easily and untroubled, taking his time as he went along and taking his fun with him, too.

Except for the change of a name or a date or a place here and there, the seasons of 1923 and '24 were like that of 1922. The club finished in sixth place. That was about all there was to those years, all but the first signs of Dodger Daffiness. About noon one day, all the players were loaded into buses and driven to Lakeland for an exhibition game with the Indians. On their arrival, they found Tris Speaker and his players sitting on the porch of their hotel enjoying a siesta. The Indians, coming slowly out of their coma, looked at the Dodgers in surprise.

"What are you guys doing over here?" Speaker asked.

"Why, we came over to play you fellows this afternoon," Robbie said.

Tris shook his head.

"Nope, you're wrong, Robbie. The game's tomorrow."

There was a vague disturbance in the Dodger ranks at the start of the 1924 season. The veteran Zach Wheat, a fixture since 1909, had clubbed the ball for a .375 average in 1923 and seemed to be getting better as the years rolled on. Jack Fournier had joined the team in 1923 and slammed out twenty-seven home runs to lead the league. Dazzy Vance and Grimes were having great years, but the team didn't seem to be going anywhere, that is until Robbie pulled off several trades. He got Milt Stock from the Cardinals to strengthen the infield, and the veteran spitball pitcher Bill Doak. Eddie Brown, an outfielder, was brought up from Indianapolis. Then the Dodgers started to move. They won 15 straight to take over first place by Labor Day. Dazzy had a 15-game streak. They caught the Giants, then slumped as the Giants caught on.

Overnight it seemed the Dodgers started to slide away, enough that the Giants drew away to win. The Dodgers, as Wheat, Fournier and Brown slammed out home runs, came in second, a game-and-a-half behind the Giants. Vance won twenty-eight games and lost six and Grimes won twenty-two, lost thirteen. Wheat hit .375, Fournier hit .340 and Brown hit .308.

Shortly after his return from Clearwater in the spring of 1925, Charlie Ebbets became ill and his doctor ordered him to bed in his suite at the Waldorf Hotel. He died early in the morning of April 18. His heart simply stopped beating.

The Dodgers were playing their bitter rivals, the Giants, at Ebbets Field that day, opening a three game series. The McKeevers and Robbie decided to go on with the games.

"Charlie wouldn't want anybody to miss a Dodger-Giant series just because he died," Robbie said.

The next day, the day of Charlie's funeral, it ws cold, gray and blustery and as the mourners stood beside the open grave, Ed McKeever complained of the cold. The next day he was in bed with pneumonia. Within a few days he was dead.

Steve McKeever was, as sole remaining original owner, the logical choice to become president of the club. But the Ebbets' heirs, including Charlie's son, who controlled 50% of the stock, voted for Robbie. And so Robbie became President of the Dodgers.

Robbie appointed Zach Wheat acting manager, but after twenty-one tangled games, Robbie returned as manager. It was a dismal season as the Dodgers finished in their favorite spot, sixth place, tied with the Phillies.

There were few bright spots that season. Dazzy Vance was outstanding. Zach Wheat hit .359; Babe Herman arrived and promptly hit .317 and slugged 11 home runs.

As president of the Dodgers, Robbie never did have a grasp on the front office operations of a ball club. There was an amusing story at the 1925 draft meeting. Then as now, there were severe penalties for "covering up" players in the minor leagues. The St. Louis Cardinals drafted Paul Richards, a Brooklyn protegee who was thought to be safely hidden in the Eastern Shore League.

"They can't do that," Robbie thundered.

"Why not?" asked Commissioner Landis, presiding over the meeting.

"Because I've got him covered up," protested Robbie.

When the roar of laughter subsided, Commissioner Landis remarked, "That's what you thought, Robbie."

As Robbie's influence in the front office waned, so did his influence among his players. Discipline was practically non-existent among those wild men of the 1930's. And there were some very good ball players to come up from time to time—Jumbo Jim Elliot and Watson Clark, pitchers; Charley Gelbert, a fine third baseman; Johnny Frederick, a hard-hitting outfielder. But the Dodgers had finished sixth four years in a row and finally in 1930 Robbie was relieved of his presidency.

That was a strange National League campaign that year. Robbie had players like Babe Herman, Del Bissonette, Glenn Wright, Johnny Frederick, Gilbert. A fine catcher in Al Lopez. There were such pitchers as Dazzy Vance, Adolpho Luque, Ray Phelps and before anyone knew what had happened, the Dodgers were in first place by the middle of September and it looked like Robbie had pulled another rabbit out of his hat.

Then the Cardinals came to Brooklyn prepared for a do-or-die battle with the Dodgers in a 3-game series that would, to all intents and purposes, be the deciding series. The Cardinals' Bill Hallahan beat Dazzy Vance 1-0 in a ten-inning battle that had all of Brooklyn screaming with anguish; then the Cardinals swept the series with Andy High, whom Robbie had traded away, wrecking the Dodgers with his hot bat. The Cardinals won the pennant and the Dodgers slipped into a fourth place finish.

Max Carey was appointed to replace Robbie during the 1931 season and Robbie went on to Atlanta to become President of that Southern Association club.

In the summer of 1934 Robbie was attending a baseball meeting in Atlanta and suffered a stroke. In falling he fractured an arm, severely. The shock was too great and he passed away in a few days with his beloved "Ma" at his bedside.

And so passed away one of baseball's great figures.

Dazzy Vance in 1925, when he won 22 and lost 9 for the Dodgers.

Uncle Wilbert Robinson and Babe Herman

George Napolean "Nap" Rucker was an outstanding Dodger pitcher for 10 years. From 1907-1916 Rucker won 135 games. His finest year was 1911 when he won 22 and lost 18.

Otto Miller caught some of the most famous Dodger pitchers, from 1910-1922.

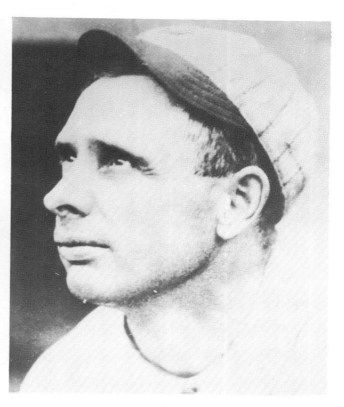

"Gentleman" Jake Daubert, so named because of his sporty attire, was Brooklyn's first batting champion. Jake hit for a .350 average in 1913, and over .300 in seven out of eight seasons. He was a solid line-drive type of batter and in his 15 seasons with the Dodgers hit for a .303 lifetime average.

George Cutshaw was an outstanding second baseman for the Dodgers from 1912 to 1917. His best year was in 1912 when he batted 280.

Zach Wheat, Hy Meyers, and Casey Stengel. This outstanding trio of stars led the Dodgers of 1916 to the National League pennant.

It was August, 1915 and the Dodgers were battling the Giants and Braves for the pennant. Wilbert Robinson, the Dodgers' manager, needed some pitching help desperately and corralled the 10 year New York Giant star Rube Marquard from the Giants. But Marquard could only deliver 3 victories for the Dodgers as they fell to third place behind the Braves. However, 1916 was another year, and Rube responded by winning 14 games, while losing 6. It was enough to win the pennant for the Dodgers . . .

John Tortes "Chief" Meyers had been Rube Marquard's battery-mate, when Rube was a Giant star. The Dodgers had acquired Marquard in 1915 and when the Chief joined the Dodgers, Robbie felt that the club could go all the way in the pennant race. Chief Meyers caught 110 games and contributed both on offense, with some timely hits, and with his catching which was superb . . . as the Dodgers scrambled, fought, and clawed their way to the pennant.

Jimmy Johnston (left) was a Dodger star from 1916 to 1926. He was a versatile ball player and played both infield and the outfield. A lifetime .294 hitter, Jimmy had 3 fine years when he hit .300 or better.

Pitcher Larry Cheney's best year was in 1916 when he won 18 and lost 12 as the Dodgers went on to win the pennant.

The 1916 pennant-winning Brooklyn Dodgers get together at Yankee Stadium for a reunion, October 5, 1949, as guests of Dodger President Branch Rickey.

Fred Merkle, a tall, rangy defensive first-baseman with the Giants for ten seasons, hit .299 in 1915. Manager Robinson of the Dodgers thought Fred could be the man to plug up the Dodgers' infield so he dealt for Merkle during the 1916 season. Merkle , however, slumped badly, played in only 23 games for the Brooks and was traded to the Cubs in 1917.

One of the hardest hitters of the deadball era, Zach Wheat batted over .300 13 times during his 19-year (1909-27) career and his lifetime .317 average is the highest ever compiled by a Dodger player. Zach was the National Leagues batting champion in 1918 with a .335 average but he twice batted as high as .375 in a season. Zach also led the NL in slugging percentage in 1916 with a .461 mark. He was elected to the Hall of Fame in 1959.

Hy Meyers was a Dodger stalwart from 1909-1922. He was a fine hitter with a lifetime average of .281. He hit .300 or better in 4 seasons and led the League in triples in 1919 and 1920.

In 1930 the Dodgers behind the great offensive thrust of Babe Herman, Johnny Frederick, Del Bissonett, Jake Flowers and Al Lopez finished the season in 4th place. The Dodgers were in first place through most of the summer, but fell back. It was their best finish in years and they attracted a record attendance of 1,100,000 fans to Ebbets Field. Herman had the greatest year in Dodger history, slugging the ball for a .393 average and belting 35 home runs. Johnny Fredericks hit .334 with 17 home runs. Al Lopez hit .309, Jake Flowers hit .320 and Del Bissonett hit .336 with 16 homers. Here are those five dynamite Dodgers of 1930 (left to right).

Clarence Arthur "Dazzy" Vance was turned down by the New York Yankees in 1915 and again in 1916. Yankee scouts who watched Vance pitch said "He wasn't a big-leaguer." So the Brooklyn Robbins signed Vance in 1922 and all he did that first year was to win eighteen games for the sixth place Brooks. In 1924 Dazzy won 28 games and lost but 6 and was voted Most Valuable Player in the National League. He was to go on to a memorable big league career that lasted 16 years. Here is Dazzy at the height of his career in 1926.

In a game with the Chicago Cubs, June 13, 1928, the Dodgers' great Dazzy Vance struck out a record number of Cubs—15 in all. Here is the Dazzler striking out slugger Hack Wilson for the third straight time.

Floyd Caves "Babe" Herman, better known to Dodger fans as Babe, was one of the most colorful Dodgers to ever suit up. In the spring of 1926 Babe reported to the Dodgers training camp in Clearwater, Florida as a first baseman. He was so awkward at first that Robbie placed him in right field, where he became one of the Dodgers all-time heroes. From 1928 through 1930 Babe's batting averages were: .340, .381, .393. John J. McGraw called Herman the hardest hitter he ever saw in the major leagues. But Herman's reputation had another twist. A story has it that the Babe hit into a triple play in one game; in several other games he was skulled by high fly balls. In another tight game with a runner on first, Babe drove a screaming liner to right center and, rounding first base, he headed for second. Running head down, Babe failed to note that the man who had been on first base, thinking the ball would be caught, whirled sharply as Herman neared second base, and charged back, with the result that he wound up on first base and the Babe on second. Thus, not only had a runner passed another on the base line, but two runners had passed each other, going in opposite directions.

The Dodgers' Babe Herman and the Yankees' Babe Ruth were baseball's mightiest sluggers in 1930. That year Ruth hit for a .359 average and slugged 49 home runs. Brooklyn's Babe hit 35 homers and an average of .393. In 1938 Ruth had been out of baseball for three years when Larry MacPhail, President of the Dodgers, gave him a job as a coach for the Dodgers. At year's end Ruth had had enough and quit.

Manager Casey Stengel talks to catcher Zack Taylor during spring training in 1935 The Dodgers, under Stengel's guidance, would finish 5th in 1935. Taylor, who played for several teams—including the Dodgers from 1920-1926 and the New York Yankees in 1934—was to retire following the 1935 season. His decision to retire was made easier, no doubt, by his .130 batting average for the Dodgers in 1935.

Max Carey (1932-1933)				
Year	G	W	L	FINISHED
1932	154	81	73	3
1933	157	85	88	6

Casey Stengel (1934-1936)				
Year	G	W	L	FINISHED
1934	153	71	81	6
1935	154	70	83	5
1936	156	67	87	7

Burleigh Grimes (1937-1938)				
Year	G	W	L	FINISHED
1937	155	62	91	6
1938	151	69	80	7

3
WE SHOULD HAVE DONE BETTER

1932-1938

The seven year period from 1932 to 1938 was frustrating for both the players and the management of the Brooklyn Dodgers. The pieces of the pennant puzzle appeared to be in place, but they just never seemed to fit together. Occasional spots of greatness and individual performances stood out, but as a team the Dodgers never reached their potential. After their third-place finish in 1932 the Dodgers slipped into mediocrity, and for the next six years failed to finish above fifth place in the National League. The Dodgers went through three managers and a long list of players, trying to find both the correct mix of talent and the man who could get the most out of that talent. With players like Lefty O'Doul, Hack Wilson, Waite Hoyt, and Van Lingle Mungo and managers like Max Carey, Casey Stengel, and Burleigh Grimes, these Depression Era Dodger teams *should have been better*.

The 1932 season began with new faces on the Dodgers. The "boys from Flatbush" had several new players and a new manager. Max Carey took over the reins from Uncle Wilbert Robinson on October 31, 1931. Carey was a native of Terre Haute, Indiana, and had spent 18 years in the major leagues as a player before moving into the spot as manager of the Dodgers. He had spent 1911 to 1926 with the Pittsburgh Pirates and

played his final two years with Brooklyn, hitting .247 while playing center field. Manager Carey and captain Glenn Wright opened the Dodgers' training camp on February 22 in Clearwater, Florida. Their basic philosophy was that the players were able to play baseball and it was the manager's job to get them into the best physical shape possible. Physical conditioning would allow players to best utilize their individual talents. Del Bissonette (1931 starting first baseman) was coming off a shoulder operation, and there was some question about his ability to recover. He had signed his contract on February 19 and the Dodgers intended to use him at the first base spot. By the end of February the Dodgers had signed heavy-hitting outfielder Ike Boone, Bobby Reis from Astoria, New York, and Cy Moore. The pre-season was off to a good start and optimism ran high in the Clearwater camp. Manager Carey posed for the *New York Times* with his corps of Dodger hopefuls (including Vickers, Mungo, Mattingly, Jones, Gallivan and Krider) just before they finished a vigorous game of volleyball. (Volleyball was introduced by Manager Carey as a form of conditioning and a break from the sometimes tedious practice sessions.)

The results of the 1932 season were not dramatically different from the previous one, but the cast of characters was. Six of the eight nonpitching starters had changed. Kelly (1B), Cuccinello (2B), Wright (SS), Stripp (3B), Wilson (RF), and Taylor (CF) had all replaced regulars from the 1931 team. Only Lefty O'Doul (LF) and Alfonso Lopez (C) remained at the normal spots. The pitching corps remained fairly constant except for the welcome addition of Van Lingle Mungo. The Dodgers finished the year with 81 wins and 73 losses. This record placed them third in the league behind Chicago and Pittsburgh. As a team the new infield had led the league with 169 double plays and had hit a respectable .283. Individually, Lefty O'Doul led the league in hitting with a .368 average. He also had 219 hits (third) and a .555 slugging average (fourth)—an exceptional performance by any standards. Hack Wilson, newly installed in right field, also had a good year at the plate. He placed fifth in the league with 23 home runs and tied for fourth in RBI with 123. In the pitching side of the ledger, Watty Clark finished second in the league with 20 wins and Jack Quinn led the league with eight saves. Given the number and scope of the changes from the previous year, 1932 was a fair year for manager Carey and the Brooklyn Dodgers. They finished only nine games off the pace and everyone looked forward to the next season.

As nine pitchers (Mungo, Lucas, Heimach, Phelps, Quinn, Ryan, Schwenk, Clark, and Van Dermer) and one catcher (Sukeforth) reported to the Coral Gables, Florida, camp on February 27, 1933, some serious questions faced the Brooklyn Dodgers. Alfonso Lopez was a holdout; Del Bissonette was attempting to recover from a foot injury that had sidelined him the entire 1932 season; and Jack Quinn was recovering from an off-season illness. Dazzy Vance had been traded to the Cardinals in the off-season and Joe Humphries was hopefully recovered from a broken leg suffered while playing with Hartford in the minor leagues. The 1933 season started with doubts that came true.

The Brooklyn Dodgers finished with 65 wins and 88 losses. This placed them in sixth place, 26½ games behind the crosstown Giants. Brooklyn did not lead the league in a single category; instead, the Dodgers placed in the middle of the pack in nearly every category. The mediocrity was overwhelming. The closest they came to either end of the spectrum was a second-place finish in stolen bases with 82. The season proved to be the last for Max Carey.

The rumors about Casey replacing Max Carey as manager had been circulating around New York for several weeks. On February 21, 1934, Casey Stengel was summoned to Brooklyn from his Glendale, California, home. The very next day, general manager Bob Quinn announced the firing of Max Carey. The following day, Charles Dillon Stengel accepted the job as Dodger manager. He was given a two-year contract to manage the Brooklyn franchise and opened the press conference by announcing his "set" positions for the upcoming season. Mungo, Beck, Benge, and Carroll would be the four starting pitchers; Leslie, Cuccinello, Frey, and Stripp would be the infielders; and Taylor would play left field. He concluded the press conference by saying, "Every one of the gentlemen directing this club wanted me to be manager. I will be the manager too. Darned if I don't think I know a few things about baseball and I think I can teach baseball." He opened the training camp on March 4, 1934, in Orlando, Florida.

True to his word, Manager Stengel started Leslie, Cuccinello, Frey, and Stripp in the infield. They promptly responded by leading the league with 141 double plays. Van Lingle Mungo led the league in innings pitched with 315.1. Young Danny Taylor was fourth with 12 stolen bases and newcomer Len Koenecke was third in the league with 70 bases on balls. Despite these individual performances, the Dodgers finished with 71 wins and 81 losses, not a significant improvement over the previous season. Brooklyn trailed first-place St. Louis by 23½ games at the conclusion of the season, was third in runs scored, fourth in team batting average, fifth in team slugging average, and fifth in ERA. Again, the Dodgers had completed a lackluster, mediocre season that contained some individual outstanding performances. The Dodgers looked forward to Stengel's second contract year with the anticipation that only baseball can muster.

Training camp for the 1935 season opened on February 25 in Orlando. Gordon Phelps, a newly acquired, good-hitting catcher, sparkled on the first day of camp by hitting several balls over the left-center-field fence; he was expected to challenge Lopez for catching duties. Each pitcher threw to the hitters for five minutes and was cautioned by Stengel to avoid curve balls at this early stage of the campaign. The next day Stengel began two-a-day workouts for everyone. Van Lingle Mungo reported to camp with renewed enthusiasm and still remembering the death blow he had dealt the crosstown Giants the previous September. Johnny Babich, another pitcher whom Stengel was counting on heavily, reported to camp 20 pounds overweight. Stengel demonstrated his faith in the pitching corps by announcing to the press the following day that Mungo, Benge, Leonard, and Babich would be his starters of the upcoming season.

Babe Phelps put added pressure on Lopez by becoming the first player in history to ever hit a ball out of Tinker Field in right field. The fence was 423 feet from home and the individuals who saw Phelps' towering blast said it must have traveled at least 450 feet.

The 1935 Brooklyn Dodgers finished the season with 70 wins and 83 losses to finish in fifth place. This uneventful season found the Dodgers leading the league in only one category: saves (20). Dutch Leonard accounted for eight of these, which placed his first mark in the league. On the other side of outstanding performances, Lonnie Frey led all shortstops with 44 errors. The Dodgers seemed to be mired in the middle of the pack; they were fifth in runs scored, fifth in team batting average, sixth in strikeouts, and fifth in team ERA. Excluding Leonard's league-leading saves and Mungo's third-place finish in strikeouts, the Dodgers did not place a single individual in any of the top five for any batting, baserunning, or pitching category. It began to seem as though they were slipping rather than moving ahead. Despite the disappointing finish and fan discontent, the front office renewed manager Stengel's contract for another year.

The 1936 season brought a change of scenery for the Dodgers as they returned to Clearwater, Florida, for their training camp. The field had been completely renovated; it had been plowed under and freshly seeded with 1,500 pounds of Italian grass seed. The players commented that the outfield grass resembled the green on a golf course. On February 21 the New York Giants bought Sam Leslie from the Dodgers for $20,000. Leslie had been one of only three Dodgers to hit over .300 during the 1935 season. In order to replace Leslie, the Dodgers bought Buddy Hassett from the New York Yankees farm club at Newark. They paid $35,000 for Hassett and two other minor league players. Hassett, 6'0", 175 pounds, 24 years old, had been a prep star at Manhattan Prep High School and both a baseball and basketball star at Manhattan College. The Leslie-Hassett deal marked the first time in history that a three-way deal had been completed between the three New York baseball franchises. Tom Zachary signed his contract for his 18th major league season on February 26, but Van Mungo was a holdout. He had been offered a raise to $11,000 but felt that his services were worth at least $12,000.

The 1936 Dodgers completed the season with 67 wins and 87 losses while finishing seventh out of eight teams in the National League. Despite this dismal finish, the pitching staff far outdistanced the opposition with a total of 654 strikeouts. The problem obviously lay at the other end of the offense-defense continuum. The Dodgers finished seventh in runs scored. Individually, Babe Phelps finished second in hitting with an average of .367, losing out to Pittsburgh's Paul Waner by eight percentage points. Van Lingle Mungo led the league with 238 strikeouts and amassed 18 wins. Unfortunately, he also was credited with 19 losses. Buddy Hassett had some problems adjusting to the big leagues. He hit a respectable .310 and led the league's first basemen with 121 assists, but also paced the first basemen with 26 errors. Lonny Frey also set a league mark for shortstops by committing 51 errors. By contrast, Joe Stripp and Johnny Cooney set the fielding standards for their respective positions at third base and in center field. The 1936 season proved to be the last for Casey Stengel as the Dodgers kept searching for the right pieces to fit the puzzle.

The 1937 season brought a new manager to the Dodgers, and with him, a new spirit. Manager Burleigh Grimes announced the new philosophy: "Players must battle to the finish." He vowed at the opening press conference: "I won't predict where this team will finish, but I'll hustle 10 more winning ball games out of this bunch." The changes were more than philososphical. Roy Henshaw, acquired from the Chicago Cubs in a trade for Frey, and Luke Hamlin, a right-hander from the draft, joined the pitching corps. Gilbert Brack was acquired in a trade from Louisville for cash and Ray Berrea to bolster the outfield crew. Van Mungo and Fred Frankhouse were holdouts, but the front office anticipated little trouble in signing Frankhouse. The problem lay with Mungo. They had offered him a $1,400 raise above his $12,500, 1936 salary, but he balked.

Still bouncing about between fifth- and seventh-place finishes, the 1937 Dodgers placed sixth with 62 wins and 91 losses. Again the pall of mediocrity hung over the team as they led the league in none of the batting, fielding, or pitching categories. Individually, Buddy Hassett continued to lead the league in assists with 116, but also led first basemen with 20 errors. Van Mungo justified his salary increase by leading the league in allowing the fewest hits per nine innings (7.60) and most strikeouts per nine innings (6.82). Except for Mungo and the base-stealing talents of Lavagetto and Hassett, the Dodgers were unable to place any of their players in the top five in any of the batting, baserunning, or pitching categories. The fans hoped that the new manager and players were going through a period of adjustment and the following year would finally see the Brooklyn team start some movement out of the second division of the National League.

In another search for the pieces of the pennant puzzle, the Dodgers moved their 1938 camp to Hot Springs, Arkansas. The talk around the new camp was about National League's new baseball, which had more stitching and a thicker cover. Both changes were designed to aid the pitcher. On February 23, 1938, Executive Vice President Larry McPhail announced that 24 Dodgers were already signed, leaving only seven unsigned for the upcoming season. Lavagetto had already signed, but the contract had not been received in Brooklyn, and the team seemed close to signing Butcher, Hamlin, Durocher, English, and Hassett. The lone problem lay with Heinie Manush. As the Giants and other clubs worked out, the Dodgers used a novel conditioning technique—they hiked the mountains surrounding the Hot Springs camp and soaked in the warm natural springs each day.

Manager Grimes moved Buddy Hassett to left field during the 1938 season to make room for Dolf Camilli at first base. Camilli responded by leading the league in walks with 119, finishing fourth in home runs with 24, and placing third in runs scored with 106. Furthermore, he only committed eight errors at first base. Johnny Hudson, the new second baseman, and the displaced Cookie Lavagetto paced the league for errors at their respective positions with 27 and 28 errors. Rookie shortstop Leo Durocher and Goody Rosen won fielding honors. As a team the Dodgers led the league in triples with 79 and stolen bases with 66. This new speed and daring baserunning relieved some of the cries about mediocre baseball in Brooklyn, but it couldn't completely stem the tide of change. It was Burleigh Grimes' last year as manager of the Dodgers.

The Depression Era period from 1932 to 1938 paralleled the search of the nation to somehow wrest itself from the grasp of a force it couldn't completely explain. The Dodgers continued to shuffle the deck but repeatedly were dealt bad hands. The following season would see a change and finally some progress out of the rut that seemed to be the Dodgers' home for the past seven years. A young shortstop named Leo Durocher was to emerge as that elusive piece of the puzzle that had been missing for so many years.

Van Lingle Mungo pitched for the Dodgers for eleven seasons (1931-1941). The righthanded hurler won over 100 games for the Dodgers, including 18-win seasons in both 1934 and 1936.

In the twilight of his great career, Hack Wilson played for the Dodgers in 1932, 1933 and 67 games in 1934. The man who was elected to baseball's Hall of Fame in 1979 hit 23 homers for the Dodgers in 1932.

Ernest Gordon "Babe" Phelps was acquired by the Dodgers from the Chicago Cubs prior to the 1935 season. Nicknamed "Blimp" because of his prodigious size (6'2", 225 lbs.), Phelps played for the Dodgers for seven seasons. He had his best year in 1936 when he hit .367 as the Dodger starting catcher.

Johnny Cooney played three seasons for the Dodgers (1935-1937). As a starting outfielder in 1936 and 1937, Cooney hit .282 and .293 respectively.

First baseman Buddy Hassett hit .310, .304 and .293 for the Dodgers in 1936, 1937 and 1938 respectively. He suffered with deficiencies in the field, however, was traded to the Boston Braves prior to the 1939 season.

Hall-of-Famer Burleigh Grimes won 158 games for the Dodgers as a 175-pound righthanded pitcher during the period 1918-1926. Nicknamed "Ol' Stubblebeard," Grimes managed his former team — the Dodgers — for two unproductive seasons (1937-1938).

Tony Cuccinello came to the Dodgers from Cincinnati in a bombshell of a deal that sent widely-admired Babe Herman to the Reds in 1932. Cuccinello served the Dodgers as a capable second baseman from 1932 to 1935. Along with George Kelly at first base, Glenn Wright at shortstop and Joe Stripp at third, he gave the Dodgers a fine all-around infield. Cuccinello's best year was 1935 when he hit for a .292 average.

The 1932 Dodgers finished in 3rd place, some 14 games behind the Cubs. It was the Dodgers' best showing since 1924, when they finished second. High spot of the Dodger attack in the '32 season was the tremendous hitting of Lefty O'Doul. The California clouter hit .368 for the year with 21 home runs. O'Doul later was to tutor another California youngster — Joe DiMaggio.

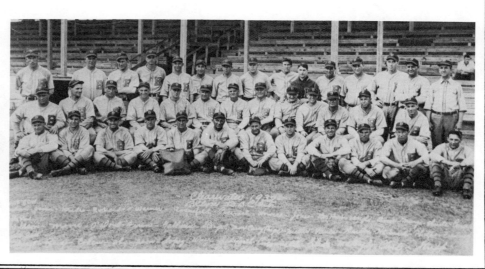

The Phillies' Morrie Arnovich is about to be tagged out by the Dodgers' Paul Chervinko on an attempted steal of home in 1938 at the Phillies' home field—Baker Bowl. Earl Browne is the batter and Dolly Stark is the umpire.

Harry Arthur "Cookie" Lavagetto played for seven years for the Dodgers. He began his career as a second baseman, but the Dodgers switched him to third base after the 1937 season—a year in which he hit .282 as Brooklyn's starting second baseman. His greatest moment as a Dodger came in 1947 when his two-out, bottom-of-the-ninth inning hit broke up Bill Beven's no-hit bid and gave the Dodgers a dramatic victory in the fourth game of the World Series.

Bert Haas started his 9-year major league career with the Dodgers in 1937. Toiling for five different teams, Haas had a lifetime average of .264. In 1937 in only 25 times at bat, Haas had 10 hits for a .400 batting average.

Freddy Fitzsimmons, a great pitcher for the N.Y. Giants from 1925-1937, was traded to the Dodgers midway through the 1937 season. He went on to play over six seasons for Brooklyn. During the 1943 season, he left the Dodgers to assume the managerial reins of the Philadelphia Phillies—a job he was to hold without distinction.

Infielder John Hudson played five seasons for the Dodgers (1936-1940). Hudson demonstrated his versatility by playing short, second and third for the Dodgers. He had his best year in 1938 when he hit .261.

Outfielder Art Parks played two seasons for Brooklyn (1937 and 1939). In limited action, he hit .313 in 1937—his best year.

Waite Hoyt was a legendary pitcher with the Yankees of the Babe Ruth era. In 1927 and 1928, he won 22 and 23 games respectively. Early in his tenth season with the Yankees, Hoyt was traded to the Detroit Tigers. His Tiger tour was followed by stops (however brief) in Philadelphia, Brooklyn, New York (Giants) and Pittsburgh. After pitching in 11 games for the Pirates in 1937, he was traded to Brooklyn for his second stint with the Dodgers. Here he is shown in 1937 pitching a 3-0 shutout for the Dodgers over the Philadelphia Phillies at Ebbets Field on August 20, 1937. Hoyt finished the year with seven victories as the Dodgers stumbled to sixth place. In 1938, Hoyt retired at the end of the season after pitching just 16 1/3 innings. Hoyt's remarkable 21-year-career earned his induction into baseball's Hall of Fame in 1969.

Charles Dillon Stengel.

The year was 1939, and the 34-year-old firebrand Leo Durocher was named to manage the Brooklyn Dodgers. As the team's regular shortstop in 1938, Leo hit a puny .219, but he was all over the infield making tough plays. In 1939, as playing manager for Brooklyn, Leo hit a strong .277 and led the Dodgers to a third-place finish in the National League race. Twenty-two years later, in 1961, when Leo had been out of baseball for five years, he was appointed to assist Dodger Manager Walt Alston with the Los Angeles Dodgers. Within a week after taking over his job, Leo was suspended for kicking umpire Jocko Conlin.

4

THE LEO DUROCHER ERA

1939-1946

The Cardinals of 1935 had the misfortune to be pennant contenders the same time their bitter rivals, the Chicago Cubs, put together an amazing twenty-one game winning streak in September to nose out the high-flying Redbirds in the chase for the National League flag.

But for the fiery play of shortstop Leo Durocher, the Cards would have finished in second division. His amazing skill at short, his spirit and hustle and even some timely base hits, drove the Cards on to victory after victory. At the plate Leo drove out eight homers when they were needed, and he wound up the season with a solid .265 batting average. "High enough," he said recently, "that it could bring me one of those million dollar contracts today."

LEO DUROCHER
MANAGER 1939-1946
(part of 1948)

Year	G	W	L	FINISHED
1939	157	84	69	3
1940	156	88	65	2
1941	157	100	54	1
1942	155	104	50	2
1943	153	81	72	3
1944	155	63	91	7
1945	155	87	67	3
1946	157	96	60	2
1948	75	37	38	5

There was, however, one serious situation, insofar as Leo was concerned; it was the widening rift between Leo and the manager of the Cardinals, the great second baseman, Frankie Frisch.

"I was riding high with the Cardinals for four-and-a-half years," said Leo, "and alongside the Dean brothers, Pepper Martin and Frisch, they were my best friends. Frisch had been my pal. Frank and I roomed together, we played golf together. We were real pals, I thought, until—

"One day in 1937, after our spring training chores for the day were over, Branch Rickey called me over. Rickey was the president of the Cardinals and my favorite guy.

'You and Frisch had a fight?' he asked.

'No , sir,' I said. 'We hit if off great.'

'Well, he wants me to trade you,' snapped Rickey.

"My jaw dropped. 'Trade me? That ungrateful rat! I've been holding him up for years and now he's out for my neck, eh? Well, what are you gonna do about it?'"

After that Frisch and Durocher drifted apart and were hardly talking to each other, except to exchange insults. The break came when Frisch fined and suspended Durocher for the rest of the season.

Leo learned of the trade, his departure from the Cards, when he picked up an afternoon paper. He was to go to the Brooklyn Dodgers for Joe Stripp, Johnny Cooney, Roy Henshaw and Jim Bucher.

Durocher was wild with rage. From a pennant contender to a team fighting to keep out of the cellar. Leo was pacing his hotel room, threatening all kinds of torture and revenge when Rickey walked in. He puffed a cloud of smoke at Leo and smiled.

"I didn't think you were worth four very good ballplayers. Imagine, Leo, four players for you."

"Four players!", sneered Leo. "Four washed-up old men. So Frisch finally sold you a bill of goods!"

"Easy now, boy," Rickey soothed.

"Easy, my foot" Leo bellowed. "It's bad enough you're trading me—but to Brooklyn!"

"Great guns, boy!" Rickey shouted. "Don't you ever see farther than your own belligerent nose? You have ambitions beyond being just a player, haven't you?"

"Right then," said Leo, "it didn't sink into my head because I was mad. Later it developed that Rickey had ideas about my managing and really wanted to give me a break. I wasn't all through; he could have made a better trade for me with another club. But he picked Brooklyn and for a good reason."

"You've made a fine team captain for the Cardinals, and I'll bet my shirt if you keep free of those strange friends and entanglements of yours," Rickey said, "you'll be the new manager of the Dodgers."

Burleigh Grimes, the Dodgers' manager, could hardly have suspected that he was bringing to his daffy Dodgers the one man who would soon replace him—and change the entire spirit and atmosphere at Ebbets Field.

Leo Durocher wasn't the only bombshell to hit Brooklyn in 1938. The harried board of Directors of the Brooklyn club, faced with another miserable season, poor attendance and a dejected ball club, and faced with possible bankruptcy, brought in Larry MacPhail as General Manager of the Dodgers. Larry MacPhail played a church organ in Detroit. When he graduated from high school, he received an appointment to Annapolis, but he went instead to Beloit College, then to Michigan, finally to George Washington University, where he graduated with a law degree and began to practice law.

When World War I started, Larry enlisted, saw action at the front and was gassed. Larry proved to be a first-class soldier and soon was promoted to the rank of Captain. When the war ended, he was stationed near Metz. It was there that he joined in a plot, hatched over a couple of bottles of wine, to cross the border into Holland to kidnap the Kaiser, who had sought refuge at Amerongen in Holland. By January 4, Larry and Colonel Luke Lea, a 30-year-old U.S. Senator and six other officers reached the castle where the German ruler lived, but 200 German soldiers frustrated the kidnapping. MacPhail escaped with the Kaiser's ashtray as a souvenir.

After the war, Larry moved around. He ran a glass factory, sold autos, refereed football games. Finally he purchased an option on the Columbus team, which he later sold to the Cardinals, and in 1933 was appointed General Manager of the Cincinnati Reds. Larry breathed new life into the tottering Cincinnati team. He traded players right and left, cleaned and painted up Crosley Field, instituted night baseball, hired the fabulous Red Barber to broadcast the Red's games and soon the crowds started to pour through the turnstiles, even though the team continued to lose as many games as they won.

By 1937 Larry was bored with his job and jumped at the opportunity to get into New York, via Brooklyn; and the minute he saw the Dodgers' tiny Ebbets Field Offices, he began to take the place apart. He enlarged and re-decorated the offices, painted and cleaned-up and re-decorated the ball park.

And after he spent about $250,000 he started to spend money on ball players. He bought first baseman Dolph Camilli from the Phillies for $50,000 and then brought in Leo Durocher. He hired Red Barber to broadcast the Dodger games. He hired Andy Frayne to set up a first-rate uniformed corps of ushers, who would direct ticket holders to their own seats. Heretofore groups of young thugs would take over a section of seats and even the police couldn't or wouldn't move them. He brought in Babe Ruth as a coach and even introduced night baseball.

The season was only a few days old when the Dodgers started their skid. They lost six in a row and went down into sixth place, seventh place on May 15. The team finished in seventh place and MacPhail immediately started to make more changes.

The World Series ended October 9. On the tenth, Larry announced that Grimes was out as manager

Leo Durocher as the NY Yankee shortstop in 1928.

of the Dodgers. And on the thirteenth, he announced that his new manager would be Leo Durocher.

Larry MacPhail had promised some new faces in 1939 and he brought pitchers Whit Wyatt and Hugh Casey. Pete Coscarart came up from Nashville to play second base. He obtained Dixie Walker from the Tigers, and the Dodgers started off by dropping three staight to the Giants. But Leo struggled and juggled his lineup. He moved players around like a chess-master and the team started to win. Pee Wee Reese and Coscarart started to make the double-plays; Dixie Walker started to hit and the Dodgers took 15 out of their next sixteen games and the fans began to jam the park. More than a million fans paid their way into Ebbets Field in 1938 and even though the club had to beat the Cubs in the last three games of the season to finish in third place, the fans enjoyed the fast and furious baseball they had seen and they were aching for next year. It was the highest finish for a Brooklyn club since 1932.

Nobody worked harder than Durocher to get a team ready for a season in 1939. He brought a kid up from the farm system, Harold Reiser, the best looking young hitter in spring training, and with Joe Vosmik and pitcher Tex Carleton and Reese at shortstop, the Dodgers were ready to roll.

The Dodgers broke away swiftly, rolling up nine straight wins and they were in first place, In a game against Cincinnati, Carleton, supposedly all through, pitched a no-hit game that fired up the club even more. Late in July, Larry MacPhail called Leo and told him that he had made a deal with

October 13, 1938, a new era began for the Brooklyn Dodgers as President Larry MacPhail (left) congratulates Leo Durocher after announcing Durocher had been appointed the new manager of the Dodgers, replacing Burleigh Grimes.

Branch Rickey and had bought the Cardinals slugger, Joe Medwick, for $125,000.

The deal was hailed all over Brooklyn and the fans were screaming pennant. The newspapers joined in the enthusiastic battle and now the ball park became a madhouse. Brooklyn was in full battle cry a couple of days later when Medwick was beaned and knocked unconscious; he was rushed to the hospital and in a few days was back in the lineup. But he was never the same aggressive hitter he had been before he was beaned.

All the new excitement, jammed ball park, fighting and feuding couldn't bring the pennant to Brooklyn that year. But the Dodgers made a great fight and finished in second place, twelve games behind the Reds...and throughout all of Brooklyn, the battle cry ..."Wait til next year!"

MacPhail didn't wait too long to add the final pieces to his ball club. He made his first move and bought Kirby Higbe from the Phillies for $100,000. Kirby had won 14 games in 1940 for a last place club. Then Larry called Branch Rickey. "How about a deal for that young catcher of yours, Mickey Owen," he asked, "I want $60,000."

"You're on," Larry said, and Mickey Owen became a Dodger.

The 1941 season opened with bright hopes, but were dimmed immediately by the Giants, who slugged the Dodgers in three straight games. Gradually the pieces of this great Dodger club started to jell. And when MacPhail made a deal for Billy Herman, who had been a Cub star for ten years, pennant fever hit Brooklyn overnight. The club started to win ball games. All over the nation, baseball fans were becoming Dodger fans and were listening to the dulcet tones of Red Barber on the radio. Everyday seemed like a world series as Leo and the Brooks battled with the Giants, the Reds and the Cardinals, as each team jockeyed and fought for first place. The only thing that kept the Dodgers going in those frantic days was their fighting spirit.

Leo looked like a bedraggled hobo by September. He had worn the same slacks, sport coat and the same tie for nearly three weeks. He hadn't shaved during that time either. As long as the Dodgers held the lead, he wasn't changing clothes. He didn't intend changing his luck.

There was a Sunday doubleheader in Philadelphia, in September and the Dodgers jumped on the Phils quickly and won the first game, and between the games Dodger scout Ted McGrew popped into the Brooklyn clubhouse.

"I got a message for you, Leo, from MacPhail. He said for you to pitch Luke Hamlin in the second game."

Leo exploded. "I've been doing pretty well up to now without him picking my pitchers. Tell him to go to hell. I'll pitch whoever I want to. He's probably going to take charge now, and take credit for winning the pennant."

Leo calmed down a bit after McGrew left. After all, why not let Hamlin pitch? MacPhail was still the boss. So he pitched Hamlin and in the very first inning Luke loaded the bases, then came in with a fast pitch to Danny Litwhiler, who promptly hit the ball over the fence for the ball game. Leo was angry. So were the rest of the Dodgers.

It was the final two games of the year in Boston. The Dodgers won the first on Dixie Walker's big triple in the eighth inning. But, now Durocher was worried. He lay sleepless in his bed and tossed and turned and worried. Reese had booted another tough play. It had almost cost the game. Should he replace him? It might kill the kid's spirit. What to do? Who to pitch?

A bleary-eyed Durocher staggered down for breakfast the next morning. Over his coffee, he read the sports pages. All he saw about the Dodgers was "If". If the Dodgers won today and the Cards lost, Brooklyn had the pennant. Leo called on his ace, Whit Wyatt, to sew up the flag for the Dodgers. Wyatt had won 21 games. Had beaten Boston in five straight games that season. Wyatt, sensing the gnawing anxiety eating away at Leo, patted him on the back, "Just get me one run today, Leo," he said. "That's all I am going to need."

The Dodgers picked up that one run in a hurry. Walker singled, went to third on two infield outs and scored when Medwick singled. In the second inning, the Dodgers picked up another run and again in the third frame the Dodgers scored, to give them a 3-0 lead. Pete Reiser homered in the seventh and now it was 5-0. And from the press box there was word that the Cardinals were losing 3-1. A Dodger player jumped up and yelled, "This is it." But Durocher shut him up. It was too soon.

In the ninth inning, Wyatt set down Boston in order, while the press box yelled to the Dodgers that the Cards had lost.

As Wyatt got the last out, every Dodger on the bench leaped off the bench to a man, and, together with the players on the field, carried Wyatt and Durocher on their shoulders to the clubhouse. The locker room was a bedlam; with flash bulbs exploding, players laughing and shouting and drinking champagne.

In New York, Red Barber on the air over W.O.R., announced the time that the team would be arriving at Grand Central, not realizing that all of Brooklyn would take off to meet the team.

The train ride back to New York on a special victory train was one long, hysterical, mad party. Some of the players suggested that they get off the train at 125th Street to avoid the crowds that might gather. Leo vetoed the idea.

"I don't care if the mob is there and they tear the clothes right off your back. We belong to those fans, and we're not going to cheat them out of this. I gave the conductor orders not even to stop at Grand Central."

In the spring of 1938, the Dodgers signed free agent Pete Reiser for a $100 bonus. It was one of the biggest bargains in baseball history for Pete was to become one of the all-time Dodger heroes. Starting in 1938 in his first spring training camp, Pete hit a towering home run. Then in his next 12 times at bat that spring, he reached base 12 times, on three homers, five singles and four walks. After watching him for a few days, the Yankees offered $100,000 for Reiser to Larry MacPhail—the general manager of the Dodgers. The offer was rejected. Pete was sent to Elmira, where he set the league afire with his play. In 1941, his first full season with the Dodgers, Pete, despite several crippling injuries, hit .343 and became the first rookie to win the National League batting championship. He led the league in triples, runs scored, total bases and tied Johnny Mize with 39 doubles. Back from the Armed Forces in 1946 and again severely injured, Pete hit .277 including 11 home runs. During the season, Pistol Pete set a major league record by stealing home seven times. In 1949, he was traded to Boston. In the hearts and minds of every Dodger fan, however, Pete Reiser will always be remembered as one of the most exciting players in Dodger history.

Leo never found out that MacPhail had hopped a cab to 125th Street to meet the train. Larry waited impatiently on the platform. He would board the train, congratulate Leo and the team and ride in triumph to Grand Central. But the train roared right on through the station, leaving a furious MacPhail standing there enveloped in dust and mad as a hornet.

Leo thought it was a good joke on MacPhail, but he changed his mind when Larry summoned him to his hotel suite.

"Who gave the order to run the train through 125th Street?" he demanded.

"I did, Larry. Why?"

"Didn't you get my wire that I was going to meet you there and board the train?"

"No, I didn't," snapped Durocher, who was rapidly losing his temper. He was on edge, tired from the bitter tension of the pennant race. Now, instead of congratulating him, MacPhail was bawling him out.

"You're through, Leo!" Larry yelled. "Fired!"

A.J. Laveque presents Leo Durocher with a bag containing 2500 pennies collected by Dodger fans to pay a $25 fine. The fine was imposed by baseball commissioner Ford Frick after Leo's fight with the Giant's first baseman, Zeke Bonura, in a game July 8, 1939.

In 1940, Mickey Owen cost the Dodgers $50,000 in a deal with the Cardinals. In 1949, he was traded to the Cubs.

In 1937, Dolph Camilli was one of baseball's leading hitters. Playing first base for the Phillies, Dolph drove out 27 home runs and slugged the ball for a brilliant .339 average. Larry MacPhail, newly appointed President of the Dodgers, wanted Camilli to shore up that position with his hapless sixth place club. Larry shelled out a great deal of money for Dolph, but it didn't immediately help the ball club. In 1941, however, Camilli blasted 34 home runs, a career high, and helped the Dodgers capture the National League flag...

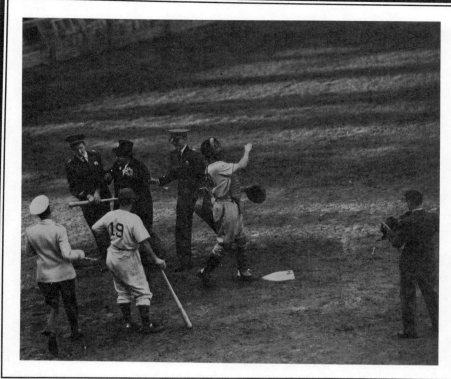

It could only happen in Brooklyn. Eddie Bettan, one of the all-time great Dodger fans, wanted to salute the Dodgers 100th victory. And so on Sept. 19, 1941, with formal attire, including top hat, Eddie waited for the proper moment in the 8th inning of the game between the Dodgers and Phils. He picked up a bat and wanted to hit a pitch off Rube Melton. The ushers, however, promptly escorted Eddie, formal garb et al, off the field and into a box seat to view the rest of the game.

P.S. The Dodgers won the ball game with Eddie's support.

'41 Series

On a certain day in 1941, The Borough of Brooklyn in the City of New York was bursting with bliss. Perfect strangers on the busy streets of Flatbush were smiling at each other for the first time in history. The grass seemed a little greener in Prospect Park. Williamsburgh was excited as people chatted with each other on the streets. Greenpoint was delighted. Brownsville was alive with excitement as kids raced around telling of the great news. Coney Island was alive with a carnival spirit.

The occasion of all this joy was the fact that the Dodgers—Brooklyn's gift to the world of baseball—had clinched the National League pennant by defeating the Boston Braves. For the first time since nineteen twenty, the National League pennant flew over Ebbets Field.

Little did it matter to the joyous Brooklyn fans that the Dodgers would have to meet those bruising Bronx Bombers—The Yankees—in the World Series. They were sure that "Pistol Pete" Reiser would match anything Joe DiMaggio did—that "Dixie" Walker hit as well as "King Kong" Keller—that Pee Wee Reese was every bit as good as Phil Rizzuto—and the Dodgers pitchers, Whit Wyatt, Curt Davis, Hugh Casey, Kirby Higbe, would be a match for Atley Donald, Red Ruffing, Marius Russo and Spud Chandler.

The first two games were played at Yankee Stadium and the Brooklyn mob came across the bridges and through the tunnels and flocked into Yankee Stadium for the opening game of the series

on October 1, even outnumbering the Yankee fans, so that the louder cheers welled up from the stands as the Dodgers trotted onto the field. Hilda Chester was there with her huge cow bell, and the four-piece band with all the characters so familiar to fans at Ebbets Field. You would have thought, had you been there, that the Dodgers, not the Yankees, were the home club.

Manager Leo Durocher startled the baseball wisen-heimers by starting Curt Davis in the first game, a natural expectation being that he would start Whitlow Wyatt, the top pitcher on his staff. But Davis was plenty good, and smart and cool, and perhaps just the pitcher to handcuff the Yankees. Joe McCarthy opened with cunning Red Ruffing and the game was under way. In the second inning Joe Gordon slammed a home run; and in the fourth Keller walked and scored on Bill Dickey's long double. In the sixth, the Yankees scored once more; Keller walked, went to third on Dickey's single, and scored the Yankees 3rd run on a single by Joe Gordon.

The Dodgers did manage to score twice, on Reese's single, Mickey Owen's triple, then once more in the sixth inning, when Lavagetto beat out a hit to short, Pee Wee singled him to third and Reese scored when Rizzo pinch-hit for Owen and singled. But Ruffing held the Dodgers after that and the Yankees won, 3-2.

Durocher countered with Whit Wyatt in the second game. And once again the Yanks took the

Leo Durocher gets a big kiss from his mother just before game-time, Sept. 24, 1941.

lead, scoring on a hit by Spud Chandler, a pass to Gordon and single by Keller. They scored another run in the third on a double by Tom Henrich and a single by Charley Keller. But the Dodgers roared back. They filled the bases on a pass to Dolph Camilli, a double by Joe Medwick and a walk to Cookie Lavagetto. Reese forced Cookie, but Camilli scored. Mickey Owen drove a single to left scoring Medwick and the score was 2-2.

In the sixth inning, Spud Chandler was pulled out when Dixie Walker beat out a hit. Billy Herman slapped a single to right and the Dodgers went ahead 3-2 and that was how the game ended.

Newspapermen visiting the Dodgers' dressing room after the game walked into a scene that is usually reserved for a World Series victory.

"We've got em now!" the Dodgers yelled. "Wait till we get in Brooklyn! We'll murder the bums!"

They were singing in the showers, throwing wet towels at each other, and generally acting as though all they had to do was to go home and wait for the Baseball Commissioner to send them their World Series checks. In the Yankees dressing room the players calmly talked over the game as they dressed slowly and Fred Logan, their clubhouse man, packed the uniforms for shipment to Ebbets Field.

In the third game the Dodgers were victims of a cruel break. Freddy Fitzimmons, a lion-hearted pitcher with years of experience, put on a terrific battle with Marius Russo, the Yankees' young left-hander.

In the seventh inning of a scoreless game, Russo smashed a drive right back at Fitz. The ball smashed into Fitz's left knee and popped into the air, and an alert Reese caught the ball for the out. But Fitz had to leave the game and Hugh Casey came in to pitch. Four singles in a row by Rolfe, Henrich, DiMaggio and Keller gave the Yankees two runs. The best the Dodgers could do was to score one run in the seventh, on a double by Walker and a hard single by Reese and the Yanks were on top 2-1.

The fans streamed away from the park, storming and cursing against the evil fate that had befallen Fitzimmons and cost the Dodgers the game, just when it seemed safely in the bag.

The fourth game was set for Sunday. This was the one that Brooklyn had to win to get back in the series. Fans by the thousands stood in line all night at the bleacher entrance—the reserved seats had been sold out for days.

Joe McCarthy started Atley Donald, a tall right-hander with a great, hopping fast-ball. Durocher started Kirby Higbe, but the Yanks jumped him for a run in the first inning and two in the fourth and he was through. French, a husky southpaw, came in to relieve Hig. The Yanks were out in front 3-0.

The faint-hearted Dodgers fans were just about ready to give up the ship with the Yanks 3 runs up; but the Dodgers were just beginning to fight back. In the fourth inning, Owens walked, so did Coscarort, in at second base for Herman. Jim Wasdell, batting for French, doubled off the left field fence and two runs were in. Dixie Walker doubled and now the crowd was up and screaming. And they went nuts, pure, plain nuts, as Pistol Pete Reiser hit the ball out of the ball park and the Dodgers were out in front 4-3.

Dixie Walker is safe at first as Joe Gordon's throw pulls Yankee first baseman Johnny Sturm off the base in the 2nd game of the 1941 World Series. Dolph Camilli's hit scored Dixie in the 6th inning for the winning run as the Dodgers won 3-2.

The play was tense and tight now. The Yanks could not hit Casey. Hugh was curving them. Cross-firing them, never giving the Yanks a good ball to hit. The seventh inning, eighth inning rolled on and it was still Dodgers 4-Yanks 3.

The Yankees came to bat in the top of the ninth. Johnny Sturm was out on a grounder. Red Rolfe hit to Casey and was thrown out. Two down, one to go, and the series would be tied up. Casey worked carefully on smart Tommy Henrich; the count went to three and two. The stands were still, for the moment. Ready to burst with joy. But they wanted that last out.

Casey curled in for his windup. He broke in with a sharp curve, and Tommy swung and missed, and the game was over. A scream rose in 35-thousand Flatbush throats. But wait! The ball slipped through Owen's glove and spun off to the right of the plate—and Henrich raced to first base beating Owen's frantic throw.

The crowd was stunned. So were the Dodgers. The Yankees had new life and now broke through. DiMaggio singled. Keller doubled scoring Henrich and DiMag. Dickey walked. Gordon doubled, scoring Keller and Dickey. Finally Johnny Murphy made the third out. But the Yanks had scored four runs and now led seven to four.

As in a trance the Dodgers went out in order in their half of the ninth inning. The Yanks had pulled out the game 7-4. The following day the Yankees behind Tiny Bonham beat the Dodgers 3-1 for the Championship.

Even the loss of the World Series could not dim the bright achievement of the Dodgers that year. They had won a pennant for the first time in twenty-one years, had played to a record 1,200,000 people and over one million on the road. And they now had the players that both Larry MacPhail and Durocher knew would bring more glory, perhaps a World Series victory in the near future.

The third strike that got away from Dodger catcher Mickey Owen in the ninth inning of the 4th World Series game at Ebbets Field in 1941 is shown. It is one of the most dramatic pictures ever taken. Tom Henrich has taken his 3rd strike and missed. Umpire Goetz is giving the out sign. The sign doesn't mean a thing, however, as Henrich got to first and the Yankees went on to win the game.

The Dodger heavy hitters tested their skills in Yankee Stadium prior to the first World Series game in 1941 against the Bronx Bombers. (Left to right) Dolph Camilli, Pete Reiser, Dixie Walker and Joe Medwick.

Leo Durocher with two of his 1941 Brooklyn Dodger stars, (left to right) Dolph Camilli and Billy Herman. Camilli hit 34 home runs and had an average of .285 for the pennant winning Dodgers, while Herman hit .291. Everybody is all smiles as the Dodgers take their first pennant in 21 years.

ed house of 33,476 Dodger fans are jammed into Ebbets Field, May 8, 1942, to watch the opening flag-raising
nies prior to a Dodger-Giant game. Dodger players are lined up at attention while a Navy band plays the National
n. The Dodgers are lined up along the first base line.

John "Spider" Jorgensen played for the Dodgers for 3+ seasons. In 1947, he hit .274 as Billy Cox' predecessor at 3rd base for the Dodgers. The Dodgers obtained Cox from the Pittsburgh Pirates during the 1947 off-season, relegating "Spider" to part-time duty for the next two years. Eventually, the Dodgers traded Jorgensen to the N.Y. Giants.

Bobby Bragan, who went on to manage four different teams—three in the National League and one in the American League, played four years for the Dodgers as a utility player. His best year was 1944 when he hit .267.

Joe Vosmik hit .282 as a semi-regular outfielder for the Dodgers in 1940.

On July 1, 1943 at Ebbets Field, Dixie Walker makes history as he sings a song, "My Buddy" for the War Relief Game.

Dixie Walker's finest year was in 1944 when he hit for a .357 average.

At age 69, Dixie Walker still looks trim as he appeared in 1980 at the Dodgers Old-Timers game in Los Angeles.

Fred "Dixie" Walker
(The People's Choice)

Another season . . . another 1st game . . . another 1st ball being thrown out.

A close game on June 12, 1939 as the Dodgers battled the Reds. Johnny Hudson dashed home from 3rd base on a sacrifice fly. The ball and Hudson arrived at home at the same time. Hudson crashed into home plate and knocked the ball out of Ernie Lombardi's hand. Hudson's heads-up play tallied the winning run for Brooklyn.

Joe DiMaggio (5) seldom responded to any taunts or had harsh words in his lengthy career as a Yankee. But in the 1941 World Series between the Yankees and Dodgers, Joe and Dodger pitcher Whit Wyatt exchanged several verbal non-pleasantries. Finally in the 5th inning, DiMaggio rushed to the mound and attempted to fight Wyatt. Dodger and Yankee players broke up the exchange before any fisticuffs. DiMaggio complained that Wyatt had consistently thrown at his head during the game. Of course, Wyatt denied it was intentional. But angry pushes and shoves were exchanged. The Yankees took game 5, 3-1 as Bonham of the Yanks outpitched Wyatt. The Yankees eventually won the World Series 4 games to 1.

It rained April 11, 1942, in Brooklyn, so the Dodgers exhibition game was called off. Leo Durocher took the opportunity to call his Dodgers together for a brief pep talk in the Dodger dressing room.

The late Charley Dressen, famed actor Robert Wagner, Leo Durocher, and the late Danny Goodman, at one of the Dodger's ever-popular, annual Hollywood All-Star games.

Twenty-two years after he had been appointed playing-manager for the Dodgers in 1939, Leo has been out of baseball for five years. In 1961, he was appointed to assist manager Walt Alston with the Los Angeles Dodgers. Within a week after taking over with the LA Dodgers, Leo is suspended for kicking umpire Jocko Conlan.

Second baseman Eddie Stanky, fiery Dodger second baseman (center) signs his 1947 contract with president Branch Rickey of the Dodgers (R) as manager Leo Durocher (L) looks on. "We'll win it all this year," said Stanky. "Thanks for the raise." Stanky was right...The Dodgers won the pennant in 1947.

5

THE BRANCH RICKEY STORY

1943-1950

It was April 9, 1947. Spring and baseball were in the air all over the nation and with the opening games just a few days away, there was a furor at the Dodger offices on Montague Street in Brooklyn.

President Branch Rickey, Leo Durocher, Branch Jr., traveling Secretary Harold Parrott and three Dodger coaches were discussing the club's roster, trying to come up with a combination that could win the pennant after several disastrous seasons. The Dodgers had not won a pennant since 1941; had come mighty close in 1946, just three games back of the St. Louis Cardinals.

Rickey, a cigar in his teeth, tilted back in his swivel chair and turned to Durocher. "Well, what do you think, Leo?"

Durocher nodded without hesitation. "Bring up Robinson now, Branch. He's ready. He had a great season. He and that big Greek kid, Campanis were the talk of the League. They won the Championship. And Robinson did it. We need him. If we had him last year, the Cardinals wouldn't have come close. It's a helluva situation, but hell...bring him up. He could be the big difference this year."

Branch Rickey had had more training and experience to take over as general manager of the Dodgers than any man in baseball.

Once a ballplayer himself, he had managed the St. Louis Browns and the Cardinals, and during the past twenty years, from 1923-1943, had achieved tremendous stature as vice-president and general manager of the Cardinals. He was the architect of baseball's first farm system. A lawyer, Branch had graduated from the University of Michigan. He was a scholar, a sound businessman and had an almost uncanny knack to judge raw baseball talent. He had taught Larry MacPhail most of the baseball Larry knew, and when Larry went into the Army in 1942, Rickey was the most natural choice of the Directors to take over in 1943.

Now it was 1947 and Rickey, always sensitive to the pulse of the nation in sports, had seen the "color line" begin to waiver. Times were changing. A war had been fought to bring more, rather than less, freedom to the world. Branch wasn't planning a crusade. His interest was in keeping baseball the top American game. There was a situation here that lent itself to his purpose of building a better ball club. Maybe he couldn't help thinking in terms of fairness, but he did not start out with any grand notions of being a great emancipator.

It was a monstrous step Rickey was taking in signing Jackie Robinson and he made the importance of it clear in a long, day-long session with the ball player.

"Remember Jack," he said, "you are doing more than signing a contract to play ball. You are breaking ground for all other youths qualified by skill and ambition to become major league players. If you fail—not through lack of ability, but for any other reason—your failure will have a far-reaching effect. But if you succeed, there will be other Negroes ready to play big league ball."

On October 23, 1945, Branch Rickey, president of the Brooklyn Dodgers, called a press conference at the Dodger's Office for a historic announcement. "The Brooklyn Dodgers", said Rickey, "have signed to a contract with their Montreal club twenty-six year old Jackie Robinson. And if he performs well," said Branch, "he will be brought up to the Dodgers". All Jackie Robinson did that year was to hit .349 to lead all hitters in the International League and inspire his team (the Montreal Royals) all season long to the league championship. On opening day, 1947, Jackie Robinson was promoted to the Brooklyn Dodgers.

1947 was a year to remember in Brooklyn base-ball. There were no Daffy Dodgers in '47, yet it was one of the most tumultuous years in all of baseball.

Leo Durocher was suspended without warning by the baseball commissioner, Happy Chandler, "For conduct detrimental to the game." Burt Shotton was named to manage the Dodgers. Under Shotton's direction the team played a conservative type of game, completely different from the Durocher style, which consisted of a free-wheel-ing, gambling-for-the-big-inning type of baseball. The Dodgers, under Shotton, started to win.

One of the biggest baseball stories of the year (1948) was the day Branch Rickey, President of the Dodgers, announced that Leo Durocher was no longer the Dodger's manager. Leo was switching over to the New York Giants and Burt Shotton would take over the Dodgers. Leo in his new Giant uniform and Shotton pose on July 27, 1948.

Burt Shotton was a pretty fair outfielder for the St. Louis Browns and the Cardinals during a four-teen-year period as a major leaguer. Burt had become Rickey's right hand man in St. Louis, when Branch managed the Cardinals. Shotton managed the Cardinals on Sunday, when Branch absented himself from the ball park. Branch never went near the park on Sunday. Burt managed at Syracuse, then managed the Phillies for six years, then to Rochester and Columbus for Rickey. He was a solid, mature, knowledgeable baseball man and in a short period of time, Shotton had the team moving.

Jackie Robinson put together a 21-game hitting streak and was a flash of brilliance on the base paths. Once he reached first base, Jack was a chal-lenge to every pitcher, as he danced back and forth across the bag, daring a throw, and most often darting to second at the first opportunity. Ralph Branca was a big winner and Dixie Walker, Pete Reiser, Carl Furillo and Robinson hit the ball all season long at around the .300 mark.

It was brilliant baseball and at last on September 22, it was all over. The Dodgers did not play. But the Chicago Cubs beat the Cardinals and the Dodgers backed into the pennant.

BURT SHOTTON MANAGER 1947-1950				
Year	G	W	L	FINISHED
1947	154	93	60	1
1948	79	47	32	5
1949	156	97	57	1
1950	155	89	65	2

The World Series opened at Yankee Stadium and a record crowd of 74,000 fans attended the first game. Ralph Branca was untouchable for four-and-a-half innings and retired the first twelve Yankee batters, but the Yanks broke through Ralph in the fifth inning, scored five runs and that was the ball game. The final was 5 to 3.

In the second game Vic Lombardi faced the Yankee ace, Allie Reynolds, and Reynolds held the Dodgers and struck out 12 to win, going away, 10-3.

There were 33,443 fans at Ebbets Field for the third game, but there are at least half-a-million who claim to have seen this strange, exciting and dramatic game.

There were two out in the last half of the ninth inning as Cookie Lavagetto stepped up as a pinch-hitter for Eddie Stanky. The Yankees were out in front by a 2-1 score and Bill Bevens of the Yanks was but one out away from a no-hit game...the first in Series history.

Shotton had sent in Gionfriddo and Miksis to run for Reiser and Furillo. Both men were walked by Bevens, and now Lavagetto was up. Cookie had been out of the lineup most of the year, sitting on the bench and utilized mainly as a pinch-hitter.

Most of the year he was unhappy, dejected, because he did not play very often.

Now he was up and the crowd was screaming. Cookie had his big bat ready, when Bevens threw his fastball on the outside corner and Cookie slammed the pitch high and far and he could follow the ball as he ran to first. The ball drove into the wall as Tommy Henrich leaped high into the air in right field, but the ball caroomed off the wall and the two Dodgers, Gionfriddo and Miksis, crossed the plate with the tying and winning runs. The Dodgers were swept up by the wildest, craziest, mob of Dodger rooters, trying to get to Lavagetto, Miksis, Robinson—anybody they could lay hands on.

The Dodgers had gotten but one hit...but that was more than enough to win one of the most dramatic games in World Series history, by a 3-2 score.

The fifth game was a normal one for these two teams. Rex Barney pitched well for the Dodgers, but DiMaggio's homer gave the Yankees a 2 to 1 win and an edge in the series with three wins.

In a wild and wooly sixth game the Dodgers finally got to Joe Page and slammed him around for an 8 to 6 win. The star of this game was Al Gionfriddo, a tiny outfielder, who was only five feet five inches tall. But he was tall enough to make one of the unforgettable World Series plays in the sixth inning. Joe DiMaggio with two men on base, rifled a pitch some 415 feet to deep left field. Gionfriddo raced to the fence and caught the ball just as it appeared that the ball would go into the stands. Al's back was to the plate as he made the catch.

In the Series finale, Joe Page limited the struggling Dodgers to one base hit in the final five innings as the Yankees applied the crusher with a 5 to 2 win.

So once more the Dodgers had won a pennant and had been knocked off in the World Series. Yet by winning the flag, they had exceeded all expectations and Shotton proved himself a top-notch manager.

On December 5, 1947, there was a terse announcement to the press, from the offices of the Brooklyn Dodgers.

"The 1947 contract of Leo Durocher has been renewed for 1948 by the Brooklyn Baseball Club—Branch Rickey."

When Durocher's suspension was over, Rickey refused to abandon his principles, even in the face of tremendous pressure and rehired Durocher to manage the team.

Leo found himself in a peculiar position in taking over a Dodger team that had won the pennant in 1947 under Burt Shotton. If the Dodgers won again in 1948, that was to be expected. If they lost, critics would jump all over him, would say he ruined a great ball club.

Jackie Robinson after his "Rookie of the Year" season in '47, reported some twenty-five pounds overweight. Jack had been on the banquet circuit, had played in numerous exhibition games and had a great time all winter. He was slow and puffy and

Phil Rizzuto, Yankee shortstop, puts the tag on the Dodgers' Pete Reiser after Pete tried to steal second base. Play was in the first inning of the 3rd World Series game between the Yankees and the Dodgers in 1947. The umpire is Bill McGowan.

The Dodgers are going crazy at home plate, dancing and jumping for joy as Eddie Miksis slides home with the winning run in the ninth inning of the Fourth Game of the 1947 World Series at Ebbets Field. Reese (1), Al Gionfriddo (30), who scored the tying run ahead of Miksis and Gene Hermanski (left) celebrate the winning run that gave the Dodgers a stunning 3-2 victory and evened the series with the Yankees at two games all. Yogi Berra, the Yankee catcher, is at upper right.

Ralph Branca

Harry "Cookie" Lavagetto

Here is that dramatic smash by Cookie Lavagetto. Cookie is on his way to first as the tying and winning runs come across the plate.

DI MAGGIO   PINELLI   STIRNWEISS   HENRICH   McQUINN   McGOWAN

RIZZUTO   GIONFRIDDO   MIKSIS   PITLER

BEVENS   BERRA

LAVAGETTO

BLADES   GOETZ

Dodger pinch-hitter Cookie Lavagetto is at bat with a count of one strike on him. There are 2 outs. It's the 9th inning of the 4th World Series game between the Dodgers and Yankees in 1947. Bill Bevans of the Yankees is pitching no-hit ball. There are 2 men on base and the Yanks lead, 2-1. Cookie smashes a vicious drive off the right field wall to score Gionfriddo and Eddie Miksis, to give the Dodgers the most dramatic World Series win in the 44-year history of the classic. The 3-2 victory enabled the Dodgers to tie the Yankees at 2 wins each in the Series. Game was played on Oct. 3, 1947 at Ebbets Field.

his game suffered. It was June before Jack was in condition and had taken off all that excess weight and Leo seemed to take Jack's lack of condition as a personal affront and they were cool to each other.

Eddie Stanky had held out for a better contract and was then traded to Boston. There were some bright spots...Roy Campanella hit 13 home runs for St. Paul and was brought up by the Dodgers in mid-May. Duke Snider was impressive in the early weeks and so was another new comer, husky, free-swinging Gil Hodges at first-base, hitting the ball well. They were to form the nucleus for the great Dodger teams to come, along with Pee Wee Reese, Furillo, Billy Cox at third base. Rex Barney, one of the best fast-ball pitchers in baseball, was beginning to find himself and his control problems, at least for the moment, were licked. He now looked like the best pitcher on the staff. But there was something missing as the season started and the team sagged badly. Durocher was not as aggressive, not as decisive as he had been in the past, and the Dodgers lost game after game and by June were floundering in sixth place.

Leo waited for the axe to fall. But Branch Rickey, slow at firing managers, was hoping Leo would resign. Rickey hadn't lost faith in Leo, but the constant carping of the fans and the press had reached the stockholders. Attendance had dropped to an alarming low. Here was a pennant-winning team morassed in second division: A change would have to be made and soon.

Leo was unhappy with the team. So was Rickey. Something was due to happen and soon. One day Horace Stoneham, president of the Giants approached Rickey at the All-Star break and said, "Branch, I'd like your permission to talk to Burt Shotton about a job managing the Giants. I've got to replace Mel Ott."

"No," said Rickey, "I have certain plans for Burt."

"Does that mean that I have your OK to talk to Leo?"

"You have my permission."

On the morning of July 15, league president Ford Frick phoned Rickey and asked him to come to his office that afternoon. Horace Stoneham wanted to work out certain details with him.

Rickey hurried over to the National League offices in Radio City and found the Giant's owner waiting for him.

"Branch, Mel Ott has resigned as manager of the Giants and I'd like to hire Durocher."

Rickey puffed his cigar energetically, "Very well, I'll have him flown back to New York immediately. He's with the team."

The very next day a bewildered and apprehensive Leo Durocher sat alone with Rickey in the Dodgers' Montague Street office.

"Leo, I want to get right to the matter at hand. We need to make a change. I've had some discussions with Horace Stoneham and he asked me if you were available to manage the Giants."

Jackie Robinson signs a new contract for 1949 for $17,500. Top salary in baseball at that time was Bob Feller's $40,000 at Cleveland. At left is Burt Shotton, the Dodger manager. On the right is Branch Rickey, the president of the Dodgers.

"What did you tell him?"

"I told him he has my permission."

"Does that mean that I'm fired?" Leo spat.

"No, it doesn't mean that at all. But it may well be that, Leo. The team is sagging badly. They're not going any place. Besides that, you're in an impossible spot here. With the Giants you will have a new and fresh start. A new challenge that you can respond to. And perhaps a great deal more security."

"That's all I wanted to hear, Branch," Leo said. "I'll call as soon as I get through talking to Stoneham."

It happened just like that. The Dodgers released Durocher from his contract and Leo was the new manager of the Giants. Burt Shotton came out from retirement, once more and took over the Dodgers.

The news of Leo's departure hit like a bombshell. It was front-page news all over the country. But the fans took the switch in stride, after the first shock had hit.

The Dodgers under Shotton seemed to shake off the lethargy and started to play sound baseball. Under Durocher the Dodgers had played .500 ball. They won 36 games and lost 35. Under Burt Shotton, the Dodgers won 48 games and lost 33 and finished in third place behind the Cardinals in second, as the Boston Braves under Billy Southworth won the pennant.

In 1949 Branch Rickey and Burt Shotton fielded a Dodger team that some experts call the finest Dodger team ever assembled. Jackie Robinson was incredible. He more than made up for the mistakes of a year ago. He appeared at Vero Beach in great condition and proceeded to tear the league apart once again. He had the pitchers crazy with his base-stealing antics and as the season neared end, hit .342. The newcomers, Gil Hodges and Duke Snider responded with a slashing home run spree. Gil drove out 23 homers, while Duke hit the same amount, 23. Campanella handled the pitchers beautifully and hit 22 homers. Even Pee Wee Reese broke into the home run circle with 16, and Newcombe with 17 victories, Preacher Roe came in with 15 wins, Branca with 13 and Joe Hatten won 12. And the Dodgers nosed out the Cardinals to take the pennant by a single game.

In the World Series against the Yankees, the Yankees took four of the first five games to once again easily defeat their cross-river rivals 4 games to 1 to win another World Series.

Branch Rickey and one of his boys, Duke Snider (1960).

A GREAT YEAR . . . 1949
THE DODGERS WIN THE PENNANT . . .

Ralph Branca had just beaten the Giants 2-1 at Ebbets Field and Jackie Robinson rushes over to shake big Ralph's hand. It is 1949 and the Dodgers are on their way to a pennant. Branca, who won 21 games in 1947 and 14 in 1948, would win 13 big games in '49. Pee Wee Reese has just congratulated Branca and Billy Cox, the incomparable fielding third baseman of the Dodgers nonchalantly trots into the dugout...

Tommy Henrich has just homered in the 9th inning off Dodger pitcher Don Newcombe, which gave the Yankees a 1-0 victory over the Dodgers in the first game of the 1949 World Series at Yankee Stadium. Carl Furillo walks away dejectedly after the drive landed over the 344-foot wall.

Jackie Robinson heads for home as Gil Hodges is on his way to first base after singling in the second inning of the 2nd game of the 1949 World Series between the Dodgers and the Yankees at Yankee Stadium. Jackie's run is the first run of the game. The Yankee catcher is Charlie Silvera. The umpire is Cal Hubbard. The Dodger 3rd base coach is Milt Stock.

Dodger pitcher Preacher Roe (C) is congratulated by teammates Paul Minner (L) and Ralph Branca after he pitched a 6-hitter to beat the Yankees in the 2nd game of the 1949 World Series at Yankee Stadium.

It's the top of the 9th inning in the 5th game of the 1949 World Series between the Yankees and the Dodgers at Ebbets Field. The field lights are turned on. Phil Rizzuto is at bat. It was the first time in Series history that lights have been used. The Yankees won their 12th World Championship with a 10-6 win over the Dodgers. The game was played on Oct. 9, 1949.

Roy Campanella—one of the greatest catchers ever to play the game. Campanella averaged 24.2 home runs per year for his 10-year career which was cut tragically short by an autombile accident. He was inducted into baseball's Hall of Fame in 1969.

Catchers for the 1949 All-Star game at Yankee Stadium were (from left) the Dodgers' Roy Campanella, the Yankees' Yogi Berra, the Red Sox' Birdie Tebbetts and the Phillies' Andy Seminick.

Walter O'Malley, the late President of the Dodgers.

6

THE O'MALLEY STORY

1950-

Once again, as in the past, the pennant effort of the Dodgers carried to the final day of the 1950 season, but this time they lost. The most traumatic experience of the year came six weeks after the Phillies, Dick Sisler's 10th inning home run destroyed Brooklyn's hope of a second straight championship.

On October 26, at Brooklyn's Hotel Bossert, a group of newspapermen, photographers and radio men gathered early and patiently waited for the bearers of important tidings, entertained by a bartender who busily mixed things from interesting bottles. Walter O'Malley walked into the room looking quite relaxed. After a few moments, Branch Rickey followed. He seemed his usual happy self. Then in came the rest of the Dodgers' directors. Rickey took a seat at the end of the conference table, rapped for attention. Then he rose and smiled.

He stabbed at a biblical quotation for starters.

"Comest thou here," he asked, "to see the reed driven in the wind?"

Getting to specifics, he announced that he (Rickey) had offered his resignation as president of the Brooklyn ball club and that it had been accepted. He said that it was his pleasure to now introduce the new president of the Dodgers, "a man of courage, a youthful man, a man of enterprise, a man you all know, Walter O'Malley."

"I have developed," said O'Malley, "the warmest possible feelings of affection for Mr. Rickey as a man. I do not know of anyone who can approach Mr. Rickey in the realm of executive ability in baseball. I'm terribly sorry and hurt personally that we now have to face this resignation."

The legend goes that Brooklyn is a place where anything could happen and Ebbets Field is where it usually did. It is a durable piece of folklore, accepted without reserve by those sympathetic to baseball. That is why the elevation of Walter O'Malley to the presidency of the Dodgers seemed too incongruous a move when it happened in October 1950, after the Dodgers had blown the pennant.

O'Malley was a man, who for twenty five years had been a very successful engineer, an attorney with a huge practice and a Tammany politician. He was a man with a fabulous business background. Besides owning 37 percent of the Dodgers, at that time O'Malley also was sole owner of the New York Subway Advertising Company, worth about $7 million, was co-owner of J.P. Duffy & Company, a $5 million outfit making building supply materials, was one of a syndicate of seven which owned the Brooklyn Borough Gas Company, a $7-1/2 million public company, owned 6 percent of the Long Island Railroad, was half-owner of a $200,000 building block company in Port Jefferson, Long Island and was a director of several banks and corporations.

The 1950 Dodgers. Manager Burt Shotton is shown wearing a Dodger jacket (2nd row from the bottom, sixth man from the left). On September 19 the Dodgers trailed the Phillies "Whiz Kids" by nine games. By Oct. 1 the two clubs were playing a game that would give the Brooks a tie for first place, if the Dodgers won. The game went into the 10th inning tied 1-1. The Phillies' Dick Sisler slammed a drive with two men on to win the extra-inning game 4-1 to end the season for the valiant Dodgers as the Whiz Kids took the pennant.

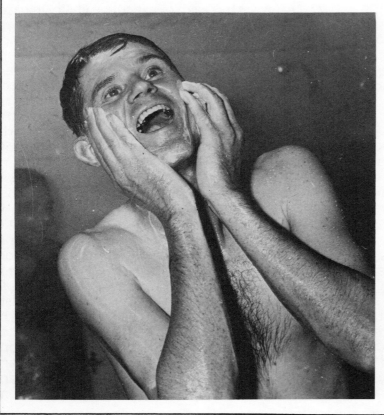

Elwin (Preacher) Roe had his greatest season in 1951 when he recorded a 22-3 mark and was named the finest pitcher in the National League by The Sporting News. In 1950 Preacher was the best pitcher on the Dodgers squad with a 19-11 mark. Roe began his big-league career with the Pirates in 1944 and was traded to the Dodgers in 1948 where he remained until 1954. Preacher was showering in the Dodgers clubhouse when he was informed that he was selected as the top pitcher of 1951.

CHARLIE DRESSEN				
Named Manager (1951-1953)				
Year	G	W	L	FINISHED
1951	158	97	60	2
1952	155	96	57	1
1953	155	105	49	1

Taking control of the Dodgers, O'Malley immediately installed his people within the Dodger organization. Buzzie Bavasi and Fresco Thompson who had been in the Dodger organization for a number of years, were installed as Vice Presidents, and Charlie Dressen was named to replace Burt Shotton as manager of the Dodgers.

Charlie was born and brought up in Decatur, Illinois, and in the 1920's was an outstanding athlete. Charlie was a fast, shifty and aggressive quarterback of the old Decatur Staleys, one of the pioneer pro football clubs and on several occasions tangled on the gridiron with the fabulous Jim Throp.

Charlie was a third baseman for the Cincinnati Reds for several years; he was one of those great infielders with a "good field, no hit," label, but he was one of the most aggressive players ever to suit up.

Prior to the start of the 1951 season, Charlie Dressen, one of the sharpest baseball men in the game, was named to manage the Dodgers. Here he is with his ace pitcher Don Newcombe, who won 20 games while losing but 9. The manager and his pitcher are wishing each other good luck with a wishbone and a horseshoe.

Charlie then turned his skills to managing and became manager of the Nashville team in the Southern Association. He was with the Giants briefly, then managed the Reds and became a Dodger coach, when Larry MacPhail took over as president.

Dressen and the Dodgers got off to a horrible start in 1951. That is to say, it was horrible after August 12. Until then, the Dodgers had a comfortable 13-1/2 game lead over the Giants.

Jackie Robinson, playing as if possessed by the devil, was incredible. He could not be stopped, either at bat or on the base paths. He hit for a .338 average and once he was on base, he would be off and running on the very first pitch. On bloop singles, Jackie usually would wind up at third base. Once there he was a constant threat to steal home. Along with Jackie's marvelous play, Gil Hodges, the strong man, clubbed 40 home runs. Roy Campanella, caught up in the mad dash for the pennant, played as if he was on fire. Campy slugged the ball for 33 homers and a batting average of .325. The Duke was not idle, either. Snider patrolled center-field like the All-Star he had become, and slammed out 29 home runs; Andy Pafko hit 18 homers, Furillo drove out 16. Don Newcombe was one of the league's top pitchers with 20 wins against 9 losses. Roe won 22 games, and Erskine came in with 16, King won 14 and Ralph Branca won 13.

But all of a sudden Dodger bats were silent; the pitchers were losing hard-fought, close games and the big lead dwindled down, down, down until at the end of the regular season the Giants, who were playing miraculous baseball under Leo Durocher, tied the Dodgers for the lead.

In the playoff series, both teams won a game. In the third and deciding game, the Dodgers led, 4-2, in the ninth inning. But with one run in and one out for the Giants, Bobby Thomson slugged one of Ralph Branca's fast balls into the stands in the Polo Grounds and the Giants won the pennant.

Dressen and the Dodgers had the satisfaction of winning pennants in both 1952 and 1953, but it was the same old story in both World Series—too much Yankees. Carl Erskine, who had pitched a non-hitter in 1952 and repeated in 1956, set a Series record by fanning 14 Yankees.

Spring practice called on account of rain, as Roy Campanella (C) holds a huge umbrella for some of his Dodger teammates in 1951 at Vero Beach, Florida.

Dodger first baseman Gil Hodges has just homered in a game at Ebbets Field and blows a kiss to his wife as he crosses the plate.

Jackie Robinson has just slammed a game-winning home run in the 14th inning against the Phillies. In the dressing room, Manager Charlie Dressen grabs Jackie's hands to congratulate him. The game was played in Shibe Park, Philadelphia, Sept. 30, 1951.

The Polo Grounds in New York were jammed with fans as they watched one of those dramatic Giant-Dodger games in 1951.

In the 1951 combination of Newcombe pitching and Campanella catching for the Dodgers was enough to worry any National League manager. Big Don had a marvelous year, winning 20 games, while losing only nine. For Campy, it was a great year. He slugged 33 home runs and hit for his best average in the major leagues, .325.

The scene shifts from Brooklyn and Ebbets Field to Los Angeles. It is 1981 and Campanella, after a terrible auto accident in 1957, has been confined to a wheelchair. Don Newcombe, having conquered an acute case of alcoholism, works as a Community Development Director with the Los Angeles Dodgers . . .

Carl Daniel Erskine was better known as "Oisk" in Brooklyn Dodger circles. He came up to the Dodgers in 1948 and by 1951 was one of the mainstays of the pitching staff. The likeable "Oisk" won 20 games in 1953 while losing only 6. Erskine continued to pitch outstanding ball for the Dodgers until 1956, when his arm began to trouble him. Carl was 13 and 11 in 1956, but tailed off in 1957 and won but 5 games. In 1952 Erskine pitched a no-hitter against the Cubs and repeated with another no-hit game against the hated Dodger rivals—the Giants, on May, 1956. When the Dodgers moved to Los Angeles in 1958, "Oisk" went west with the club and won 4 games for the LA Dodgers. In 1959 Carl voluntarily retired from the game. He won a total of 122 games for the Dodgers during a 12 year career and appeared in five World Series.

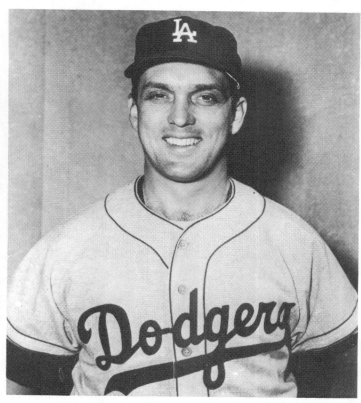

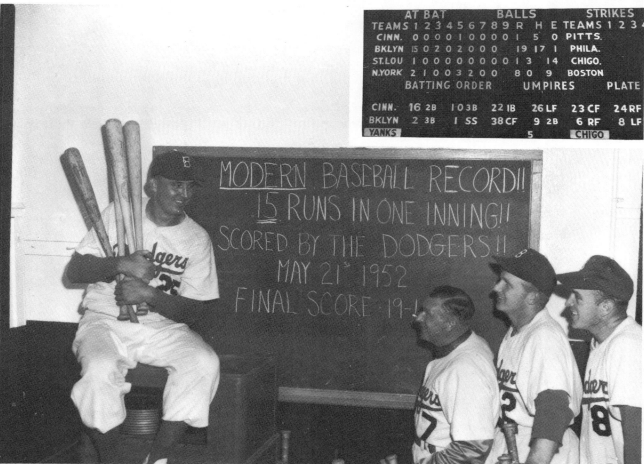

The May 21, 1952 Dodger scoreboard tells the story. The Dodgers scored 15 runs in the first inning against the Reds. Chris Van Cuyk, the Dodger pitcher, got 4 hits in 5 trips to the plate. Manager Chuck Dressen, Bob Morgan and George Shuba gaze at Chris and his 4 bats while the scoreboard tells the story of the Dodger hitting massacre.

Dodger shortstop Pee Wee Reese and Dodger manager Chuck Dressen (behind Reese) got together with National League President Warren Giles and Reese's National League teammates for the 1952 All-Star game (from the left: Murry Dickson, Enos Slaughter, Curt Simmons and Robin Roberts).

The Dressen-Dodger Mascot "Bonnie" in 1952.

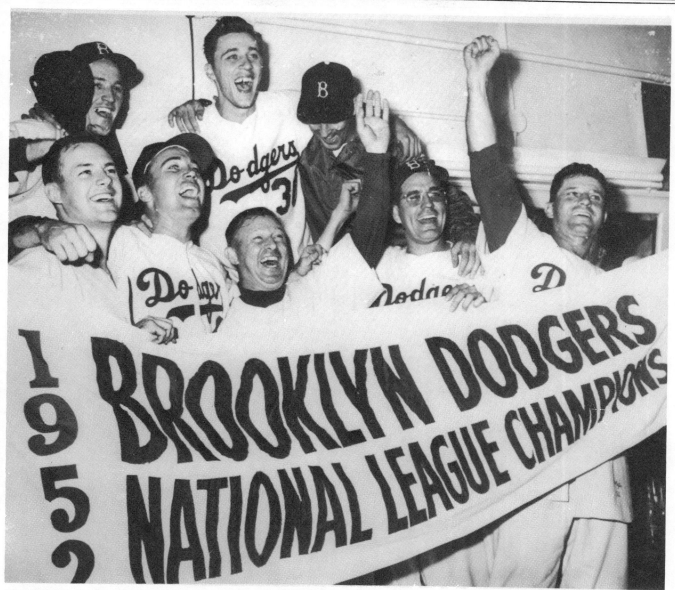

The 1952 Dodgers easily won the National League pennant over the Giants by 6-1/2 games and then came within a game of defeating the Yankees in the World Series. Here are the delirious Dodgers celebrating after winning the pennant. Manager Chuck Dressen (center) leads his happy Dodgers in a rip-roaring celebration.

Prior to Game 1 of the 1952 World Series, Dodger manager Chuck Dressen shakes hands with Yankee skipper Casey Stengel.

AP/World Wide Photos

Billy Loe's first pitch of the sixth game of the 1952 World Series was called a ball by umpire Art Passarella. The hitter—the Yankees' Gil McDougald—proceeded to ground out to third. The Dodgers' catcher is Roy Campanella.

THREE GREAT DODGER CATCHES...
BUT THE YANKEES WIN THE
1952 WORLD SERIES; 4 GAMES TO 3

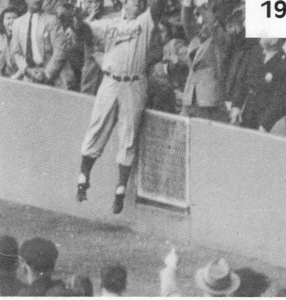

At Ebbets Field, Brooklyn. In the second inning of the fifth game of the 1952 World Series, Andy Pafko makes a great leap and steals a home run off the bat of the Yankees' Gene Woodling.

Duke Snider comes up with one of the most sensational catches ever in the 4th inning of the 4th game of the 1952 Dodger-Yankee World Series. Duke makes a leaping grab of a 400-foot drive off Yogi Berra's bat. In the photos on the left and in the center Duke leaps high to grab the ball in front of the scoreboard. In the right photo, Carl Furillo runs up as Snider tumbles. The Yankees won the game, however, 2-0.

Carl Furillo leaps high into the air in front of right field stands to snare a tremendous drive by Johnny Mize in the 11th inning of the 5th World Series game at Yankee Stadium, Oct. 5, 1952. Mize's drive would have tied the score at 6-6. Dodgers won the game, 6-5. In the foreground is Duke Snider, Number 4.

Carl Erskine pitches to Yankee pinch-hitter Don Bollweg in the ninth inning of the third game of the World Series at Ebbetts Field, Oct. 3, 1953. Erskine struck out Bollweg and also fanned the next hitter, Hall-of-Famer Johnny Mize, to set a new strikeout record of 14 in a World Series.

AP/World Wide Photos

Dodgers' second baseman Billy Cox bounds high over sliding Granny Hamner of the Phillies in the second inning of the game on July 3, 1954, as Cox gets off a throw to first baseman Gil Hodges in an attempt to complete the double play. At left Dodgers' shortstop, Don Zimmer, yells encouragement.

Having won two pennants in a row, Dressen, hoping to emulate Durocher, asked Walter O'Malley for a two-year contract. O'Malley offered him the usual one-year deal. Mrs. Dressen got into the act by sending O'Malley a letter that fairly sizzled. It annoyed the hell out of O'Malley and Dressen was released. Then O'Malley brought in Walter Alston as the new manager.

Alston had to settle for second place in 1954, but made Dodger history in 1955, when the Dodgers romped home by 20 games over the Milwaukee Braves to win the National League flag.

In the 1955 World Series, the Dodgers came from behind to defeat the New York Yankees four games to three to win their first World Series in Dodger history after seven failures to win the flag—the last five at the hands of the Yankees.

In his new job as president of the Dodgers, O'Malley moved quickly and ruthlessly when he was under pressure. He could, however, be fair and lovable, under the proper conditions. Alston was not O'Malley's choice to manage the Dodgers in 1954. His two Vice Presidents, Buzzy Bavasi and Fresco Thompson, and scouts Andy High and John Corriden were all in favor of Alston. O'Malley had another man in mind but he went along with the majority. Then he spoke to Alston.

"I want you to feel," he said to the new Dodger manager, "that the job is yours as long as you are happy with it and we are happy with you. There will be no one looking over your shoulder while you are doing your job. This is no interim job. No Brooklyn manager was ever fired by us for losing."

This formula of sweetness paid off for the Dodgers after O'Malley took over the club in 1950. It paid off at the box office where the per capita paid at the gate rose from $1.07 in 1950 to $1.29 in 1954 without any increase in ticket prices. It also paid off in those first few years in player-fan-management relations.

How did O'Malley do it? Harold Parrot, the team's business manager at the time said, "Walter wrapped up the Dodger rooters and their heroes in one emotional sandwich."

Walter O'Malley was 47 when he became president of the Dodgers, and from the very first day, he exhibited a determination to make the franchise richer than it had ever been before. Initially he sought to improve Ebbets Field, originally built for 18,000 fans, and enlarged it so that in 1950 32,000 fans would be accommodated.

O'Malley commissioned Norman Bel Geddes, a famous architect, to draw up plans for a great new modern stadium in Brooklyn, but finally concluded that the expense would far outweigh the gain. The chief problem was that Ebbets Field occupied an entire city block. There was no way to enlarge the quarters. There were also few facilities for parking.

O'Malley suggested he would locate a new park at and around the Atlantic Avenue depot of the Long Island Railroad. That was and still is a lamentably depressed area. The city fathers either would not or could not act upon his suggestion.

Just when the idea dawned that Walter might move the Dodgers to another city is not known. It may have even preceeded 1953, when the Boston Braves moved to Milwaukee and achieved spectacular success. Perhaps it was then that O'Malley began to look about for a brighter tomorrow for his Dodgers.

He sold the ground beneath Ebbets Field to a real estate operator who announced he would erect an apartment building "when the Dodgers obtained a new park."

In 1956 O'Malley got the league's permission to transfer 10 home games to the unused International League Park in Jersey City. And now the signs were plain to read, but New York's City Hall found it more expedient to sidestep the problem. The city fathers' official reaction was that O'Malley was bluffing.

O'Malley was the first official in baseball to realize that the imminent emergence of jet air travel from coast to coast would bring California into the orbit of the major leagues. And with part of the proceeds of the land sales in Brooklyn, he persuaded Phil Wrigley to sell his Pacific Coast League park in Los Angeles.

Now the direction of O'Malley's thrust was obvious. Within days Mayor Norris Poulson of Los Angeles and a large party of important Angelenos arrived at the Vero Beach spring training base to begin planning O'Malley's deal for the old Spanish land grant called Chavez Ravine in exchange for Wrigley Field in Los Angeles. The next move was to point out to the mayor of San Francisco what a coup he could score by bringing the Giants from New York, thus transferring one of baseball's great natural rivalries of the Giants and Dodgers to California.

San Francisco officials had little trouble convincing Horace Stoneham that he might starve if he stayed behind in New York after the Dodgers left. At a special meeting in May, 1957 the National League voted to approve the relocation of the Dodgers and Giants, that is if the two clubs requested "permission" to move to Los Angeles and San Francisco respectively.

Throughout the summer the Dodgers maintained the pretense of holding out hope that Brooklyn might still save its ball club, presumably by filling Ebbets Field for every home game. "My roots are in Brooklyn," said O'Malley. Roots or no roots, if the final papers had not actually been signed, the arrangements to move had been agreed upon.

Fewer than seven thousand customers were on hand the night of September 24, when the last game was played at Ebbets Field. Danny McDevitt shut out Pittsburgh 2-0. Gladys Gooding, their very talented organist, played nothing but old sentimental songs, ending with "Auld Lang Syne." And the Dodgers were gone from Brooklyn.

Ebbets Field

**CALIFORNIA
HERE
WE
COME**

The Dodgers come to Los Angeles on horseback, led by Walter O'Malley.

Chavez Ravine
O'Malley Builds A Ball Park

The baseball tree that grew in Brooklyn is now flourishing in Los Angeles, but chances are that if Walter O'Malley had known, when he drafted the territory, how much legal spadework remained before he could turn a shovel of dirt in Chavez Ravine, he might have thought twice.

After the Dodgers announced their westward move on October 8, 1957, President O'Malley jokingly telegraphed Mayor Norris Poulson:

"Get your wheelbarrow and shovel. I'll meet you at Chavez Ravine."

Only the day before, the Los Angeles City Council had voted, ten to four, approving its contract with the Dodger baseball club.

It was not until September of 1959 that O'Malley and Mayor Poulson finally met in Chavez Ravine for groundbreaking ceremonies. And it was not until October 19, 1959, when the United States Supreme Court upheld the validity of the contract, that the final obstacle was cleared. In those two years there had been a favorable public referendum; an adverse superior court decision; two reversing actions by the State Supreme Court; a challenging state legislative bill which Governor Pat Brown vetoed; and an eviction incident which attracted nation-wide attention.

Chavez Ravine was an arid, hilly expanse of more than three hundred acres of real estate—most of it not on the tax rolls—that city authorities had with futility tried to put to use for many years.

Except for a few ramshackle dwellings, the land was occupied by jack rabbits, gophers, possums and skunks. Its seldom-used roads and trails were littered with tin cans. In 1938 plans were made to hold a world's fair there, but the war stopped that. Then the Federal Housing Authority took over and proposed to build $33,000,000 worth of apartments in the area. By 1951, after most of the land owners had been bought out and the church and a school had been abandoned, it became apparent the need for a low-rent housing area no longer existed.

It was then that Los Angeles bought the property with an eye toward increasing its park and playground areas; but the funds were not readily available, and nothing was done about it.

Even before this time, newspaper writers and other public-spirited citizens were beating the drums for major league baseball in Los Angeles. In fact, there is a possibility that the St. Louis Browns, dying of attendance anemia, might have come to Los Angeles, but just as the owners were about to ask permission of the American League, Pearl Harbor was bombed. That was in 1941.

Halfhearted attempts were made to get the Browns' franchise, which went to Baltimore, and get the Philadelphia Athletics, which went to Kansas City. "Los Angeles didn't put its money where its mouth was," said the late Del Webb, a local resident and former co-owner of the Yankees, about the St. Louis deal. "We were led to the altar only to be jilted," said Mayor Poulson when Kansas City got the Athletics. That was in 1954. Bill Veeck had been here the year before, trying to make a deal for the Browns. The next year P. K. Wrigley of the Chicago Cubs hired him to come to Los Angeles and spearhead a move for major league baseball.

In 1955 a $4,500,000 bond issue to erect a park for major league baseball failed. Veeck and Wrigley apparently had given up and now Calvin Griffith of the Washington Senators was sending feelers west. This was in 1956.

It was in April of that year that Governor Harriman of New York signed legislation authorizing the mayor of New York to appoint a three-man authority to study the problem of property condemnation and the issuance of up to $30,000,000 in bonds for a new Brooklyn ball park. Mayor Robert F. Wagner of New York named a special committee and set aside $25,000 for its study. O'Malley was quoted at the time as protesting that this was not enough.

Los Angeles officialdom perked up its ears when, on February 1, 1957, Wrigley announced he had sold the Los Angeles franchise in the Pacific Coast League and Wrigley Field in Los Angeles to the Dodgers for $2,500,000.

Mayor Poulson and Kenneth Hahn, member of the Los Angeles County Board of Supervisors, along with President John Gibson of the city council and half a dozen others, organized an official junket to Vero Beach to meet O'Malley at the Dodgers' spring training camp. What they promised the Dodgers never became public, but it is apparent they proposed the sale of Chavez Ravine and the erection of a ball park. After their meeting, Poulson and Hahn triumphantly announced, "We've got the Dodgers!"

New York writers at Vero Beach with the ball club began to express fear that this might be true. Some even pressed the panic button.

O'Malley played it straight. He wouldn't say "yes" and he wouldn't say "no." "My roots are in Brooklyn," he kept insisting.

In the meantime San Francisco started making its big pitch for the New York Giants. It already had passed a $4,500,000 bond issue to build a ball park.

Then came a period of much talk and no action. New York apparently didn't take the Giant threat seriously; its city park commission made a weak offer of a seventy-eight-acre tract in Queens for the Dodgers; and Los Angeles politicians seemed content to just take bows.

O'Malley arrived in Los Angeles on May 1 to inspect his Pacific Coast League holdings. Inevitably, he talked again with city and county officials but nothing was announced. Two weeks later Abe Stark, president of the New York City Council, charged the mayors of Los Angeles and San Francisco with "organized piracy."

"I resent strongly," he said, "the organized piracy of the mayors of Los Angeles and San Francisco in attempting to take business away from New York. It is an unsportsmanlike attack."

More than a straw in the wind was the announcement from Chicago on May 27 that the club presidents of the National League had granted permission to the Dodgers and Giants to draft the Los Angeles and San Francisco territories of the Pacific Coast League. Ten days before, the New York City Council had suggested it might enlarge Ebbets Field to 50,000. O'Malley, who had been fighting for the property at Atlantic and Flatbush avenues, said to that proposal: "President Stark continues to add confusion to what would have been a simple solution had he shown some initial support."

It was not until late in July of 1957 that Los Angeles took a positive official step. The city council appointed Harold C. (Chad) McClellan, a local paint manufacturer, to negotiate with O'Malley.

McClellan had no particular sports background. A former president of the National Association of Manufacturers, he had made an impressive name for himself in Washington circles as assistant secretary of commerce for international affairs, a post he had left on July 1.

McClellan went to work immediately. After discussing legal problems with Roger Arnebergh, the city attorney, and Samuel Leask, Jr., the city administrative officer, he started planning a contract with Dodger officials. Then, in mid-August, the Giants announced they were moving to San Francisco.

With the Giants now lost, the panic in New York was great. Two prominent industrialists, Sinclair Robinson and Louis Wolfson, among others, offered to buy the Dodgers to keep them in New York City. The New York Board of Estimate met in mid-September to again study O'Malley's request for the land at Atlantic and Flatbush Avenues. Even Nelson Rockefeller, later to become governor of New York, stepped into the picture. He came up with an offer of financial aid to raze the existing structures at the site: let the Dodgers use the property rent free for twenty years while building and operating a new stadium there.

"We want to make Angels of the Bums," was Mayor Poulson's reaction in Los Angeles, "but we can't play Santa Claus like some of the big names."

On September 16, the Los Angeles City Council, spurred on by the revived New York City action, voted a resolution to accept McClellan's document as a basis of final contractual negotiation with the Dodgers. The passage wasn't unanimous, as had been expected. Certain councilmen already were talking about the Chavez Ravine deal as a "giveaway."

Two days later O'Malley met with Rockefeller and Major Wagner. He gave definite indication of not being satisfied but said he was willing to give New York a little more time. But time was running out for O'Malley, New York and Los Angeles. The National League deadline for drafting the Los Angeles territory was October 1.

Governor Harriman of New York apparently felt it necessary to say something at this time. He predicted that the Los Angeles smog would prevent the Dodgers from playing many night games there!

In Los Angeles, a series of long and tumultuous city council sessions followed the presentation of McClellan's contract. In essence, Los Angeles proposed to cede upward of 300 acres in Chavez Ravine to the Dodgers and spend up to $2,000,000 in grading, street construction, and other improvements. The L.A. County Board of Supervisors had promised to provide $2,740,000 for access roads into the hilly area.

The Dodgers were to deed Wrigley Field, value estimated at around four million dollars, to the city. They also promised to set aside forty acres in Chavez Ravine for their youth program, spend half a million dollars on facilities and improvements; and maintain it for twenty years at an annual cost of sixty thousand dollars with the city parks and playground commission controlling activities.

The city was to reserve half the mineral rights. The other half, if oil were found on the property, would go into a trust fund jointly controlled by the ball club and the city, and specifically earmarked for recreational facilities to promote the youth program of the Dodgers.

In addition, the Dodgers would agree to construct a modern baseball stadium that would seat at least fifty thousand.

Opposition immediately began to solidify. Those leading the fight against the contract charged too much property was involved. Engineers testified that the hilly terrain called for a loss of more than a third of the acreage in terracing for the ball park and parking lots.

Another battle was waged around the oil rights. The opponents shouted that the land was rich in mineral content. The defenders countered this with reports that major oil companies already had run surveys and ruled this out.

(As a matter of record, two years later when the city opened the land for oil bids, not one was forthcoming. This prompted Councilman Charles Navarro to remark facetiously, "And I had been led to believe there was a billion dollars' worth of oil there.")

After a particularly long and bitter council meeting on September 30 for the first public reading of the contract, Mayor Poulson wired O'Malley his promise that he had the necessary minimum of ten votes to pass the enabling ordinance. Apparently not completely satisfied, the National League voted to extend the deadline to October 15 for the drafting of the Los Angeles territory. The mayor's prophecy came true seven days later when the council voted ten to four in favor of the ordinance. O'Malley turned down the last New York proposals and announced on October 8, 1957, that he would move the club: "In view of the action of the Los Angeles City Council yesterday, and in accordance with the resolution of the National League made October 1, the stockholders and directors of the Brooklyn Baseball Club have met today and unanimously agreed that the necessary steps be taken to draft the Los Angeles territory."

On receipt of the telegram Major Poulson signed the ordinance.

This set off a bitter chain reaction that spanned the nation. In New York the press attacked both O'Malley and New York City officials from Mayor Wagner on down. In Los Angeles the opposition immediately put into motion the machinery to start the circulation of petitions calling for a referendum.

Undismayed, the Dodgers set up offices in Wrigley Field. By October 24, they announced applications for box and reserved seats. The response was so great that it became immediately apparent that Wrigley Field, with a capacity of twenty-two thousand, could not handle the crowds. As for Chavez Ravine, the mounting legal delaying actions made it equally obvious a ball park could not be erected there in time.

President O'Malley was greeted with a huge outpouring of civic officials and new-found Dodger fans when he landed at the Los Angeles International Airport a few days later. A great civic luncheon was held on October 28. O'Malley's charm captivated the more than a thousand who were lucky enough to purchase tickets. When he stood up to speak, the throng arose to cheer him. After it had quieted, the Dodger president said: "The next time you will be asked to stand will be when your own Duke Snider hits a home run for your Dodgers here."

O'Malley promised to visit the city council and thank "those honest gentlemen who have opposed me," as well as the others. He did, but apparently his salesmanship was lost on "the honest gentlemen" who opposed him.

O'Malley was undaunted. He went looking for a temporary site for the ball club. His engineers visited Pasadena's Rose Bowl and took measurements. He talked to Pasadena officials. He and his men studied Memorial Coliseum with its inviting expanse of over 90,000 available seats. In the end, it was decided the Coliseum was more suitable, despite a short 251-foot left field foul line. It took weeks to arrive at a contract with the Coliseum's commission.

While O'Malley was commuting between Los Angeles and Brooklyn, winding up affairs there and organizing in California, the Chavez Ravine opponents made hay. They got the necessary signatures to put the question to a vote. Fear mounted that the city might reject the council's ordinance, but O'Malley refused to enter the fight.

The Dodger baseball team went to Vero Beach for training, opened the season in defeat at San Francisco, and came to Los Angeles April 18.

The first of many new attendance records for major league baseball was set that day when 78,672, the largest crowd ever to witness an opener, came to see the Los Angeles Dodgers. The team gave them something to cheer about with a 6-5 victory.

Mayor Norris Poulson pitching to San Francisco Mayor George Christopher at the opening game in Los Angeles.

Thousands of Angelinos welcome the Dodgers to Los Angeles in ceremonies at City Hall. Dodger players enjoying the City Hall reception include: (11) Dick Gray, (7) Coach Chuck Dressen, (10) Al Walker, (9) Gino Cimoli, (2) Randy Jackson, and (26) Fred Kipp.

Sports writers from every New York newspaper and many from other parts of the land crowded the press box. Mostly they denounced the Coliseum as a playing site, and many took their best verbal shots at O'Malley for selecting it.

While the crowds kept coming, the Dodgers were proving to be far from artistic on the playing field. On the day that Los Angeles voted in favor of the ordinance, the team returned from a sad road trip and dropped an 8-3 game to Cincinnati. The Dodgers were now ten games back of the leader, deep in the cellar. This was June 3, 1958. The balloting had been 351,683 for and 325,878 against. Although the margin was comfortable (nine of the city's fifteen districts had voted in favor), the fight for Chavez Ravine had only begun.

Several taxpayer suits already had been filed. These were heard before Superior Judge Arnold Praeger. At approximately the same time O'Malley's engineer, Captain Emil Praeger of New York, was running surveys on Chavez Ravine.

It came as a blow to O'Malley and also Dodger proponents when Judge Praeger ruled the contract was invalid on three counts. That necessitated carrying the case to the State Supreme Court. Captain Praeger went back to New York.

Not until January 13, 1959, did the higher court act. Chief Justice Phil S. Gibson announced it had ruled affirmatively on the constitutionality of the city's contract. The score was a shutout, 7-0, among the voting judges.

Opposition attorneys appealed. The Dodgers were in their second season when, on April 21, 1959, they won their second legal shutout, and by the same score. On June 3 the City of Los Angeles and the Dodger baseball club formally signed the contract, although the opposition had not yet given up.

Attorneys for the suing taxpayers bundled up thirty pounds of legal documents and went to Washington to press their suits with the United States Supreme Court. In the meantime, Governor

In the first game ever played by the Los Angeles Dodgers, the Dodgers defeated their hated rivals, the Giants of San Francisco, by a 6-5 score as more than 78,000 fans jammed the Coliseum. No. 1, Pee Wee Reese, Captain of the Dodgers, is selecting his bat before going up to the plate to hit. There are literally dozens of Hollywood's most famous screen and TV stars at the star-studded opener. In the upper right portion of the photo in his shirt sleeves is the popular actor Edward G. Robinson, a great baseball fan.

Brown squashed legislative opposition by vetoing an assembly bill that charged the City of Los Angeles with "damage to urban development" by its contract.

The end came on October 19, 1959, when the United States Supreme Court dismissed the appeals against the contract. By that time Dodger officials had drawn up a plan of development. Bulldozers had been tearing away at "O'Malley hill" and the two million cubic yards of earth that had to be moved. The plan presented to the city council called for such interesting items as a car wash, auto service center and other commercial enterprises that had nothing to do with baseball. Another row resulted, Dodger officials were ordered to eradicate these before they came back. They did, and on November 5, 1959, the council voted nine to five to approve parking and commercial zoning.

While the legal mills were grinding slowly in favor of the Dodger occupancy of Chavez Ravine, a disconcerting incident occurred in the very heart of it. Away back in 1951, when the land still was being considered as a federal housing project, the family of Manuel Arechigas had started a fight against eviction. The contention at the time was that its property was worth more than the $10,500 approved by the court. The Arechigas had lived there unmolested and without paying taxes from

that time to May 8, 1959, when Captain Joe Brady of the Los Angeles sheriff's office and a group of deputies descended with storage van and bulldozer to make them comply with the law. The melee that followed was spread across the land by scores of photographers, writers, newscasters and TV cameramen. Mrs. Aurora Vargas, a thirty-eight-year-old daughter, was carried away kicking and screaming. Children wailed hysterically. Mrs. Victoria Augustian struggled fiercely in the grasp of deputies. Mrs. Avrana Arechigas, the seventy-two-year-old matriarch, hurled stones at the officers. For several days public sympathy mounted. The Arechigas came back to live in a tent supplied by friends, and a trailer company lent them the use of one of its best.

Then the bottom dropped out of the sob story. A reporter from the **Los Angeles Mirror** ran down the fact that the Arechigas were not being dispossessed from their only property. They owned eleven other dwellings in the city, valued at around seventy-five thousand dollars.

After that the last occupants of Chavez Ravine submitted to the writ of possession and stole quietly away. Chavez Ravine had earned its rightful place among the many daffy chapters in the amazing history of the Dodgers.

There were a number of influential people who helped Walter O'Malley bring the Dodgers to Los Angeles in 1958. Mayor Norris Poulson was one, so was famous comedian Joe E. Brown. No one was more vocal in the Dodger's behalf than an ex-sports announcer for the Chicago Cubs. He had been a leading Hollywood star, and at that time was a spokesman for the General Electric Company—Ronald Reagan. By 1969 President Reagan was Governor of California, but still found the time to see his favorite Dodgers play. Here the then Governor and his wife Nancy applaud as they watch the Dodgers defeat the N.Y. Mets 1-0 in a sensational game at Dodger Stadium.

Greeting Dodger President Walter O'Malley.

Welcome signs were up all over Los Angeles.

Chamber of Commerce and LA Booster signs welcoming the Dodgers were all over town.

Storefront help.

The merchants went all out to welcome the Dodgers. And it seemed that every store had a good luck sign.

Chavez Ravine, now the home of the Los Angeles Dodgers, is one of the most beautiful ball parks in the nation. It seats more than 55,000 fans, in the most comfortable setting ever seen. But in 1959, Chavez Ravine was an arid, hilly expanse of some 300 acres with some ramshackle dwellings, skunks, jackrabbits, gophers occupying the land. On June 3, 1959 after the City of Los Angeles and the Dodgers had agreed on a contract that would cede Chavez Ravine to the Dodgers, the bulldozers began tearing away at the two million yards of earth that had to be moved. On September, 1959, O'Malley and Mayor Poulson of Los Angeles broke ground for Dodger Stadium.

Dodger Stadium
A View from Center Field

*Dodger Stadium
A view from left field.*

The Dodgers and Giants in action at the Coliseum, 1958.

The late Walter O'Malley and his wife.

Dodger President Peter O'Malley.

Manager Walter Alston
Brooklyn Dodgers 1954-1957
Los Angeles Dodgers 1958-1967

	Year	G	W	L	FINISHED	Year	G	W	L	FINISHED
Brooklyn	1954	154	92	62	2	1968	162	76	86	7
	1955	154	98	55	1	1969	162	85	77	4
	1956	154	93	61	1	1970	161	87	74	2
	1957	154	84	70	3	1971	162	89	73	2
Los Angeles	1958	154	71	83	7	1972	155	85	70	3
	1959	156	88	68	1	1973	161	95	66	2
	1960	154	82	72	4	1974	162	102	60	1
	1961	154	89	65	2	1975	162	88	74	2
	1962	165	102	63	2	1976	158	90	68	2
	1963	163	99	63	1					
	1964	164	80	82	6					
	1965	162	97	65	1					
	1966	162	95	67	1					
	1967	162	73	89	8					

7

THE WALTER ALSTON ERA

1954-1976

When the Dodgers' President Walter O'Malley introduced Walter Alston as the new manager of the Brooklyn Dodgers, on November 24, 1953, at a hastily called press conference at the Dodgers' offices on Montague Street, one of the sports pages of a leading newspaper read: "Walter Who?"

That was the initial reaction when the one-time college science professor and Ohio farmer, a man who batted just once in the big leagues—and struck out—succeeded street-wise Charlie Dressen as the Dodger manager.

On September 27, 1976, the 64-year-old Alston, Dodgers' manager for 23 years and the only pilot to direct the club in its entire Los Angeles existence, announced that he had been at the job long enough and now it was time for him to step down in favor of a younger man.

Walter O'Malley, chairman of the board of the Dodgers and the man who hired Alston and kept him on as manager for 23 seasons, was at the side of his manager.

"This is not a very happy moment for me," said O'Malley. "All of the Dodgers' greatest victories have come with this man as the manager. I had the privilege of signing Walter 23 years ago and when I think of all the managers who have come and gone throughout the major leagues, I know without hesitation I would hire him again."

When Walt Alston played first base in the St. Louis Cardinals chain, he won four home run titles, but the Cards kept him in the minor leagues because they had during his time such first basemen as Rip Collins, Dick Siebert (who later coached baseball at Minnesota and discovered Dave Winfield) and Johnny Mize. Conceivably he might have made other big league clubs, but he never got the opportunity, for he was bound to the Cardinals. He spent 14 years as a minor league manager, traveling through the small towns, bumping along the bus trails, before he was called up by Walter O'Malley in 1954 to manage the Brooklyn Dodgers.

"They had me pictured as a quiet and dead kind of a guy," Alston said, not complaining but just stating fact. "Everybody seems to think I'm pretty easygoing and I probably am...when things are going right. But I hate to lose as badly as anybody; Dressen, Durocher. But I always had the feeling that if I did the very best that I knew how and the very best that I could do, things would come out eventually.

"I always heard the fans in Brooklyn, back when I first took over, were really tough," said Walt, "but when the 1954 season was over and we finished in second place behind Durocher and the Giants, I felt the fans were even better to me than they might have been.

"When I came here in 1954," Alston said, "I didn't apply for the job. Mr. O'Malley and his staff knew what I could do, and I just bided my time, and they did send for me. They knew all about me and they knew what I could do and had done for the 14 years I worked for the organization.

"I had always gotten along with the fans and players wherever I worked, and I had many of the Brooklyn players in the minors. I had always gotten along with them and anticipated no problems."

Alston—who taught science, biology and industrial arts and coached baseball and basketball as well in his home town of Darrtown, Ohio—meted out learning and discipline with equal authority during his scholastic years. Once he spanked a seventh-grade boy for "fooling around the water cooler".

"But you can't get away with that in Brooklyn," he smiled. "To be a good manager you have to have good players. That's 100%, and I've been lucky. Very much so. The Dodgers with Robinson, Reese, Hodges, Duke Snider, Campanella, Moon, Gilliam, Wills, Koufax, Drysdale, Garvey, John, Sutton and all those other first rate men were professionals and all you do is try to come up with the right combination of players—each day, try to get them to work together for the good of the team. With little or no

injuries and lots of good luck—you wind up the winner."

"Back in 1955, my second year in Brooklyn," said Walt, "people said I was changed. I managed in a different way. I didn't think so. The big difference in 1955 was that we had great pitching: Newcombe with 20 big wins; Erskine came in with 11; Johnny Podres won 9 big games and the biggest of them all in the Series against the Yankees; Labine won 13; Billy Loes won 10; Bessent and Roebuck had good years. And the hitters were just great; there was Duke with 42 home runs and hitting .309, and that Furillo with 26 home runs and a .314 average. And Campanella played like a demon all year and he never got hurt. Roy hit 32 home runs and hit for a .318 average. And Captain Reese with 10 homers and a .282 average and he pulled that team together, when it was rough. Jackie Robinson was great all year at third base, and spunky Don Zimmer hit 15 home runs. Hodges hit 27 home runs and was a giant at first base and Sandy Amoros won some big games," said Walt. "And when you put all of that together...in one big season you come out on top. And then you win the World Series for the first time in history. That's a marvelous feeling."

1955 — "A Vintage Year and a World Series"

The Dodger "brain trust". Manager Walt Alston and his coaching staff were ready for the 1955 season. (L to R) Coach Jake Pitler, Alston, Joe Becker and Coach Billy Herman.

The Dodgers assembled for their first spring training drills of the 1955 season, and as the days passed, there was a growing air of excitement and confidence in camp. Through the exhibition games, the excitement grew as the players executed flawlessly in the field and hit the ball hard at the plate. There seemed to be a feeling in the air that said, "This is the year of the Dodgers".

ROBINSON STEALS HOME IN 1ST GAME OF '55 SERIES

One of the great thrills of the 1955 World Series came in the eighth inning of the first game as the Dodgers' Jackie Robinson surprised the Yankees with a steal of home. (Top left) Robbie starts his slide as Yogi Berra awaits the pitch from Whitey Ford. Dodger hitter, Frank Kellert (12), a pinch hitter, stepped aside as Jackie slid under the tag attempt by Berra. Umpire Bill Summers called Jackie safe.

THE WALTER ALSTON ERA **119**

...YOGI DISAGREES

But the Yankees won the game, 6-5.

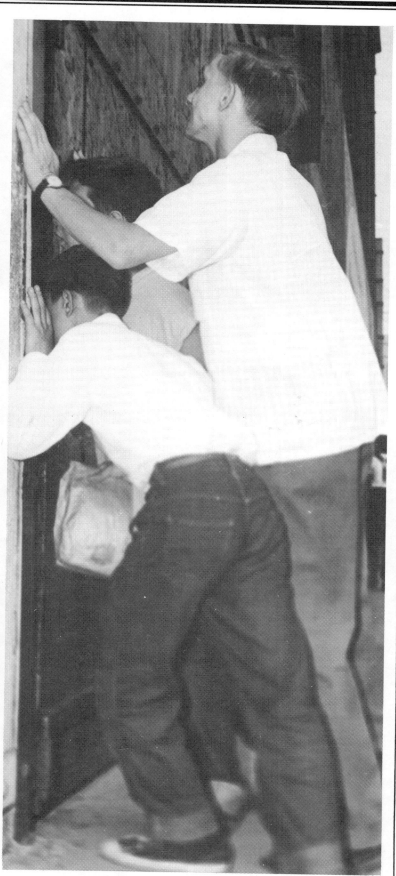

In 1955, if you couldn't raise the 75 cents for a bleacher seat, you just peeked through a hole in the fence at Ebbets Field and brought your lunch.

SORRY BILLY...

A daring attempted steal of home by the New York Yankees backfires as Dodger catcher Roy Campanella blocks plate and piles atop second baseman Billy Martin to tag him out in sixth inning of 1955 World Series opener at Yankee Stadium in New York City, Sept. 28. Umpire Bill Summers raises hand to signal out as pinch-hitter Eddie Robinson of Yanks watches. Martin tried the steal from third as Dodger relief pitcher Don Bessent faced Robinson.

Here's Pee Wee Reese sending a signal to a baserunner.

It was a happy day for Dodger southpaw Johnny Podres at Ebbets Field in Brooklyn, N.Y., Sept. 30, in more ways than one. Podres, 23 years old Sept. 30, celebrated his birthday by pitching Brooks to an 8 to 3 victory over the New York Yankees in the third game of the 1955 World Series. Here the sequence catches Podres on the mound as he rears back and cuts loose with a delivery. Johnny allowed seven hits, struck out six and walked only two. It was his first World Series win.

Big Don Newcombe is greeted at home plate by Carl Furillo (6), Don Zimmer (23), Jim Gilliam (19), and the bat boy after slugging a 3-run home run in the fourth game of the 1955 World Series against the Yankees.

At Last!

Here's how the sequence camera recorded Dodger left fielder Sandy Amoros' spectacular and maybe game-saving catch in the sixth inning of the final World Series game in 1955 at Yankee Stadium. With two men on base, Sandy raced into the left field corner to grab the ball hit by Yogi Berra and get it back to first base to double up Gil McDougald at first base. The Dodgers won the game, 2-0, and their first World Series in history.

AT LAST...

Dodger President O'Malley congratulates Manager Alston.

History Making Dodgers...Brooklyn Dodgers' pitcher Johnny Podres yelled and jumped happily as he was grabbed by catcher Roy Campanella after final out of seventh and deciding game of the 1955 World Series. Running up behind was Dodger third baseman Don Hoak. The 2-0 win, in which Podres held Yankees to eight hits, gave Brooklyn its first baseball championship in eight tries.

A grinning Sandy Amoros and Duke Snider clown in the locker rooms after the World Series win in 1955.

The Dodgers had just defeated the vaunted Yankees in the final game of the 1955 World Series and they were The Champions. It was the first World Series triumph for the Dodgers. In the locker room, in the halls, and on the field, the celebration is wild. Champagne flew freely over Duke Snider and big Don Newcombe. It was chaos as the partying went on all night all over Brooklyn.

"I knew it all the time!"
Walter Alston

A great moment of victory for President Walter O'Malley, Clem Labine (L), Coach Jake Pitler (R), Dixie Walker and Billy Herman.

AT LAST...

The Dodgers' great star, Johnny Podres, is given a lift by teammates Gil Hodges (L) and Carl Furillo (R) after Podres' great pitching beat the Yankees 2-0 in the final game of the 1955 World Series, giving the Dodgers their first World Series Championship.

The Dodgers are champs in '55. Pee Wee Reese (L), Ford Frick (C), President of the National League, and Gil Hodges celebrate the win over the Yankees.

Pee Wee Reese (left) and Manager Walt Alston prepare to hoist the 1955 World Championship banner above Ebbets Field.

1955 was an incredible year for the Dodgers as they captured their first World Series. After the game a happy Carl Furillo (6), who slammed out 8 hits against the Yankees, and an equally happy Carl Erskine, arms around each other, trot into the Dodger victory celebration in the locker room at Ebbets Field.

AT LAST...

The Dodgers sym-phony at Ebbets Field.

Baseball Commissioner Ford Frick shows the 1955 World Series rings to Dodger Captain Pee Wee Reese (L, center) as Duke Snider (L), Warren Giles, President of the National League, Jackie Robinson, Carl Furillo and Manager Walter Alston (24) look on.

AT LAST...

The Dodgers parade through the main streets of Brooklyn after winning their first World Series. A motorcade of 28 convertibles toured the Boro of Brooklyn, as a crowd estimated at 500,000 packed the route and cheered the Dodgers.

The big parade was led by Manager Walter Alston and coach Billy Herman.

In the more sedate residential areas, the players parked their cars and paraded on foot. Here they are led by batboy Charley DiGiovanna.

The parade finally wound up at Brooklyn's Borough Hall where a crowd of some 50,000 cheered each individual Dodger. Borough President John Cashmore declared this day Dodger Day and declared a city-wide holiday.

Alston entrenched himself in 1956 when the Dodgers won out after a desperate and final stretch duel with the Milwaukee Braves. Thus a third place finish in 1957 did not incite the fans to violence.

After the migration to Los Angeles, Alston had to start all over to prove himself...and it wasn't easy. Sincere and straight-shooting, calm and dispassionate in the heat of the long, hot summer, he had the local press on his side, but the fans, disappointed when their ball club hit the downslide and stayed there, yelled for his dismissal. Either Alston relieved his pitchers too soon, or left them in too long. He had his batters bunting, when they should have been going for the short fence in left field, or he was generally fouling things up by not ordering the squeeze play. He had never heard such second-guessing in his life, not even in Brooklyn.

As early as mid-June, O'Malley found it necessary to give his manager a "vote of confidence," which is generally the kiss of death in baseball circles. There was no dancing in the streets when Alston was rehired after the disastrous 1958 campaign, which saw the ex-Brooklyn Dodgers in seventh place.

In 1959 Alston kept his team in contention although injuries hit a number of key players. Gil Hodges' home run bat was out of action for an entire month, just as the pennant race was heating up. Sore knees kept hard-hitting Carl Furillo on the bench for more than 1/4 of the season. Duke Snider was in and out of the lineup for the same reason and Sandy Koufax and Johnny Podres missed important pitching starts because of injuries. And big Don Drysdale suddenly became ineffective.

The Braves challenged the Dodgers with Warren Spahn and Lou Burdette, who won more than forty games between them. Eddie Mathews was the home run champion of the League and Hank Aaron was the batting champion.

Willie Mays and Orlando Cepeda combined to hit 61 homers and to drive in 209 runs for the Giants. Johnny Antonelli, Sam Jones and Jack Sanford came in with a total of 55 games won to keep the Giants near the top.

Los Angeles had nobody to match these prodigious feats, yet Alston, moving his men about like a field marshall, put together aging veterans, solid performers and swift-moving ambitious rookies to mold the best team in baseball.

The balding, forty-eight-year-old grandfather was called too conservative. But when necessary Alston pulled out all the stops. Back in Brooklyn, when he had all the Dodger stars in their younger years, the only change in the daily line-up was the pitcher. In '59 he didn't have the young and the swift.

In 1959 the all-important No. 4 position in the lineup was occupied by seven players, Snider, Hodges, Don Demeter, Furillo, Rip Repulski, Chuck Essegian and Norm Larker. When he was healthy, Duke Snider was the No. 4 hitter, but Alston didn't hesitate to juggle his lineup if he felt that Snider was off his stride.

Casey Stengel, who broke even with Alston in two World Series (1955-1956), covered the Dodgers-White Sox World Series in 1959 for a national magazine. He carefully scrutinized every move that Alston made and he also analyzed every move made by Al Lopez, manager of the White Sox. When the Series was over and the Dodgers were World Champions, Stengel commented, "This fella Alston is great. And he gets better every time I watch him. He makes moves like a magician. He is one helluva manager."

The managers, Walt Alston and Casey Stengel exchange pleasantries prior to game 1 of the 1955 World Series.

"When I went back home to Darrtown," said Alston, "after the 1955 season, and looked over the record of the club and how the fellows performed, and asked myself what we could do to continue winning. I thought about the choices and what moves to make and how and when to make them. Sometimes you make the right moves and you're a hero, next day you make almost the same moves and you lose a game. You've lost some of that shining armour.

"As far back as I can remember," said Walt, "I wanted to play ball. That was the big and important thing. We lived on a farm near Morning Sun, Ohio, and there was nobody to play with, neighbors or anything. When my Dad wasn't out there to play catch with me, I was bouncing the ball against the barn door. That's how I got that nickname, Smokey, 'cause I used to have a really live fast ball.

"We moved to Darrtown when I was in the seventh or eighth grade. I sold my pony and bought a bicycle. In Darrtown, there was a big vacant lot, sort of a commons. Some man kept it real nice and grassy and we'd play ball there. My Dad was interested in baseball and he supplied the balls and bats for us. I'd get kids together and we would play some games. I think that kind of thing went on when I went to High School. I was organizing things and I was the pitcher and hitter on the team. At college, I switched to playing shortstop, so I could hit more."

After graduation from college, Alston broke into organized baseball as a third baseman for the Greenwood club of the East Dixie League. He batted .326 and in seven of the next dozen years of his playing career, Walt Alston hit above the .300 level.

To augment his modest minor league salary, Alston taught high school classes in biology and mechanical drawing and coached basketball during the winter months. For six years he was an instructor at New Madison High School, then transferred to another Ohio hamlet, Lewiston, where he taught until 1949—the year he won his first pennant as manager of the St. Paul Saints of the American Association.

Alston had become a player-manager in the lower minor leagues in 1940, but his masterminding was rather unspectacular until he hit the jackpot at St. Paul. There he captured two pennants and a play-off championship, and later two pennants and a Little World Series triumph at Montreal. His record with the Dodgers includes seven National League pennants and four World Series Championships.

Walt Alston was successful in Brooklyn but he never became a big city feller. He achieved greater success in Los Angeles, but he wouldn't even know what "going Hollywood" means. He remains the first citizen of Darrtown, Ohio, although he probably would deny it.

Walt Alson is not a man given to introspection, but there must be times when Alston wonders about what he has done and what he is doing. When he was going to college, his driving ambition was to become a teacher and coach. We think he succeeded beyond any description.

WHAT PEOPLE

His wife, Lela: "Walt was the high school hero. People were already looking up to him for direction. He would never be quiet, but on bad days he didn't ever talk baseball when he was managing."

A New York sportswriter, upon learning that the Dodgers had hired the unknown (at the time) Walter Alston to replace Charlie Dressen: "The Dodgers do not need a manager and that is why they got Alston."

Outfielder Tommy Davis: "He's a straight guy. . .really straight I respect the man."

Hall-of-Famer Dixie Walker: "Walt treated his players like men."

Former Dodger coach Danny Ozark: "Walt was a great handler of men."

Walt Alston, on his personal philosophy of managing: "I did it the way I had to, right or wrong. I couldn't do it Durocher's way and he couldn't do it mine."

HAVE SAID ABOUT WALTER ALSTON

Jackie Robinson: "In 1954 he let me know he was going to do the bossing, whether I liked it or not. The fact that he did it made him gain stature in my eyes."

Duke Snider: "Walt was a very easy going man. He left you on your own until you started to go bad and then he'd try his best to get you on the right track."

Don Newcombe: "All I ever wanted to do was pitch and help the ball club, but I didn't figure in his plans then and I wanted to know why. Of course the papers made a mountain of our little squabbles but it wasn't exactly nothing."

Roy Campanella: "He was not the holler type guy like some of the fellas we're used to, but he has his way of getting things done. When he had a beef he would sure let you know."

BEGINNING AGAIN, 1956

February 23, 1956...The right handed members of the 1955 World Champion Brooklyn Dodgers were getting their pitching arms in shape for the torrid 1956 pennant race at spring training headquarters, Vero Beach, Florida. From left to right: Don Newcombe, Billy Loes, Carl Erskine, Don Bessent, Clem Labine and Roger Craig.

Highlight of the 1956 New York Chapter of the Baseball Writers dinner at the Waldorf Astoria in New York was the "Player Of the Year Award" to the Dodgers' Duke Snider. The Award is presented annually by the New York writers and more than 1,000 persons attended the affair honoring Duke. (Left to right) Warren Giles, President National League, Duke Snider, Manager Walter Alston, Comedian Phil Silvers.

Jim Gilliam beat out a hit in the first inning of a game versus the Giants at Ebbets Field at the Polo Grounds in New York, July 4, 1956. Giant pitcher Windy McCall (10) raced Gilliam to the base. Umpire Dascoli called Jim "Safe". The Dodgers went on to swamp the Giants, 15-2 in first of a holiday twin bill.

Junior Gilliam, the Dodgers' second baseman, is safe stealing second base as the Phillies' second sacker Ted Kazanski tries to put a late tag on Junior. The ball (visible below Gilliam's right hand) dropped out of Kazanski's glove. The theft by Gilliam (on August 17, 1956) was one of 21 on the year for Junior.

On October 1, 1956, the Dodgers were at home against the Pirates. They were in first place and just needed 1 win to clinch their fourth pennant in five years. Duke hit a three-run homer in the first inning and another one later on. Sandy Amoros hit two home runs and relief pitcher Don Bessent shut down the Pirates to win the game, 8-6 and capture the pennant. As the game ends, fans mob the team. Here is Sal Maglie grabbing Bessent's right arm and hugging him as Walt Alston (left) wards off the mob of fans (upper photo). Below, fans mob the Dodgers after the game.

Don Newcombe

1956 was Don Newcombe's year. He was the finest pitcher in baseball with a 27-7 record and received the recognition he had been seeking for years. He won the Cy Young Award and was voted the Most Valuable Player in the National League (for the 1956 season).

The great circus clown Emmett Kelly shakes hands with Gil Hodges at Ebbets Field, 1957.

THE N.Y. YANKEES DEFEAT THE BROOKLYN DODGERS IN THE 1956 WORLD SERIES, 4 GAMES TO 3.

Despite a barreling slide by Hank Bauer of the Yankees, Pee Wee Reese gets the ball to Gil Hodges at first for a double play in the first inning of the 6th World Series game, Oct. 9, 1956. The game was won in the 10th inning by the Dodgers, 1-0, to even the Series at 3 games each.

Dodger pitcher Clem Labine sits down for a rest at second base, during a time-out in the 8th inning of the 1956 World Series between the Yankees and the Dodgers. During the time-out, Stengel confers with Yankee pitcher Bob Turley. Umpire Larry Napp suggested that sitting down in the World Series is bush. However Clem sat until play resumed.

In May, 1956 the Dodgers, battling tooth and nail with the Milwaukee Braves for first place, acquired 39-year old Sal Maglie, the one-time pitching ace of the Giants. Maglie had been waived to Cleveland the year before but had not been very effective in the American League. But, from the first day he put on a Dodger uniform, Sal was a new pitcher, managing 13 victories from his great pitching arm. On September 25th, as the pennant race between the Braves and Dodgers grew tighter, Sal inspired the Brooks with a no-hit game against the Phillies.

February 27, 1956...Randy Jackson defied gravity as he went high into the air, as he posed for a publicity shot at the Dodgers spring training camp at Vero Beach. Acquired from the Cubs in 1956, Randy played a smooth third base for the Dodgers in 1956 and 1957 before being traded to Cleveland where he appeared in just 29 games before being shipped to the Los Angeles Dodgers in 1958.

Walt Alston, manager of the 1957 National League All-Star team, with several of his stars. (L to R) Curt Simmons, Jack Sanford of the Phillies, Alston, Gino Cimoli, Clem Labine and Gil Hodges of the Dodgers.

HELLO CALIFORNIA!

"What in hell are you wearing, Pee Wee?," said Roy Campanella in the Dodger clubhouse. That date, November, 1957, the Dodgers announced their move to Los Angeles for the 1958 season. "I'm gonna wear this stuff in Los Angeles next year", said Pee Wee Reese. That's what they wear out there."

The First Decade in California 1958-1968...

The first week with the Dodgers in Los Angeles in 1958. (Upper Left) Motion picture star Joe E. Brown, one of the leading figures in the move to bring the Dodgers to Los Angeles, introduces Manager Walt Alston (R). The Los Angeles Dodgers line up for introductions. (Lower Left) Packed crowd at the Coliseum. (Lower Right) The team parades through downtown Los Angeles.

TEMPORARY HELP

"Big Jim" Gentile came to the Dodgers in 1957. In 1957 and 1958 Jim played in just 16 games and was traded to the Orioles. Jim hit 21 home runs in 1960 and 46 homers in 1961 for Baltimore.

Norm Larker joined the Dodgers in 1958, the first year in Los Angeles. The next season, 1959, Larker had a .289 average and was a valuable cog in the Dodger wheel that brought the World Championship to Los Angeles for the first time. In 1960, Norm hit for a .323 average and was named the Most Valuable Dodger. In 1962 Larker was sent to the Houston Astros.

Johnny Klippstein came to the Dodgers during the 1958 season and proved to be a valuable member of the Dodger's bullpen. John appeared in 28 games for the Dodgers in 1959 and posted a 4-0 record in addition to saving 2 other games for the World Champions. Overall John pitched in the majors for some 18 years with the Cubs, Indians, Senators, Phils, Twins and Tigers.

Fred Kipp broke into the major leagues with the Dodgers in 1958 and appeared in 40 games. He won six and lost six in the Dodgers' first year in Los Angeles in 1959. He was traded to the Yankees in 1960.

Elmer Valo, born in Ribnik, Czechoslovakia, was a 17-year veteran when he was traded to the Dodgers in 1957. Valo played in 81 games and hit .273. In '58 Valo hit .248 for the Dodgers and was traded to the Cleveland Indians.

The Los Angeles Dodgers new "Brain Trust" for their first year in Los Angeles in 1958 was Coaches Greg Mulleavy (L), Charlie Dressen, Manager Alston, Joe Becker and Rube Walker.

First World Series in California - 1959

It was nearing midnight and the World Series press headquarters on the nineteenth floor of the La Salle Hotel in Chicago's Loop was all but deserted.

A few blocks away, meanwhile, champagne and caviar were being dispensed by Walter O'Malley as his jubilant Los Angeles Dodgers celebrated their smashing conquest of the White Sox. The vanquished American League champions had already scattered under cover of night.

Back at press headquarters a journalistic straggler, his story long since filed to his paper, was trying to pick up a few crumbs of news and comment for a follow-up story the next day. It was his good fortune to encounter Mr. Dizzy Dean , the former pitcher, one-time sportscaster and full-time wit and raconteur.

"Well, Diz, what'd you think of the Series?" the writer asked.

"It's like this," the droll Dizzy replied, "I never saw a bunch of mice lick a cat."

Indeed, this was a shrewd appraisal of the Dodgers' four-to-two-game triumph in the 1959 post season classic. The light-hitting, opportunistic White Sox were just no match for the hard-bitten crew which clawed and scratched its way to the summit of the baseball world with the ferocity of an alley cat fighting for its life.

In shattering tradition with their improbable victory, the Dodgers became the first team ever to capture the World Series after finishing in seventh place the previous season. By the time the Los Angeles players faced the White Sox in a showdown for what was certain to be a record Series jackpot, they had been hardened by a pennant campaign as fierce as any in major league annals. First, they dashed the Giants' hopes by sweeping a three-game series in San Francisco. Then, deadlocked with Milwaukee when the regular season ended, the Dodgers demolished the defending champion Braves with two one-run victories in a play-off that was decided in Milwaukee and Los Angeles within a span of twenty-four hours.

But the real test, the moment of truth, was yet to come for the travel-weary Californians. Having already clinched the American League bunting nearly a week before, the White Sox were refreshed and enjoying the benefits of home cooking while the Dodgers winged their way east within hours after eliminating the Braves. The Windy City was agog, gripped by World Series fever. It had been forty years since their beloved White Sox had won a pennant, only to write the most dismal chapter in baseball lore—the infamous Black Sox scandal of 1919.

Time had healed the wounds of that all-but-mortal blow. The new darlings of the populace were Al Lopez and his Go-Go Sox, a cunning, resourceful team that pounced on enemy mistakes and seldom, if ever, beat itself. Many experts said it had the best down-the-middle defense in baseball in catcher Sherm Lollar, the gifted keystone combo of Luis Aparicio and Nellie Fox, and the gazellelike center fielder Jim Landis. It had A-1 pitching, personified by the twenty-two-game-winner Early Wynn, and his cohorts Bob Shaw, Dick Donovan, Billy Pierce, and the bull pen aces Gerry Staley and Turk Lown. And there was the booming bat of mastodon Theodore Kluszewski.

It was more difficult to pinpoint the strength of the upstart Dodgers. The once-feared sluggers Duke Snider and Gil Hodges appeared to be well over the hill. At shortstop was a rookie, banjo-hitting Maury Wills, and he and Charlie Neal couldn't possibly match the Aparicio-Fox double-play duo. Wally Moon was streaky. Jim Gilliam was no fence-buster. The speedy Aparicio and Landis figured to steal bases at will against Johnny Roseboro, a journeyman receiver. As for pitching, mainstays like Don Drysdale, Johnny Podres and Sandy Koufax were unmistakably erratic, and the Dodgers never would have qualified for the World Series but for some late-season successes by Roger Craig and Larry Sherry, a couple of recalled farm hands. Some people accused the quiet-spoken Los Angeles leader Walt Alston of being on the corny side when he used a well-worn cliche, "Team effort," in summing up the Dodgers' pennant victory. But Alston insisted that that was precisely what it was.

Both artistically and financially, the Series was a smashing success as records fell like autumn leaves. All financial and attendance marks compiled in fifty-five previous World Series were exceeded as the third, fourth and fifth games were staged in Los Angeles' mammoth Memorial Coliseum before crowds of 92,294, 92,550 and 92,706 on successive afternoons. Coupled with three capacity crowds at Comiskey Park, the six-game attendance of 420,784 surpassed even the record for a seven-game series, as did the total receipts of $6,626,973.44.

The combatants, of course, cut up the biggest melon of them all—$893,301.40. Full shares for the Dodgers amounted to $11,231.18, while the Chisox salved their wounds with poultices of $7,275.17.

From a competitive standpoint, the skirmishing did not run true to form. The experts were stumped when the Dodgers stole five bases, the Go-Go Sox only two. In one game, Roseboro shot down Aparicio, Fox and Jungle Jim Rivera on attempted thefts. Playing brilliantly after a shaky start, the Wills-Neal duet figured in most of the seven double plays executed by Los Angeles. The dazzling Chisox defense accounted for only two.

The most destructive batter was Big Klu, who drove in a record ten runs, with three homers, five singles and a double. Klu's .391 batting average was matched by his rival first sacker Hodges, who hammered a homer, triple and seven singles, but Gil accounted for only two runs. The surprise regular was Neal, the slender slugger whose ten hits included two king-sized homers in the second

game. Curiously, only two of the eleven round-trippers laced in the six games were recorded in the Coliseum, where the left field screen, anchored at the foul line only 251 feet from home plate, beckons tantalizingly to the fence-busting brigade. Spacious Comiskey Park proved an easy mark for Klu and the Dodger long-ball specialists, including bench-riding Chuck Essegian, who established a Series record with two pinch homers.

Dodger pinch-hitter Chuck Essegian (29) is given a hero's welcome by manager Walt Alston after his homer in the 7th inning of the 1959 World Series against the White Sox, game 2. Essegian is greeted by entire Dodger team in dugout: Larker, Zimmer, Podres, Furillo. Essegian's drive tied the game, which the Dodgers eventually won, 4-3, Oct. 3, 1959 at Chicago.

Just as curious as the paucity of Oriental homers in the Coliseum was the manner in which the White Sox scored their two triumphs. Both were by shutouts, Wynn and Staley combining to stifle Los Angeles in the opening game, and Shaw, Pierce and Donovan collaborating on another calcimine job in the fifth game.

For the first time in Series history, nary a starting pitcher was able to post a complete-game victory. And for this very reason, an opportunity was presented to Larry Sherry to win undying diamond fame. He didn't muff it. The native-born Angeleno, afflicted with club feet at birth, finished all four games won by the Dodgers. The twenty-four-year-old right-hander preserved the win for Podres in the second game and saved Drysdale's win in the

Charlie Neal crosses home plate after his 2nd home run put the Dodgers in the lead in the 7th inning of the second game of the 1959 World Series between the Dodgers and Chicago White Sox. Greeting Neal are teammates, Wally Moon (9) and Jim Gilliam (19). The second game of the Series was played October 2, in Chicago.

A fan was so intent on following the course of a homer hit by Charlie Neal of the Dodgers that he tipped his cup of beer off the wall and showered left fielder Al Smith of the Chicago White Sox. This happened in the 5th inning of the World Series, game 2. It was one of the oddities of 4-3 Dodger win over the White Sox in the 1959 Series.

Charlie Neal in 1959.

35-year old Gil Hodges connects for a tremendous home run in the 4th inning of the World Series vs Chicago. The homer gave the Dodgers a 5-4 victory and also gave the Dodgers a 3-1 edge over the White Sox in the 1959 World Series.

Here is Hodges scoring after his homer. Greeting him at home plate is teammate, Don Demeter.

third one. Iron-armed Larry was the winning pitcher in games four and six after being summoned from the bull pen to rescue Craig and Podres.

As form flew out the window, Chicago made a Roman holiday of the curtain-raiser in Comiskey Park on October 1. Rated as a good fielding, no-hit team, the Pale Hose ruined the Dodgers by a score of 11-0. In complete command, the thirty-nine-year-old Wynn fanned six Dodgers and scattered six hits before the cold weather caused his right elbow to tighten. Staley pitched the last two frames to complete the whitewash.

Meanwhile, the Sox went berserk at bat. A single by Klu and Lollar's sacrifice fly cost Craig two runs in the first inning, but that was mere child's play compared to what happened in the third round. Before order was restored, eleven White Sox strode to the plate, slammed six hits and scored seven runs, four of the tallies resulting from a complete breakdown in the Dodger defense. Two errors by Snider and one by Neal figured in the worst World Series licking ever handed a Dodger ball club. With one out, Fox touched off the explosion with a double to right, and raced home on the second of three Landis singles. Then Craig, a dominant figure in the Dodgers' stretch run, was knocked out of the box when Kluszewski lofted a ball into the right field stands. Chuck Churn, Craig's successor, found himself in trouble immediately when Moon and Snider collided going for Lollar's routine fly ball. It glanced off Duke's glove for a two-base error as a turnaway crowd of 48,013 whistled, stomped, cheered and jeered. Lollar scored the fourth run on Billy Goodman's single, and Billy came all the way around when Al Smith doubled over Moon's head. Billy momentarily halted at third, then kept coming when Snider retrieved Smith's rebounding ball and threw it toward second base, which nobody was covering. Smith took third as Hodges floundered trying to stop Duke's peg.

With Rivera at bat, the Dodger infield was drawn in. Neal fielded Jungle Jim's bouncer, only to throw low to the plate, the ball glancing off Rivera's discarded bat and skidding past Roseboro as Smith slid in. The three errors in one inning tied a Series mark. Wynn promptly improved his own position to 9-0 by scoring Rivera with a double to left center. Churn got the side out without further damage, but he fled the premises in distress in the very next inning when Landis led off with a base hit and Kluszewski's line drive struck the upper deck facade in right field for his second homer and fifth RBI of the game. Clem Labine, Sandy Koufax and Johnny Klippstein combined to hold the Go-Go Sox to one hit for the remainder of the game, but the Dodgers were a badly beaten team as they left the field.

They were taunted by joyous Chicago rooters as they silently made their way to the clubhouse. "You ain't playin' the Braves now, ya bums," boomed a beery baritone. As matters developed, the White Sox were soon to discover that they weren't playing the Washington Senators either, because the Dodgers bounced back from this unmerciful shellacking to win four of the next five games. The Sox "was dead"; they just didn't know it.

Dodger power, held in check for thirteen consecutive innings by Chisox pitching, asserted itself in the fifth inning of the second game when Neal lined a home run into the left field stands. But thanks to two first-inning runs off Johnny Podres, Bob Shaw, the youthful pride of Chicago's mound corps, still boasted a 2-1 lead as Los Angeles came to bat in the seventh inning.

With two away, Alston made a bold move. He sent Essegian in to bat for Podres, who had been pitching very effectively. On a three-and-one count, the muscular Essegian, a former Stanford football star, powered a home run deep into the upper stands in left field to tie the score. Unsettled, Shaw walked Gilliam and then was knocked out when Neal unloaded a tremendous drive which Billy Pierce caught while heating up in the Chisox bull pen behind the center field fence. The 420-foot smash sent the Dodgers ahead, 4-2, for the first time in the Series. The Sox were to tally again, but the Dodgers held on for a 4-3 victory which squared the Series to the great dismay of another standing-room throng of 47,368.

With Podres in the bathhouse, Sherry made his first Series appearance. He retired Chicago in order in the seventh inning, but found himself in deep trouble in the eighth when the redoubtable Klu opened with a bloop single and took second as Lollar lined a single off Gilliam's glove. Earl Torgeson was sent in to run for the lumbering Ted. If there was one major turning point in the Series, it arose in the next few moments. After misfiring on a bunt attempt and taking a second strike, Al Smith delivered a full-count double between Moon and Snider. Torgeson had no trouble scoring, of course, but Moon cagily faked a catch although he knew he couldn't get to the ball, and Lollar, completely fooled, slowed up as he approached second base. When Sherm saw that the drive was going for extra bases, he turned on the gas again, and as he rounded third base he was waved on in by Coach Tony Cuccinello. But shortstop Wills took Moon's throw and fired a perfect relay to Roseboro at the plate. Lollar was out by at least ten feet and didn't even attempt to slide. Meanwhile, Smith took third base.

The White Sox, however, now had one run in, a man on third and one out, instead of having two runs in, a man on second and nobody out. Heartened by this lucky break, Sherry struck out pinch hitter Goodman and retired Rivera on a weak foul pop-up to Roseboro. Sherry breezed through the ninth round to present Podres with the win.

Saturday, October 3, brought a cessation of hostilities as the teams, club officials, wives, newsmen and fans flew to the Pacific Coast where play would resume the next day. Los Angeles fans, who had supported their heroes more than two million strong during the regular season, were in a tizzy of expectancy. Scalpers demanded—and in some cases got—triple the official prices for good seats.

The first World Series game ever played west of St. Louis was also one of the strangest. The Dodgers won it, 3-1, on Carl Furillo's seventh-inning pinch single which just eluded the belated grab by Aparicio. This sent an all-time Series record crowd of 92,294 into flights of rapturous ecstasy. Famed as opportunists, the White Sox literally frittered away the contest as Los Angeles assumed an important 2-1 Series edge. The Sox made twelve hits, but only one run, leaving eleven runners stranded. And Aparicio, their All-Star shortstop, was the goat. Meanwhile, the rough-and-ready Dodgers cashed in on only five hits, four of which were singles.

It was a strange pitching duel between Drysdale and Donovan. The towering Dodger hurler did a tightrope act, constantly falling behind the hitter and yielding at least one hit per inning, while Donovan, Chicago's sinker-ball ace, pitched to an absolute minimum of nineteen batters before he blew up with one out in the fateful seventh stanza. It was the rifle-armed Roseboro who kept the Chisox at bay on at least three occasions as he threw out Rivera, Aparicio and Fox trying to steal second base.

Neal, hero of the second game, launched the seventh-inning winning rally with a one-out single off the screen, moving along as Fox threw out Moon. Then the fading Donovan issued his only two walks of the game, passing Norm Laker on four straight pitches and Hodges on five serves to load the bases. Here was another two-out situation, one in which the Dodgers thrived, for they scored nineteen of their twenty-one runs in the Series under these conditions. At this point Al Lopez replaced Donovan with thirty-nine-year-old Staley, his most reliable fireman. Alston met that move by sending Furillo in to hit for Don Demeter.

"All I wanted was a base hit," Alston explained later. "If I'd needed the long ball, I'd have used Essegian instead of Furillo."

On Staley's second pitch, Furillo, a money player from way back, pounded the ball through the box. Aparicio broke to his left a bit tardily, and the ball took a little hop over his outstretched glove behind second base and rolled out into center field as Neal and Larker raced homeward. Aparicio was to say

later that he "lost" the ball momentarily in the dazzling background provided by the oceans of white-shirted fans jammed on the slopes of the huge saucer. At any rate, the ubiquitous Sherry relieved Drysdale in the top of the eighth after Klu and Lollar led off with singles. Larry loaded the bases by plugging Goodman with a pitch. A run scored as Smith grounded into a double play but two more Pale Hose runners were left high and dry when Rivera popped up meekly. Maury Wills' single and Neal's two-bagger in the same frame made the final score 3-1.

It was Sherry's turn to take some credit for himself in the fourth game, and he did it with the timely aid of Hodges' tie-breaking homer in the eighth inning which gave Los Angeles a 5-4 verdict, its third straight over the enemy. This was a game in which the White Sox made three errors, with the Dodgers enjoying their biggest inning of the Series thus far. They achieved this by attacking Wynn for four runs in the third inning on consecutive singles by Moon, Hodges, Larker, Demeter and Roseboro—again after two were out.

But another whopping crowd of 92,550 had cause for alarm when the plucky Pale Hose came back to shell Craig to cover in the seventh after he had pitched six scoreless innings. Roger staggered through the inning but was tagged by Lollar's homer, with Klu and Fox aboard, which capped a four-run rally. Sherry faced only seven batters in the last two innings, his task made more enjoyable when Hodges' homer saddled Staley, the fourth pitcher employed by Lopez, with the defeat.

Now the Dodgers boasted an almost insurmountable advantage. Only two teams in Series history had come from behind after trailing three games to one. It was a sudden-death situation for the White Sox, and a Dodger partisan crowd of 92,706—the greatest ever to see a Series game—contributed a record gate of $552,744.77 to sit in on the kill. But the Go-Go Sox weren't gone yet. They won a classic 1-0 thriller which prolonged the suspense and sent the touring athletes back to Chicago to settle the issue. The only run of the game came off Sandy Koufax in the fourth inning when Fox and Landis hit back-to-back singles, Nellie scoring as Lollar bounced into the Dodgers' sixth double play of the Series.

Whereas the visitors had been frustrated by leaving eleven runners on base in the third game, this time the Dodgers passed up numerous scoring opportunities as they, too, left eleven aboard. Hodges failed to score after tripling off Bob Shaw with only one out in the fourth frame, and the door was slammed in the eighth after Los Angeles loaded the bases with only one out.

The most spectacular play of the Series, one which kept the White Sox's glimmering hopes alive, occurred in the seventh inning. As the lethal

Neal came to bat with two out, runners on second and third and Shaw nursing a tenuous 1-0 lead, Al Lopez made a move that smacked of sheer genius. He removed rookie outfielder Jim McAnany from the lineup, shifted Al Smith from right to left field and sent Rivera into right field. On a three-and-two count, Neal blasted the ball to right center as Rivera and Landis both took out after it in hot pursuit. Landis couldn't reach it, but Rivera speared it over his left shoulder just in front of the 400-foot marker on the fence. While the huzzahs of well-wishers rang in his ears after the game, Lopez sheepishly admitted that the reasoning behind the insertion of Rivera in the line-up "was so that I could get Smith back in left field where I figured Neal would hit the ball."

In the eighth inning, however, Lopez scored a clean-cut decision over his rival manager. The battle began with Moon being credited with a single when Landis lost his ball in the dazzling sun. One out later, Moon sped to third base when Hodges drilled a single past Fox, with Gil advancing as Landis tried to throw out Moon. Here the celebrations of Lopez and Alston could almost be felt by the frenzied fans. When a left-handed batter, Ron Fairly, was announced to hit for Demeter, Lopez lifted Shaw and sent southpaw Billy Pierce to the mound. Alston countered by replacing Fairly with right-handed Rip Repulski, so Lopez neutralized that maneuver by ordering Pierce to walk Repulski purposely.

The crowd was beside itself, and the amateur buglers were tooting the now-famous Dodger "Charge!" tune when Furillo, hero of the third game, came up to bat for left-handed Johnny Roseboro. Lopez, of course, lifted Pierce and brought in right-handed Donovan to face Furillo. Pitching deliberately, Donovan was the master of the situation. The clutch-hitting Furillo was retired on an infield pop-up and the Dodgers' hopes for a rally vanished as yet another pinch hitter, Don Zimmer, flied out.

This victory, harrowing as it was, was a great tonic to the White Sox. Even though still faced with sudden death, they felt now that the tide would turn in their favor. The Dodgers had been dealt a crushing psychological blow in losing that 1-0 game when their second World Series championship was within a base hit or two of being realized. They were worn out from the unceasing travel that had taken them to San Francisco, St. Louis, Chicago, Milwaukee, Los Angeles, Chicago, Milwaukee, Los Angeles, Chicago and back to Los Angeles again—all stops being made since September 18. And now they had to fly back to Chicago to tackle the encouraged White Sox in "the big barn," as they referred to their commodious and symmetrical ball park.

"We'll get the Dodgers in our big barn—a real ball

park," was the gist of the Chisox's remarks as they worked out in their own back yard again on Wednesday, October 7. The odds makers felt the same way about it. They established Chicago as the betting favorite to win the sixth game and square the Series at 3-3. They reckoned not with the National League champions, the hungry alley cat types who had overcome adversity, sometimes skillfully and just as frequently through sheer guts and determination.

The Los Angeles Dodgers made a shambles of the sixth game, belaboring the exhausted Wynn and Donovan in a six-run inning that left the Pale Hose hopelessly behind. The final score was 9-3, and none in that crowd of 47,653 gave their overmatched heroes a ghost of a chance after the Dodgers built an 8-0 lead.

Even when the Chisox rallied for three runs to cut into Johnny Podres' commanding lead, they sensed that it was all over because Alston played his well-worn trump card Larry Sherry a fourth time, and the one-time cripple suffocated the Chisox on three hits in five and two-thirds innings of relief to win his second decision. Possibly Podres could have survived the enemy's last defiant gesture, but the cautious Alston wasted little time in jerking Johnny after Klu hit his third homer of the classic with two mates aboard.

Inexplicably, Lopez was much more reluctant to relieve the weary Wynn, even after Duke Snider crashed a 400-foot homer into the left center seats with Moon on board in the third inning. Burly Early was still in there when the fatal fourth began, only to flee after singles by Larker and Wills, plus Podres' two-bagger over Landis' head, made the score 4-0. Donovan didn't have anything left either. He walked Gilliam, then was assassinated as Neal doubled and Moon homered on consecutive pitches. Save for Essegian's ninth-inning pinch homer, the remainder of the game was pretty dreary. The Sox couldn't solve Sherry, and the Dodgers didn't need any more runs.

"We licked 'em right here in the big barn," jeered Don Zimmer as the Dodgers entered their clubhouse after the game. Over in a corner Walt Alston, the quiet man from Darrtown, Ohio, was talking to reporters.

"It was strictly a team effort," said Alston.

And this time it didn't sound corny to anyone.

The 1959 World Series featured the brilliant pitching of Larry Sherry, the Dodgers great reliever, who pitched in 4 of the 6 games. In this photo Sherry hurls the final strikeout pitch of the series as the Dodgers defeat the White Sox 4 games to 2. He is given a bear hug by his catcher (44) Johnny Roseboro.

On Through the years...

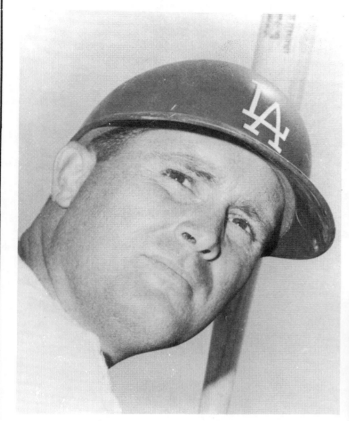

Only two seasons off the Southern California campus, Ron Fairly was retained by the Dodgers in 1959 because of Duke Snider's knee condition. It was thought that Ron would be able to spell the Duke. However, in 1960 Ron was sent back to the minors to polish his skills. He returned to enjoy an outstanding major league career that spanned over three decades. Ron's best year with the Dodgers was 1961, when he hit for a .322 average and drove out 10 home runs. He was traded to Montreal in 1969 after 11-1/2 years as a Dodger.

Norm Sherry joined the Dodgers in 1960 and provided a valuable backup for John Roseboro, the regular catcher. He had managed in the minors and was a smart baseball man. One day during a "B" squad practice game, Norm told a struggling Sandy Koufax, "When you get behind a batter, you tighten up and you use your fast ball. When you press like you do, the fast ball comes in high and the hitters tee off. Instead of the fast ball," said Norm, "go to your curve ball." "That advice," said Sandy Koufax, "made me a pitcher that very same day. I went out with Sherry as my catcher and pitched 7 innings of no-hit ball. From then on, I started to win more games than I ever had in my life."

Phil Ortega joined the Dodgers in 1960 and appeared in but 3 games. In 1961 Ortega was in 4 games. Phil was used sparingly until 1964 when he appeared in 34 games. He won 7 and lost 9 in relief. In 1965 he was traded to the Senators, where he won 12 games.

Ed Palmquist pitched in 33 games in relief in 1960, with an 0-1 record, and was traded to the Twins in 1961.

Irv Noren was acquired by the Dodgers from the Cubs in 1960. He played in just 26 games with the Dodgers and then retired.

Clem Labine tries on a new set of spikes for the start of the 1960 season.

Ken McMullen originally played for the Dodgers intermittently from 1962 to 1964 and was traded to Washington with big Frank Howard in 1964. He returned to the Dodgers in 1972 and was utilized primarily as a pinch hitter. Ken was used as a substitute for Steve Garvey, when Steve was ill and for Ron Cey, when Ron was hurt. Ken was a fine pinch-hitter and won a number of clutch games with timely home runs throughout the years, 1973 to 1975.

Tommy Davis was a marvelous basketball and baseball player at Boys High School in Brooklyn in the 1950's and had to choose between his two favorite sports. He wanted to play at Ebbets Field; it was near home. "If you play for the Dodgers in Brooklyn," said Al Campanis, "you'll be as big a hero as Jackie Robinson." And so the Dodger scout signed Tommy with a $4,000 bonus and by 1962, the 23-year old was the star of the Dodgers. He slugged the ball for 27 home runs and his .346 batting average lead the National League. Again in 1963 he was tops in the League with a .323 average. In 1965, attempting to slide into second base Davis broke his ankle and was never again to reach his top form. He was traded to the Giants in 1967 after eight wonderful Dodger years.

Everybody is waiting at the plate for Dodger rookie Tommy Davis, after Tommy slashed a two-run homer in the 11th inning to give the Dodgers a 7-5 victory over the Pittsburgh Pirates in a nip and tuck battle, July 20, 1960. Greeting Davis as he crossed the plate are pitcher Roger Craig (left), Manager Walt Alston (almost hidden) and Frank Howard, (right).

It is 1962 and Duke Snider has spent 15 years with the Dodgers in Brooklyn and Los Angeles. Chuck Connors (L), and comedian Danny Thomas are shown presenting Duke with a plaque honoring his great years, his favorite bats and Dodger shirts. Duke responds to the occasion with his usual charm.

Don Drysdale and Gil Hodges

Don Drysdale and Gil Hodges were great friends and teammates when they played together for the Brooklyn Dodgers in 1956 and 1957, and then for the Los Angeles Dodgers until 1962, when Gil went to the New York Mets. Gil then took over the task of managing the hapless Washington Senators in 1963. On October 19, 1967, the Mets' Bing Devine announced that Gil Hodges' contract had been purchased from the Senators and Gil would manage the Mets in 1968.

Maury Wills, one of the all-time Dodger stars, is shown stealing his 104th base during the 1962 season. (Upper right) Maury as he appeared ready to play in the Dodgers' 1978 annual Old-timers game at Dodger Stadium.

In January 1963 the Dodgers announced a wholesale contract signing ceremony, by inking agreements with 6 of their pitchers at the same time. Standing: Bill Singer, Bob Miller, Buzzie Bavasi, (Dodger Vice President) and Joe Moeller. Seated: Ed Roebuck, Phil Ortega and Ron Perranowski. From 1964-1972 Bill Singer won 69 and lost 76 games. Bob Miller won 29, lost 33, from 1963 to 1967. Joe Moeller won 26, lost 36, from 1962 to 1971. Ed Roebuck won 40, lost 22, from 1955 to 1963. Phil Ortega won 7, lost 13, from 1960 to 1964. Ron Perranowski won 54, lost 41, from 1961 to 1972.

Leo Durocher has been timing Sandy Koufax' fast ball. "Looks like about 92 miles per, Sandy." That year, 1963, Sandy won 25 and lost 5 games.

Tom Davis makes a leaping catch on a ball hit by Leo Cardenas of the Cincinnati Reds deep to left field. The Dodgers won 1-0 at Dodger Stadium, July 5, 1963.

Phil Ortega, Joe Moeller and Bob Miller jog around Dodger Stadium in 1963.

Dodgers vs Yankees in game 1 of the 1963 World Series, October 2, 1963 — A sweep over the Yankees — The Dodgers' disastrous loss of a long lead and the playoff to the Giants in 1962 was forgotten in 1963 as the Dodgers stormed to four wins in a row over the New York Yankees...Sandy Koufax won the first game, 5-2...Johnny Podres, with bullpen aid from Ron Perranoski, took the second game, 4-1...Don Drysdale fired a three-hit shutout in the third game, beating Jim Bouton, 1-0, and then Sandy clamped the lid on the World Series championship with a 2-1

triumph in the fourth game. No club had ever swept the great Yankees. Hitting hero of the series was Tommy Davis with an average of .400, closely followed by ex-Yankee Bill Skowron. Frank Howard and the great Mickey Mantle matched homers in the fourth game but it was Jim Gilliam who carried across the final run on a sacrifice fly by Willie Davis.

Moose Skowron (left) (14) and Dick Tracewski (44) dash to home plate to shake Roseboro's hand, then trot into dugout with John.

Los Angeles Dodgers manager Walt Alston (24) comes up on dugout steps to welcome catcher Johnny Roseboro (8) after latter had crashed a second inning three run homer against the New York Yankees in first World Series game at Yankee Stadium. Maury Wills (30) shakes Roseboro's hand. Moose Skowron (14) and Dick Tracewski (44), both of whom scored on the homer, trot to dugout. Clapping hands at left is coach Leo Durocher. The player between Durocher and Alston is Ron Fairly. The Dodgers won 5-2 as Sandy Koufax struck out 15 Yankees to set a World Series record.

Big Frank Howard is greeted at the plate by teammate Bill Skowron in the 5th inning, after Howard's long home run gave the Dodgers a 1-0 lead over the Yankees in the 1963 World Series. The Dodgers won the game, 2-1 behind Sandy Koufax, and took the World Series in four straight games.

Mickey Mantle walks back to the dugout in disgust as a strike out victim in the fifth inning of the first World Series game at Yankee Stadium, 1963. Sandy Koufax, the Dodger fire-baller, hurled 3 bullet-like strikes and the Mick was out.

Joe Pepitone, Yankee first baseman, chases the ball in the 7th inning after a throw from team-mate Clete Boyer got by Joe. Gilliam, who hit the ball to Boyer at 3rd base, raced all the way to third on the play and then scored on Willie Davis' fly ball. It was the winning run and gave the Dodgers a 2-1 win in the final game of the 1963 World Series.,

In 1963 Ron Perranoski, 26 years old, won 16 games and lost only 3. Ron (appearing in 69 games), Sandy Koufax, who won 25, and Don Drysdale, who won 19, were the three big winners of the Dodgers staff that knocked off the Yankees in 4 straight games to win the 1963 World Series.

Frank Howard of the Dodgers connects with a pitch from Whitey Ford, foreground, of the New York Yankees for a fifth inning homer in fourth game of the World Series. The ball traveled an estimated 450 feet into the second deck in deep left field, the first time a ball had been hit into that sector since the stadium was built. Catching for New York is Elston Howard. The umpire is Shag Crawford. The Dodgers won the game, 2-1, completing a four game sweep of the Yankees to win the World Series in Los Angeles, Oct. 6, 1963.

An exuberant Ron Fairly (right) leaps into the air as he joins the mob around winning pitcher Sandy Koufax on the field at Dodger Stadium in Los Angeles after the Dodgers had won the 1963 World Series by beating the New York Yankees in four straight games. Identifiable players include pitcher Don Drysdale, center-facing camera; coach Joe Becker, 33, far left; coach Pete Reiser (27), and manager Walt Alston (24).

The 1965 World Series...
Dodgers vs. Minnesota...
It Takes Seven Games...
But...the Dodgers win another.

Dodgers Stage Another Comeback Series Victory — The Dodgers lost the first two games of the 1965 World Series to the Minnesota Twins and then won in seven games. Ten years earlier — in 1955 — the Dodgers had become the first team in history to win a seven-game World Series after losing the first two contests. It was Claude Osteen who turned the tide by winning the third game, 4-0 after Dodger pitching stars Sandy Koufax and Don Drysdale had lost in the first two contests. Koufax, however, won two World Series games — including the seventh and deciding game by a 2-0 score. Lou Johnson (bottom left in above picture layout of the 1965 World Series) hit a home run in the fourth inning to give the Dodgers their first run and Jim Gilliam made a great play at third base in the fifth inning to take the steam out of a Twins threat. Willie Davis, Ron Fairly, Maury Wills and Jim Lefebvre all enjoyed standout performances for the Dodgers.

(Above) Ron Fairly greets teammate Lou Johnson as Lou charged into the Dodgers dugout after his 8th inning home run. Manager Alston is next to Fairly. The Dodgers took the game from the Twins, 7-2. It was the 4th game of the 1965 Series. Fairly and Johnson were the Series batting stars with 2 homers each.

(Left) "Sweet" Lou Johnson

From 1953 to 1965 Lou Johnson made the ball clubs in Olean, Lexington, Lancaster, San Antonio, Houston, Toronto, Denver and Spokane. He was bounced around to 17 ball clubs until he was called on to replace Tommy Davis, who had dislocated and broken his right ankle, May 1, 1965, and all Johnson did was to crack out 12 home runs, that helped the Dodgers on to the pennant and the World Series that year. In a crucial 15 inning game during the Dodgers' late drive against the Giants, Lou drove a 400 foot home run that won the game. He smacked a single in the 11th inning against the Braves to win another tight game. Clutch hits against the Reds and the Dodgers won other tight games. "He helped the club every year he was with us in '65, '66 and in 1967." In 1968 "Sweet" Lou was traded to the Cubs.

Don Drysdale held the Twins to but 5 hits and beat them 7-2 in the 4th game of the 1965 World Series. Don struck out 11 Twins. The victory evened the Series at two games for each club. Drysdale was beaten by the Twins in the opening game of the Series but got his revenge in this 4th game.

(Above) In his first year of pro ball, 18-year old Jim Lefebvre hit 39 home runs and batted .327 for his minor league club. Two years later, in 1965, he played in 157 games for the Dodgers and was selected as "Rookie of the Year," when he hit 12 homers and batted .250. In 1965 Jim slugged 24 home runs and hit for a .274 average and seemed on his way to one of the brightest futures in Dodger history. He was a most versatile player. He switch-hit, played first base, 3rd base, 2nd base and in the outfield, when Dodger regulars were injured. Unfortunately, Jim was prone to injury himself and his playing time was limited. In 1972, his 7th and last year with the Dodgers, Jim played in 70 games and hit .201. During the off-season, Jim worked with the Dodger organization and several Dodger players, including Wes Parker, visiting high schools and colleges to give anti-drug lectures.

(Left) Jim Gilliam makes a great stop of a hard smash by the Twins' Zoilo Versalles to stop a rally. Jim's play kept the ball from going through for a sure hit. Gilliam got to third base in time to force Frank Quilici, who would have scored. Dodgers won the game 2-0 behind Sandy Koufax' great pitching as the Dodgers won the 1965 World Series over the Twins, Oct. 15, 1965.

The Dodgers win the 1966 National League pennant...

(Top) Dodger rightfielder Ron Fairly makes a great one-handed running catch to get Cincinnati's Deron Johnson then rolls over on his back as center-fielder Willie Davis looks on. The great catch in the ninth inning broke up a rally that saw the Reds tie the score at 2-2. (Bottom) Winning Dodger pitcher, Claude Osteen, obviously elated, greets Fairly at the dugout after Ron singled in the winning run, in the bottom of the 9th inning. The Dodgers slipped by the Reds 3-2 at Dodger Stadium, July 6, 1966.

Don Drysdale had just shut out the Cubs, 4-0, in a game at Wrigley Field, Chicago and is congratulated by his catcher, Jeff Torberg. The victory gave the Dodgers a 2-1/2 game lead over the Pirates with a week to go to the end of the season. The game was played September 23, 1966. The Dodgers won the pennant, nosing out the Giants and Pirates.

The 1966 World Series...

Dodgers vs. Baltimore...

Oh! Oh!...Baltimore 4, Dodgers 0...

Manager Walt Alston, right, of the Los Angeles Dodgers conducts a tour of Dodger Stadium for his rival, manager Hank Bauer of the Baltimore Orioles, and a team of umpires to go over ground rules for the 1966 World Series.

Dodger outfielder Willie Davis is a force-out victim in the 7th inning of the first game of the 1966 World Series in Los Angeles. Davis is trapped as the Orioles 2nd baseman Dave Johnson flips ball to shortstop Aparicio. Davis (3) doesn't believe the call and argues. But the umpire always has the last word. The Orioles won, 5-2.

Shortstop Maury Wills of the Dodgers, goes to the air to avoid the sliding Andy Etchebarren as the Baltimore catcher was forced at second in the sixth inning of the first game, of the World Series, at Los Angeles. The play came as the Oriole pitcher tried to sacrifice and bunted to the pitcher.

Guess Who Won Yesterday — You'd never know from their expressions whose team won the opening 1966 World Series game in Los Angeles the day before as managers Hank Bauer, left, of the Baltimore Orioles and Walt Alston of the Los Angeles Dodgers get together in Dodger Stadium. As every baseball fan knows, Bauer's team won, 5-2.

Paul Blair of the Orioles is home without a play in the fifth inning of the 1966 World Series game 2 as Dodger center fielder Willie Davis dropped an Oriole easy fly and then threw wildly to third trying to catch Blair. It was a double error for Davis, whose error a moment earlier had allowed Blair to get on. Dodger catcher is Johnny Roseboro.

Dodger catcher Johnny Roseboro, swooping in at the last second, reaches over the head of first baseman Wes Parker to catch the pop fly of Baltimore's Dave Johnson in the fifth inning of World Series game No. 2 in Los Angeles.

Ron Fairly, 6, Los Angeles outfielder, dives for the bag at second base today as Baltimore's Dave Johnson, (15), gets off his throw to first to complete a double play in the second inning of the third World Series game at Baltimore. Lou Johnson of the Dodgers started the action with a tap to Baltimore shortstop Luis Aparicio. The Orioles took the game, 1-0 behind the great 3-hit pitching of Wally Bunker.

1967, 1968...Time to Rebuild

A hatless Don Sutton serves up a pitch in batting practice as the Dodgers engage in workouts at Dodger Stadium in early February, 1967. Don won 11 games in 1967.

Ron Hunt jogs around the bases after slugging his first home run as a Dodger. In a game against the Pirates at Dodger Stadium Ron smashed a towering drive over the center field fence in the fifth inning of a game won by the Dodgers, 5-1. Hunt, who brought a lifetime .282 average to the Dodgers, was obtained in a big trade with the Mets. In the deal the Dodgers traded Tommy Davis to the Mets for Hunt and Jim Hickman.

In 1967 Alan Foster became the "hottest" young prospect in the nation, when he earned his nickname, "Double-No-No" by pitching 2 successive no-hit games against Seattle in the Pacific Coast League. Dodger scouts beat everybody off with a six-figure bonus and he responded in 1969 by pitching 2 straight shut-outs over the Mets and Padres. But he never quite reached the heights expected of him. In 1970 Foster won 10 games and lost 13 and the following year was traded to the Indians. In his best year, 1973, he won 13 and lost 9 for the Cardinals.

Tom Haller came to the Dodgers in a trade with the Giants in 1968 and it proved to be one of Tom's best years. The big catcher hit .285 and was selected as "Dodger of the Year". A former quarterback at Illinois, Haller hit for a .270 average and 10 home runs in 1970. In 1972 the 11-year veteran was sent to the Tigers.

THE DODGERS STAFF, 1969

The Dodgers have one of baseball's best staffs, headed by Manager Walt Alston (24). Front Row, from left: Red Adams, Jim Gilliam and Carroll Beringer. Back from left: Dixie Walker, Roy Hartsfield, Alston and Danny Ozark.

THE DODGERS STAFF, 1969

Ted Williams, manager of the Washington Senators in 1970, and Dodger manager Walt Alston discuss their chances during spring training in Florida.

In 1969 Bill Singer had a remarkable year, winning 20 games, while losing 12. In 1970 he pitched a no-hit-no-run game against Philadelphia, on July 20. In April he contracted hepatitus and was sidelined for 2 months. When he returned on June 19, Bill won 7 out of 8 games. Medical men could not believe that Singer could recover so quickly from so serious an illness.

Wes Parker hit .350 for Albuquerque in 1963. The next year, 1964, Wes came up with the Dodgers, played 124 games and hit .257. Wes had his finest of 9 seasons with the Dodgers in 1970 when he hit .319. Parker retired as an active player in 1972, at the young age of 32. "There are other things I'd like to do with my life," he said.

5 GREAT MEN

(Above) Jack and Campy at Dodger Stadium in 1970.

Casey Stengel, Gil Hodges and Jack Dempsey are signally honored at the NY Cartoonist Award Dinner in New York City, Jan. 28, 1970.

The manager has to be everywhere and to see everything. Here's Walt Alston behind the batting screen in 1970.

Steve Yeager

Pete Richert

Eddie Solomon

Ted Gilje

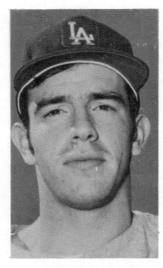

Terry McDermott

Lee Lacy

Dave Lopes

Larry Hisle

Tim Johnson

Some of the Dodger rookies who reported to Vero Beach Spring Training Headquarters of the Dodgers in 1971.

The sight of these formidable Dodger sluggers poised for action in spring training at Vero Beach was enough to strike terror to every National League pitcher in 1971. The Dodgers traded Ted Sizemore and Bob Stinson and received the hard-hitting Richie Allen. All Allen did was to drive out 23 home runs and to hit for a .295 average. Duke Sims came in on a trade with the Indians and hit .274. Willie Davis, in his 12th and finest year with the Dodgers, hit .309, Wes Parker hit .274, Bill Grabarkewitz, injured for part of the season was down to .224, and Steve Garvey recalled from Spokane hit .227, but his 3 home runs against the Giants almost won the division title for the Dodgers, as they finished 1 game behind the San Franciscans in the Western Division.

A bombshell deal in the winter of 1970 was the Dodgers-Cardinals trade in which Ted Sizemore and Bob Stinson went to the Cards for Richie Allen, one of the great hitters in baseball and one of the most controversial players. In 1970 Allen slugged 34 home runs and hit .279 for the Cardinals. For the Dodgers, in 1971, Richie drove out 23 home runs and hit for a solid .295 as the Dodgers finished a nose behind the Giants in the Western Division. The next year Richie was gone to the White Sox.

Richie Allen has just slugged his second home run of the game...A tremendous 400-foot shot that brought the crowd up roaring with excitement. But the Dodgers lost to the Astros, 5-3, despite 2 home runs by Allen and his 3rd hit a long double. Here Richie crosses home plate and his Dodger teammates greet him led by no. 28, Wes Parker. The game was played at Dodger Stadium, April 17, 1971.

Willie Davis...On The Move

With the Dodgers 1960 to 1974

At six-foot two and 185 pounds, Willie Davis was slim and graceful. Like a big cat he was, with reflexes like lightning and feet as nimble as Sugar Ray Leonard's. He covered tremendous ground with his long strides. He had all the ability a ballplayer dreamed of. During the late 1960's and early 1970's Willie put together three or four outstanding seasons for the Dodgers. He hit as high as .311 and drove in as many as 93 runs. He got six hits in one 19-inning game. He hit in a record 31 straight games (Dodger record). Willie hit over .300 five seasons and close to .280 for his 13 seasons with the Dodgers. He stole almost 400 bases. He led the National League in triples, twice. He won Gold Gloves for fielding excellence three times. "He was a big boy who never grew up," said Buzzy Bavasi, Dodger Vice President. Before one of the World Series games, Bavasi said, "If the President throws out the first ball, Willie Davis will swing at it. He was a wonderful, big kid. We all miss him."

Al Campanis rates the acquisition of Al Downing as one of the Dodgers' great trades. Obtained from Milwaukee in 1971, Downing proved to be the most consistent pitcher on the club. He won 20 games while losing 9 and was selected by The Sporting News as the Comeback Player of the Year. Downing pitched for the Yankees from 1963 to 1968 and was in two World Series with the Bombers. But he reached his peak year in 1971 with the Dodgers. He remained with Los Angeles until 1977, when the crafty lefty retired.

Dodgers At Work — The Dodgers are at work in pre-season drills at Dodger Stadium in 1972. Above, Frank Robinson takes a cut in the batting cage and then chats with Dodger coach Jim Gilliam who is in charge of the workouts. As part of the drills, Dodger trainer Bill Buhler leads the team in calisthenics.

Nicknamed "Penguin," by his Dodger teammates, Ron Cey was a Dodger All-Star at 3rd base for several years.

Chris Cannizzaro was obtained from the Cubs in 1971. He caught for the Dodgers in 1972 and 1973.

Buckner At Work—Bill Buckner headed for first base when the Dodgers opened workouts at Dodger Stadium during the 1973 pre-season drills. Buckner batted .319 for the Dodgers in 1972.

Alston and His Coaches — Dodger manager Walt Alston and his coaching staff in 1973. Monty Basgall, Tommy Lasorda, (front) Red Adams and Jim Gilliam.

On May 28, 1973, Andy Messersmith set his name in the record books when he struck out the first 6 batters in a game against the Phillies.

In his 3 years with the Dodgers, Messersmith won 14 games in '73, 20 games in 1974 and 19 games in 1975. He was traded to the Atlanta Braves in 1976.

Andy Messersmith, a former 20-game winner in the American League. Messersmith and third baseman Ken McMullen came to the Dodgers in a big off-season trade.

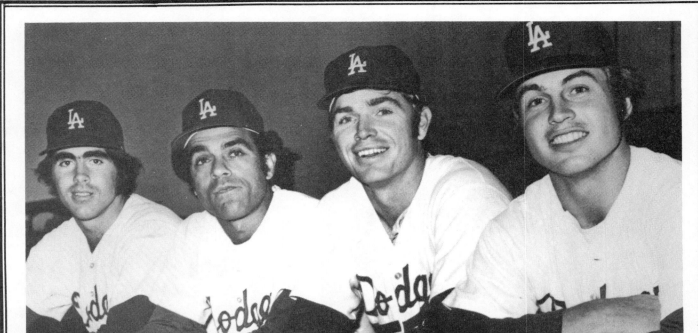

Dodger infielders: Bill Buckner, Davey Lopes, Bill Russell and Ron Cey in 1973.

When the Dodgers purchased infielder Rick Auerbach from the Brewers in the off-season of 1973, their primary thought was to have a reliable, capable defensive performer to spell shortstop Bill Russell. But Auerbach's weak hitting bothered Dodger coaches, Jim Gilliam, Monty Basgall and Tom Lasorda. It was thought that Rick, with his fine co-ordination and strength, should be a more productive batter. They had Rick practicing hitting day after day, hitting, hitting. The coaches also had films taken of Auerbach's stance and swing at the plate. The coaches worked overtime with Rick and noticed several flaws in his swing and stance. There was more work and more pictures. Was there any improvement? Well, in 1974 Rick played in 45 games and hit for an average of .342.

Dodger President Peter O'Malley and one of his favorite players, outfielder Willie Davis, in 1973.

(Above) Manager Walter Alston opens spring training in a novel way in 1974.

(Left) Dodger President, Peter O'Malley, and Walt Alston in 1974 at spring training, Vero Beach, Fla.

Stan Musial and the Dodgers' Bill Buckner exchange pleasantries before a game between the Cardinals and Dodgers in 1974.

Juan Marichal was obtained from the Red Sox in 1974. It was thought that the crafty left-handed pitching ace might still have some wins in his great arm. But the "Dominican Dandy" had had it. He pitched only 6 innings for the Dodgers in 1975. After 243 career wins Marichal was through.

Willie Crawford holds up a poster given to Dodger fans in 1974. A fine outfielder with the Dodgers since 1964, Willie was a consistent and solid performer for 11 years. His best years were in 1973, when he hit for a .295 average and drove out 14 home runs and 1974 when he slugged 11 homers and repeated with a .295 average.

"Rick Rhoden proved that he could be a starting pitcher in 1975," said Dodger Vice President Al Campanis. Rick did start 11 games and compiled a 3-3 mark. In 1974 Rick appeared in 26 games and saved 11. He is big and a Don Drysdale look-a-like.

Mike Marshall
1974 Sporting News Pitcher of the Year
and
Cy Young Award Winner

"I'm not saying Mike Marshall is the Messiah, but he's the only guy I've talked to about sore arms and throwing whose made any sense. Without Mike's help there would be no way that I could have thrown a football effectively." Those were the words of Fran Tarkenton in 1975, when he was one of the great quarterbacks of the National Football League. Marshall, who has a doctorate degree in physiology, was obtained by the Dodgers in 1973, December 5, in one of the best deals that Dodger Vice President Al Campanis ever made. Campanis sent one of the Dodger stars, Willie Davis, to the Expos for Marshall, and all Mike did in 1974 was to practically insure the pennant and a World Series spot for the team. In his record-setting performance, he pitched in 106 games, 208 innings in relief; finished 83 games, pitched in 13 consecutive games and became the first relief pitcher in 24 years to win the Sporting News Pitcher of the Year Award. He won 15 games and had 21 saves and, to top off that magnificent year of years, was awarded the coveted Cy Young Award. In 1975, Mike was not as effective, but did manage to win 9 games along with 13 saves, but injured his rib cage on several occasions. In 1976, he won 4 and lost 3 for the Dodgers and was dealt to the Atlanta Braves in mid-season. Mike Marshall, the finest relief pitcher in Dodger history.

(Left) Ron Cey had one of his greatest days as a Dodger, in a game that was played in Pittsburgh, Oct. 6, 1974. Ron hit a home run, two doubles and a single in four times at bat as the Dodgers beat the Pirates, 5-2. In the photo, Cey has just hit a pitch off Jim Rooker, the Pirates' pitcher. The ball can be seen coming off Cey's left leg. He doubled on the hit. The catcher is Manny Sanguillen of Pittsburgh. The umpire is Paul Pryor.

(Below) Ron Cey has hit another home run. Here he is on his way home as manager Lasorda pats his back. In 1974 Ron hit 18 home runs. This time it was against the Cardinals as the Dodgers go on to win, 5-0.

The 1974 World Series...
Oakland vs. Los Angeles...
Oakland wins 4 games to 1.

Herb Washington is trapped off first base in the second game of the 1974 World Series, between the Dodgers and Oakland. The play, in the ninth inning of a 3-2 game, might have cost the A's the game. Washington represented the tying run but, Steve Garvey (6) takes the throw and tags Washington for the out. The Series was tied 1-1. The umpire is Doug Harvey. The game was played Oct. 13, 1974.

Oakland's Sal Bando slams into Dodger catcher Steve Yeager as Bando tries to score from 3rd base in the 8th inning of the first game of the 1974 World Series. Both players went flying, but Yeager hung onto the ball and Bando was out. The A's won the game, 3-2, on a Reggie Jackson homer in the game played at Dodger Stadium.

Bill Buckner is out at 3rd base trying to stretch his 8th inning base hit. The play practically ended the hopes of the Dodgers in the final game of the 1974 World Series against Oakland. A's 3rd baseman Sal Bando waits for the ball (photo 1) then puts the tag on Bill (2) as umpire Bill Kunkel calls the play (3). The A's won the game, 3-2. In photo 3, the umpire calls Buckner out.

On Sunday, April 25, 1976, the Dodgers were playing the Chicago Cubs in Los Angeles. Ted Sizemore came up to hit for the Dodgers in the fourth inning when suddenly two men ran onto the field and spread an American flag on the turf. They were just about to set fire to the flag when Dodger Rick Monday dashed over, scooped up the flag and handed it to security men in charge of the ball park. 25,550 fans rose as one man and wildly cheered Monday for his magnificent patriotic effort.

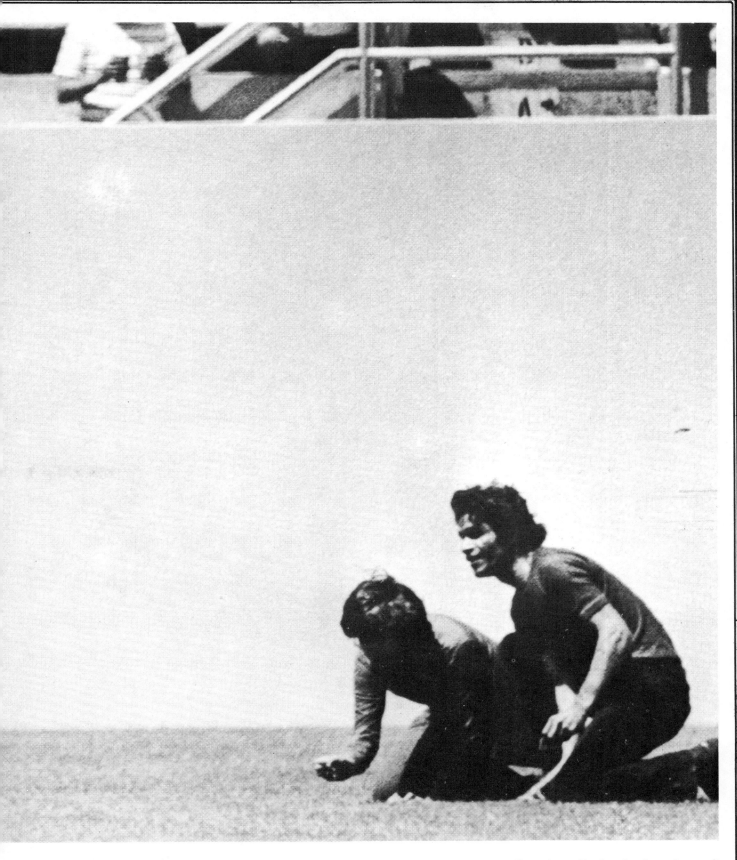

When Monday went to bat in the fifth inning, he drew another standing ovation. It was the beginning of a week that Monday will never forget. Mayor Richard Daley of Chicago invited Monday to serve as Grand Marshal of the annual Flag Day parade in Chicago. Wires, letters and phone calls poured into Monday's home and to the Dodger office and he was interviewed over countless radio and television programs.

Walt Alston managed the Dodgers from 1954 to 1976 and was one of baseball's great managers. As a player in the high minor leagues, Walt was a good first baseman but could not hit major league pitching. In his only major league at-bat, in 1936, Walt faced Lon Warneke of the Cardinals and Lon promptly struck Alston out. Here in 1974, 38 years have passed and Warneke and Alston meet at an Old-Timers game in Dodger Stadium.

Dusty Baker, the Dodgers' fleet center fielder, almost made a spectacular catch in a game against the Cubs at Dodger Stadium on July 15, 1976. In an unsuccessful attempt to catch Jerry Morales' two-run homer in the Dodgers' 5-2 victory over the Cubs, Baker leaped high and crashed face first into the outfield wall, hitting with such impact that his foot put a hole through the fence. The force of the impact left Dusty on the ground and momentarily dazed. He got up, however, and remained in the game. Two innings later, Baker further displayed his mettle by homering off Oscar Zamora.

Ready To Go — Two Los Angeles Dodgers who were plagued with injuries in 1975, catcher Joe Ferguson (top) and outfielder Bill Buckner (bottom) are ready to begin the 1976 season. Ferguson, who suffered a broken bone in his right forearm, and Buckner, who broke his left ankle, were among the many Dodgers at the annual open-to-the-public workout on Sunday, Feb. 15, 1976 at Dodger Stadium.

Home Run Smiles — Los Angeles Dodgers catcher Steve Yeager, right, is congratulated by teammate Bill Russell after hitting a two-run homer off the Pittsburgh Pirates' pitcher John Candelaria in the eighth inning of their game May 14, 1976. The home run gave Los Angeles a 3-2 lead. The Dodgers held on to win it, 3-2.

Vin Scully, flanked by Jim Gilliam and manager Walt Alston, is considered by experts as "one of the most innovative sports broadcasters in the nation." Vin started broadcasting as a sophomore at Fordham University and was actually tutored by Red Barber, the "Voice of the Brooklyn Dodgers". Barber practically adopted the young Scully and, in a short period of time, Vin became one of Red's broadcast partners alongside Connie Desmond. These men were among the most listened-to broadcasters in the nation and when the Dodgers moved to Los Angeles, Vin Scully went along with them.

Just before an Old-Timers game in Dodger Stadium, former manager Walter Alston checks his lineup with the help of Joe DiMaggio and his former coach, Dodger manager Tommy Lasorda.

Walter Alston was an action manager. In practice he would hit fungoes to his fielders and, when the season was over, Alston would retire to his home town, Darrtown, Ohio, and play ball with his grandson.

8

THE TOMMY LASORDA ERA

1977-

Year	C	W	L	FINISHED
1976	4	2	2	2
1977	162	98	64	1
1978	162	95	67	1
1979	162	79	83	3
1980	162	92	71	2
1981*	57	36	21	1
1981*	53	27	26	4
1982	162	88	74	2
1983	162	91	71	1

* Split season

Spokane 1970. A nine game losing streak leaves Lasorda's players hanging their heads. The manager walks into the silent and dejected clubhouse, realizes a pep talk is in order and tells his team that even the 1927 Yankees, the greatest team ever, which lost nine straight games, didn't get down, didn't lose its confidence. He tells his players to lift up their heads, go have a beer, go have some fun.

Spokane promptly wins nine straight, and as Lasorda and wife Jo drive home after the ninth in a row, Jo says to her husband, "Gee, honey, that story about the Yankees sure did the trick. But how did you know they lost nine straight?"

"I don't know that they did," Lasorda answers, "but it worked, didn't it?"

In one way or another, it always seemed to work for the son of a Pennsylvania steel worker, an eternal optimist who had initially spent 11 years with the Dodgers as a predominantly minor league pitcher, drafted by the Dodgers a year after receiving a $500 bonus to sign with the Phillies. Years later Lasorda encountered the Philadelphia scout and told him that if he'd only been a little more patient, if he'd waited another 15 minutes or so, "I'd have signed and given YOU the $500."

Lasorda spent more than a decade at the triple A level, winning 18 games or more on several occasions, struggling unsuccessfully to reach Ebbetts Field. A dogged left-hander who would just as soon knock down the opposing batter as strike him out, Lasorda was 0-4 with the Dodgers in 27 games over a three year span. During that period, the Dodgers featured a pitching staff of Don Newcombe, Carl Erskine, Preacher Roe, Johnny Podres, Roger Craig, Russ Meyer and Joe Black, among others.

Lasorda came close one spring. He had won 20 games at Montreal the year before and it wasn't until the final cut of March that he was returned to Montreal, making room for another left-hander named Sandy Koufax.

"One of the first things I did when I first reported to the Dodgers spring training camp," said Lasorda, "was to steal a sweat shirt with REESE written on the back of it, then I'd wear it around the park. I'd turn this way and that way so everybody would know who I was."

"One day while we were still in spring training," said Tommy, "and I was really working hard, there was a phone call for me to report to Buzzy Bavasi, the Dodgers general manager. Such a call usually means a player is being shipped back to the minor leagues."

"Tommy, I've got some bad news for you." Bavasi said.

"What's wrong, Buzz, someone in your family sick?" Lasorda said quickly.

"You gotta go back to Montreal."

"Why? I'm doing the job, ain't I?"

"Yeah, but we have to cut the roster by one more man."

"Jeez, get rid of that kid Koufax. He'll never be much of a pitcher. He can't hit the side of a barn door from 60 feet away. And you're going to keep him?"

At that time any player who had signed a bonus for over $4000 had to stay on the major league roster. So the Dodgers were stuck with Sandy Koufax, then a left-hander with speed to burn and no control. Of course, time's passage revealed Koufax as an immortal and he is now in the Hall of Fame.

Which gives Lasorda a wonderful excuse for his brief career as a major league pitcher.

"Look what I did for the organization," he would say years later. "Sandy may have gone on to make the Hall of Fame, but I was the better pitcher."

"I can honestly say that it took the greatest left-handed pitcher of all time to keep me out of the big leagues," Lasorda said.

Yet it did not prevent him from being one of the great unsung World Series heroes.

"I'm going to tell you about that." Tommy said. "It is not in the record books, sure. But every little thing can't be in the record books, can it? And this is the stuff people want to know. This is how I helped the Dodgers win the 1955 World Series."

A quick check of the baseball record books reveals that nobody named Lasorda threw a pitch in the 1955 World Series. That's because Lasorda was sitting home in Pennsylvania watching the games on television, when he got a phone call.

It was Al Campanis. He said, "Tommy, Whitey Ford and Tommy Byrne are giving us fits. Our guys can't hit 'em. Please come on up and pitch some batting practice for us." Lasorda was a left-hander with a beautiful curve ball.

"So I drove the 100 miles to New York," said Tommy, "and pitched batting practice every day—those Dodgers never saw so many good curves as I threw them—and we won the Series. Now, these damn things you won't find in the record books."

"I've got to tell you about the experience I had in the Winter League in Cuba," said Tommy. "During this one game in '53, I hit this guy in the back and I thought he was on his way to first, then all of a sudden I looked up and he was charging right at me with a bat in his hand. I didn't even have a ball to throw at him and he was so big there was just no use in trying to throw a punch. Just as he started to swing the bat, I threw my glove right into his face and then tackled him."

In fact, Lasorda did such a good job defending himself against his bigger opponent that he became a local hero. The next day Cuban soldiers escorted Tommy to President Batista, who asked, "Tommy, is there anything we can do for you?"

"No," said Tommy, "Just let me pitch to that guy again." When Lasorda got his chance, he knocked the player down again. The poor guy never said a word.

Tommy Lasorda was a man who didn't give an inch, a scrambler, a fighter, a competitor who displayed many of those same traits when the Dodgers selected him to manage in the minors.

Lasorda was ejected from his first five games as a manager and is still the only manager ever ejected from a game in the low-key Arizona Instructional League.

He was ejected so often one winter that his players had a pool on which inning he'd get it. Scout Bert Wells arrived late one day and was told that all the innings had been picked. "That's OK," Wells said. "I want the one that says he'll be ejected walking up to the plate with the lineup card."

Lasorda calls it color and says the game needs it. One of his favorite anecdotes involves the night in the Dominican Winter League when he was ejected for throwing his spikes over the fence and his shirt into the stands while arguing with an umpire.

"I had no more than reached the clubhouse," he says, "when a rifle squad marches in and takes me to jail. We were on the road and I was damn scared. But the general finally comes and says I'm not being punished, that he simply wanted to compliment me for my spirit and wishes his team had a manager who did the same."

Through it all—the 11 sometimes frustrating years as a minor league pitcher, the five years as a scout (he once sealed the signing of one of the nation's most coveted players by delivering a eulogy at the funeral of the youth's grandfather, a man he didn't even know), the seven as a minor league manager (breaking in at $6,500 at Ogden), the four as Dodgers' third base coach (elevated from the minors to serve as a liaison, a bridge between the reserved Alston and the young players Lasorda had managed in the minors)—his commitment and belief in the Dodgers only became stronger.

Lasorda rejected a number of major league coaching opportunities along with managerial feelers from Atlanta, Montreal and Pittsburgh, claiming he bled Dodger blue and worshipped the Great Dodger in the Sky. He said he wanted his tombstone to read, "Dodger Stadium was His Address, But Every Ballpark in America Was His Home."

The late Walter O'Malley, owner of the Dodgers,

got wind of Lasorda's wish and presented him with a tombstone that carried just that inscription and had drops of blood—blue blood—carved into it.

"I'm the only guy anywhere with his own tombstone," said Lasorda, who then gave it back to O'Malley and told him, "I want to go on working for the Dodgers even AFTER I die."

Lasorda became the Dodgers' 20th manager on September 29, 1976, and there were those who predicted he and the club would soon qualify for a tombstone, that the methods he employed in the minors would prove fatal in the majors, that familiarity with his players would soon breed contempt. Tommy spoke, "I have to keep remembering that marvelous day, September 28, when Peter O'Malley and Al Campanis said I was the leading candidate to replace Walt Alston. They told me they'd have their decision at 9 AM the very next morning. They told me to stay close to the phone and to expect a call.

"My wife and I waited by that phone from 6 AM on. I wouldn't even allow myself to go to the bathroom. At 9:02 the phone rang and I jumped clear across the room and had the phone in my hand. It was Al Campanis and he said the words that I'll always remember, 'You're the manager of the Dodgers.'

"The next morning when I drove to the Stadium for the press conference, I had to keep pinching myself, and kept telling myself, 'For God's sake don't speed. You'll get a ticket.'"

Lasorda stood at the podium on the day of his hiring and said he had been entrusted with the Hope Diamond, and that his hiring represented the greatest day in his life, and that he didn't intend to change his way of doing things. He said that in order to win, in order to taste the "fruits of victory," a team had to have fun and had to have togetherness. He said he would continue to hug his players, eat with them (depending on who's picking up the check), to have them as guests at his home. He said he would continue to make it a point to know the names of the players' wives and children, to exhort them with the cliches many of them first heard in Ogden or Albuquerque or at Spokane. "You've got to pay the price," he would tell his players then. And: "Let's hear some noise out there. You remind me of a morticians' convention."

A short time after the 1976 season ended, Lasorda contacted every player on the Dodgers' squad. To Steve Garvey he wrote:

"I would like to have you concentrate on home runs rather than collect your 200 hits."

He asked Davey Lopes to take over and become the team leader.

He assured Dusty Baker that the Dodgers hadn't lost faith in him, and that he was being counted on as an outfield regular.

In his first winter as manager of the Dodgers,

Lasorda was a man on the go, living up to his reputation as a communicator and motivator. Lasorda and his wife Jo, for example, began one day after his appointment as Dodger manager with an early morning appearance on the Regis Philbin television program. The Lasordas then hurried back to their Fullerton home to tape a program with a student from a college radio station. When the show was finished, they repeated the interview, because the student had fouled up the only tape he had. Lasorda hunted around, found a tape in his home and loaned it to the kid.

That evening Lasorda had just arrived at the Los Coyotes Country Club to speak at a banquet, when he received a call from a friend hosting another banquet. "Our speaker didn't show up, Tom. Would you come over?" So, Lasorda gave his talk at Los Coyotes and then rushed over the other banquet, where he spoke to another 200 persons.

An unusual day? Not really. The word of Lasorda's touch, his ability to speak anywhere at any time has gotten around.

"Look at it this way," he said recently. "If I was in any other kind of work, no one would phone me. I'm delighted. I'm thrilled if a group thinks I can help make a success of a meeting. It's a chance for me to put something back in the pot. To spread the word about baseball and the Dodgers." Lasorda has spoken to them all, from youths to senior citizens, from bridge clubs to roasts at the Friars Club.

But his most important messages have been delivered to his players. His goal has been to let each player know just where he stands and what is expected of him.

"What has happened in the past with Walt Alston, that's another time, another era. I'm concerned with this club, now. I'm looking ahead. Baseball has to be played with a relaxed and confident attitude. Putting on that Dodger blue uniform should be fun. I want a team that's aggressive, that wants to win, that hungers for victory, but I can't be naive enough to think that as the manager I'm going to win any games.

"The players do it all and my job is to stay with them, motivate them, know their strengths and weaknesses, make each player feel that he's a part of it and create a happy clubhouse.

In Lasorda's first spring as the Dodgers' third base coach, outfielder Tom Paciorek said, "I've been with him for several years. I've heard every one of his stories, his lines, and yet I laugh every time. Some men have it that way. He's a motivator, an inspirational man, but ask me to put it into words and I can't. I suppose the thing is that Tommy sincerely tries to be like a father to us. And, of course, you'd play like hell for your father."

"Yes," Lasorda said, "I want to be like a father to them. I want to be like a father, teacher, philosopher, disciplinarian. Managing is like holding a dove

The 30-Home Run Club—the first foursome in major league history to hit 30 or more home runs are: (kneeling) Dusty Baker and Ron Cey and (standing) Steve Garvey and Reggie Smith. Garvey led the 1977 Dodgers with 33 homers and Smith (32), Baker (3) and Cey (30) followed.

in your hand. Squeeze too hard and you kill it. Not hard enough and it flies away. I want to be the type manager who can say of himself, 'If I were starting my career over, I'd want Tom Lasorda as my manager.'"

The success Tom Lasorda experienced in the minors continued in the majors, even though there were those who continued to demean his skills and methods. He was needled about the hugs he gave his players when they hit home runs or made key plays, needled about the sacrilegious references to the Great Dodger in the Sky, needled about the showbusiness personalities such as Frank Sinatra and Don Rickles who frequented his enlarged clubhouse office where the walls were lined with autographed pictures of Hollywood types (Club President Peter O'Malley finally asked Lasorda to restrict the office to baseball and media personnel), needled about his expanding waistline and the variety of foods he could dish up from his clubhouse refrigerator, which contained everything from bologna to egg rolls.

If many of the players who had virtually grown up under Lasorda in the minors now found him something less than the father he had once been, there was also this measure of the man and manager. In his first five years at the Dodgers' helm the club continued to shatter all of the game's attendance records, playing to a sellout almost every night, while winning at a pace superior to any ever recorded by a new manager. There were three Western Division titles (the Dodgers missed a fourth when they lost a one-game playoff to Houston in 1980), three National League pennants and one World Championship in that time. Lasorda became only the 19th manager in major league history to win a pennant in his rookie year when the Dodgers captured the 1977 crown, and he became only the second National League manager to win pennants in his first two years when the Dodgers repeated in 1978. The World Championship of 1981, achieved only after the Dodgers had lost the first two World Series games to New York and achieved only after they had also rallied for playoff victories against Houston and Montreal, was the club's first in 16 years.

"There have been things on the line," Lasorda said in reflection. "For me and for the team. People said you can't be a big league manager and remain close to your players. They said that with today's attitudes and salaries you can't indoctrinate a feeling of loyalty and pride in an organization. I think I proved those people wrong on both counts. My players are proud to be a Dodger in the same way that players used to say it's great to be a Yankee."

In the process, Lasorda said, he and his players also disproved the 70's myth that Cincinnati was unbeatable and went on to prove that teams like Houston, Philadelphia and the New York Yankees could also be beaten. Lasorda told his team in his first spring as manager, that the Dodgers would win the National League's Western Division and put an end to Cincinnati's dominance. The Reds had won five pennants in the previous seven years, and their rivalry with the Dodgers during the 70's was baseball's best, enlivened by a verbal give and take by the respective managers, the Dodgers' Lasorda and Cincinnati's Sparky Anderson.

While the war of words between Lasorda and Anderson was thought to be in fun, part of the overall mind-games the two teams played, there was undoubtedly some emotion to it, particularly on the side of Lasorda who never forgot that, when Tom was named the Dodgers' manager, Anderson had said, "Now we're going to find out how good a manager Walter Alston was."

When the Dodgers clinched the Western Division title in Lasorda's first year, Lasorda publicly thanked Anderson for having made his job easier, for having helped motivate his team and bring it even closer together via a number of statements ridiculing Lasorda's style and implying the Dodgers would fold.

It didn't happen.

The Dodgers responded to Lasorda's spring optimism, to the change from the steady, stoic Alston, and finished 10 games ahead of second place Cincinnati in 1977. Third baseman Ron Cey set a major league record with 29 RBIs in April as the Dodgers won 22 of their first 26 games and were never headed. The players knew what their roles and responsibilities would be even before the team went to spring training because Lasorda either corresponded or met with each individually. Garvey responded with a club record 33 home runs and 115 RBIs. Dusty Baker, Reggie Smith and Cey also had 30 or more homers as the Dodgers became the first team in major league history to have four players reach that figure. The Dodgers also became the first team ever to have an entire five man rotation work 200 or more innings apiece, each producing a winning percentage of more than .600, led by Tommy John's 20-7 record. John, who had sat out the entire 1975 season while recovering from a delicate arm operation, went on to pitch a memorable, rain-soaked victory over Philadelphia that gave the Dodgers the best of five game (they won it in four) series for the National League pennant and sent them against the Yankees in the World Series.

Lasorda would say later that his team's emotions had been drained by the divisional playoff with Philadelphia and that the Dodgers were simply flat for the Yankees, who beat them in six games, the sixth and final game highlighted by Reggie Jackson's three home runs. It wasn't the way Lasorda and the Dodgers wanted it to end, but there was still the memory of an exciting summer, a summer in which both the city and team seemed to reawaken.

Despite the tough loss to the Yankees, the Dodger players were openly vocal in their support of Lasorda's managerial skills and style. Pitcher Doug Rau stated flatly that Lasorda's unrelenting display of optimism helped relax and motivate his teammates.

Second baseman Davey Lopes, who was named team captain before the 1978 season, remarked that because Lasorda was a good teacher, Tommy was able to "continually re-evaluate his methods and adjust to changing personalities, times and attitudes."

Right-fielder Reggie Smith surmised that Lasorda's rapport and ability to communicate with the team helped relax the team; furthermore, Smith felt, Tommy's door was always open to any player who wanted to see him. Lasorda was able to develop an identity with his players as a manager who cared for them as individuals, as well as ball players.

The camaraderie between Lasorda and his players has produced results where they count — on the field.

Dodgers manager Tom Lasorda, background, yells from the dugout during the World Series game with Yankees in New York. Also watching the action is Davey Lopes, foreground.

THE TOMMY LASORDA ERA 219

Tommy John put it another way, saying the Dodgers had become "mirrors of the manager." The manager, off on a whirlwind circuit of winter speaking engagements, said he was nothing more than a traffic cop.

"Maybe I helped them believe in themselves," he said, "but nothing more. They made it happen. As I told them so often...'In the minors you needed me for instruction and advice, and now I need you.' (And) they didn't let me down. I have to be the luckiest guy in the world. I'm thankful and grateful. Every time I hugged one of them it was to show them that I feel like the father sitting at the dinner table, feeling the pride and love of his family."

Some of the love dissipated in 1978 when there were periodic charges that the communicator had stopped communicating, periodic displays of unhappiness with the lineup and periodic whispers that Lasorda handled the hanging of pictures on the Sinatra wall in his clubhouse office better than he handled the late innings of close games.

The most volatile evidence of disharmony came on August 20 when two of the Dodgers' biggest names, first baseman Steve Garvey and pitcher Don Sutton, engaged in a clubhouse fight that again brought to light the envy, jealousy and distaste many of the Dodgers harbored for All-Star Garvey and the publicity he received, in part, from his All-American image. The fight ultimately led to a public apology by Sutton that failed to eliminate the lingering heat and also created additional charges that Lasorda had failed to deal with the Garvey situation both before it came to a head and once it had.

Again, however, the Dodgers and Lasorda came up winners, rallying from a deficit that was still 4-1/2 games on August 4 to win the West by 2-1/2 games over Cincinnati and again beat Philadelphia in the playoffs. The Dodgers became the first team ever to draw three million or more in attendance. Sutton won 15 games, Garvey had 46 hits in the final month to become the first Dodger ever to collect 200 or more hits in four seasons and second baseman Lopes stole 45 bases in 49 attempts. The summer statistics failed to hold up in the World Series, however, as the Dodgers played erratically in the field and again lost to the Yankees in six games, a disappointing display that was a preview of things to come.

The Dodgers simply were unable to get going in '79. A 36-57 first half that included 31 losses in 41 games prior to the All-Star break, their worst half since the move from Brooklyn, made it impossible for the Dodgers to catch Cincinnati, this despite a 43-36 second half. For the first time, Lasorda watched the World Series via television, his club having finished third in the West with a 79-83 record. Garvey (who also had 204 hits and 110 RBIs), Lopes and Ron Cey—three-fourths of an infield that would play together for 8-1/2 years, a major league

The pitch is right over the plate. It's another strikeout for Tommy John.

record—each hit 28, but the loss of Tommy John, who had won 37 games during the previous two years, to free agency, and Terry Forster, who saved 22 games in 1978, to injury, proved critical during the opening weeks. In addition, there was more discord. In midseason a number of Dodgers anonymously rapped right-fielder Smith, who was nursing shoulder and leg injuries, for having "quit on the team." An angry Smith responded by calling a team meeting in which he demanded that his accusers make themselves known. None did, prompting Lopes, a Smith friend, to resign the captaincy Lasorda had given him before the start of the '78 season.

"We shall return," Lasorda said in the wake of the disappointing year, but the next one got off equally rocky. At least for Lasorda. The manager confronted his former first base coach, Jim Lefebvre, in a Los Angeles TV studio in February, and Lefebvre responded to what he said was a name-calling tirade from Lasorda by dropping his ex-boss with a single punch.

"A sucker punch," Lasorda said.

A long-standing member of the Dodger organization, Lefebvre was fired by Lasorda at the end of the 1979 season. Lasorda implied that many of his veteran players had been unhappy with Lefebvre's work as batting instructor and that Lasorda was equally unhappy when Lefebvre went over his head and got Vice President Al Campanis' permission to employ a video system so that he could show the veterans what they were doing wrong.

The fracas served to set a controversial stage for the 1980 season in which Los Angeles, Cincinnati and Houston waged a summer-long dogfight for the Western Division title before the Astros won it in a one-game playoff with the Dodgers, a playoff necessitated when the Dodgers swept a three-game series from Houston, the final series of the regular season, at a packed and jumping Dodger Stadium. It was a dramatic conclusion that might have been avoided if Smith and shortstop Bill Russell had not been lost to second half injuries and if the Dodgers first foray into the free agent market had returned greater dividends. The Dodgers spent more than $5 million on pitchers

In a pensive mood in the dugout, Terry Forster waits word from manager Lasorda to go into action. Here he listens to his favorite music.

Dave Stanhouse and Dave Goltz only to have Stanhouse save just seven games and Goltz win just seven of 18 decisions. Similarly, pitcher Rick Sutcliff, who won 17 games and the National League's Rookie of the Year Award in 1979, slumped to a 3-9 record.

By contrast, the stretch run was highlighted by the work of pitcher Fernando Valenzuela, a portly and anonymous southpaw purchased originally from the Mexican League and recalled in September from the Texas League. Valenzuela, a screwball specialist, kept the Dodgers alive with 10 shutout relief appearances spanning 17-2/3 innings. The poised teenager (he was 19) wouldn't stay anonymous for long.

Indeed, in 1981, during a season decimated by a long strike between owners and players, Valenzuela was the toast of baseball as he continued to demonstrate an immunity to pressure and the media blitz his success brought him. With Spanish-language broadcaster, Jamie Jarrin serving as his personal interpreter, Valenzuela dispatched press conference after press conference with the cool detachment he displayed on the mound. Moved from the bullpen to the rotation by Lasorda, Valenzuela had a 2.48 earned run average and 13-7 record (the strike took 50 days out of the season). He led the

National League in innings pitched and complete games and he led the majors in strike outs and shutouts. He made eight starts in which he allowed four hits or less and he pitched before sellout crowds in 11 of his 12 starts at home.

In post-season competition expanded to include a divisional playoff because of a split-season concept adopted in the strike's wake (the Dodgers reached the playoffs by winning the first half with a 36-21 record), Valenzuela kept his club alive by winning game 4 of the best of five playoff series with Houston, won the decisive fifth game of the best of five league championship series with Montreal (decided on a dramatic home run by Rick Monday) and again kept the Dodgers alive (they were down in games, 0-2) by tenaciously winning the third game of the best of seven World Series with New York.

This last of his overall 16 wins in 1981 was the first of four straight Dodger wins as they avenged the 1977 and 1978 Series losses to New York by winning the 1981 world's championship in six games. The final out brought the 53 year old manager racing toward the mound, the final lap of a long and loyal journey for Tom Lasorda, whose arms were raised overhead in glorious salute to the Great Dodger in the Sky.

Steve Garvey at first base, poised and ready for any ball hit to him.

Dusty Baker is greeted by his teammates, headed by Steve Garvey, after slamming a long drive over the center field wall at Dodger Stadium on Sept. 5, 1977.

Late in the 1977 season, Dodger vice-president Al Campanis brought Vic Davalillo up from the Mexican League, and Vic paid off at once. In the championship series against Philadelphia, the Dodgers were behind 5-3 in the ninth inning. With two outs and the entire season up for grabs. Vic went in as a pinch-hitter and promptly bunted for a base hit.   That started a rally that gave the Dodgers three runs and a 6-5 storybook victory over the Phils.   Vic came back to play some 75 games for the Dodgers in 1978, but its doubtful that in his 20 years as a professional   Vic Davalillo ever delivered a more important hit for any team than the one in Philadelphia in 1977.

Former Dodger manager Walter Alston, now retired, returned to Dodger Stadium, June 5, 1978, for Old-Timers Day. Alston was honored, and his uniform, No. 24, was retired—only the fourth number to be retired in Dodger history. Alston is shown after his 2,000th major league win, July 17, 1976, with pitcher Rick Rhoden. Alston is one of six managers ever to win 2,000 or more games in baseball history.

The Dodgers defeat the Phillies, three games to one, for the 1977 National League Championship and the symbolic ring.

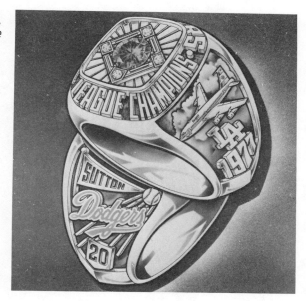

(Below) Manager Tommy Lasorda gets the full champagne treatment in the Dodgers' locker room following their 3-1 win over the Giants. The game played at Candlestick Park, Sept. 21, 1977, clinched the National League West title for the Dodgers.

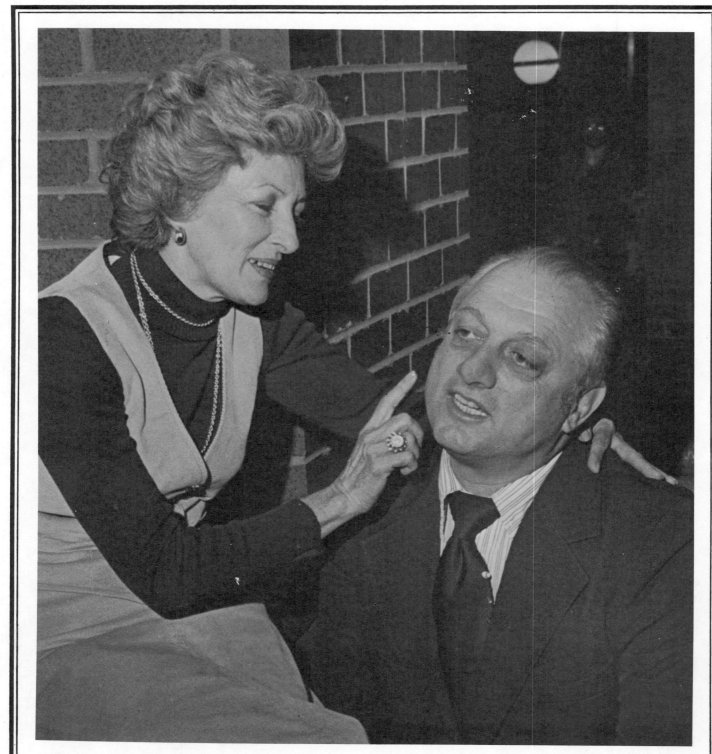

Dodger manager Tom Lasorda's wife, Jo, points to the spot where she is going to kiss Tommy after they learned he had been named the Associated Press Manager of the Year in 1977.

THE 1977 WORLD SERIES . . .
DODGERS VS YANKEES

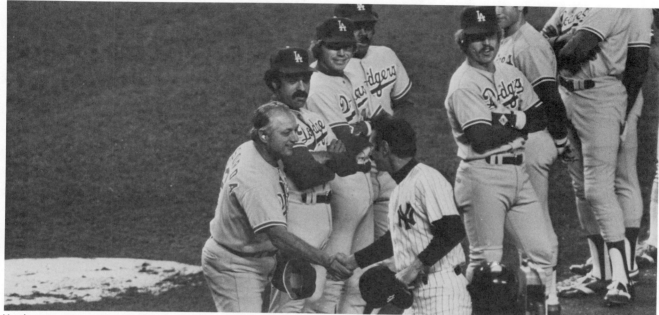

Yankee manager Billy Martin (right) shakes hands with Tommy Lasorda before the first game of the 1977 World Series at Yankee Stadium. Dodgers looking on with challenging grins are Dodgers Davey Lopes, Bill Russell and Reggie Smith (left to right). Ron Cey and Steve Garvey (right) look on grimly.

Manager Tommy Lasorda looks at photo of controversial 6th inning play from the first game of the 1977 World Series. Shot shows Steve Garvey being tagged by catcher Thurman Munson as Umpire Chylak calls the play. "Steve was safe," said Lasorda. "The ump was out of position to make a call."

(Left) Ron Cey dives in an attempt to get this line drive by Thurman Munson, Yankee catcher, in the first inning of the first game of the 1977 World Series at New York. Cey could not get the ball and Munson had a single.

Yankee catcher Thurman Munson dives for the tag as Steve Garvey slides for the plate in the 6th inning of the first game of the 1977 World Series. Umpire Nestor Chylak called Garvey out. It was a close play and may have cost the Dodgers the game. The Yanks went on to win in the 12th inning, 4-3.

Dodger catcher Steve Yeager on the ground after being hit by foul tip off the bat of Yankee pitcher Dick Tidrow (19) in the 3rd inning of the 2nd game of the 1977 World Series. Yeager stayed in the game and the Dodgers went on to win, 6-1.

Catfish Hunter was routed in the 2nd inning of the 2nd game of the 1977 World Series. The Dodgers pounded Hunter for 4 home runs as the Dodgers won 6-1.

Burt Hooton allowed the Yankees only six hits in the second game of the 1977 World Series as they beat the Yankees, 6-1.

Dodger pitcher Burt Hooton (4) pats Ron Cey (10) on top of the head as other teammates rush to congratulate Hooton, who pitched a marvelous game to beat the Yankees 6-1 in the second game of the 1977 World Series.

Burt Hooton talks to reporters after going all the way to beat the Yankees 6-1 in the 2nd game of the 1977 World Series. Hooton wears a button which reads, "I Do It Right."

A spectator holds up the excitement as he slides into home plate in the ninth inning of the second game of the 1977 World Series between the Dodgers and Yankees in New York's Yankee Stadium. Yankee catcher Thurman Munson (left), umpire Ed Sudol and an officer watch the antics.

Tommy Lasorda, Dodgers manager, plants a kiss on cheek of Gene Hooton, young son of hurler Burt Hooton, at Dodger Stadium during tail end of team workout in preparation for Game Three of the World Series against the Yankees, Friday, Oct. 13, 1977, at Dodger Stadium.

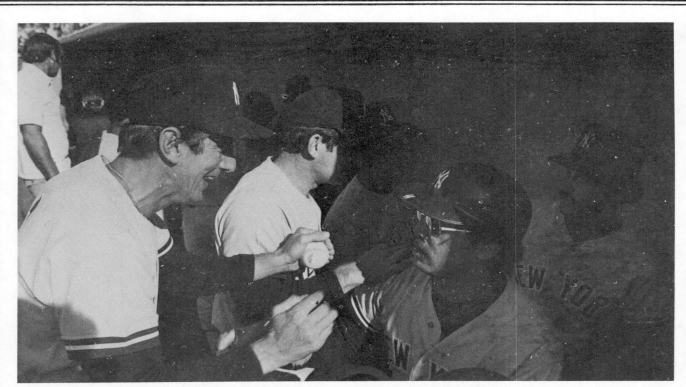

Yankee manager Billy Martin greets Reggie Jackson after the Yanks won the fourth game in the 1977 World Series. Reggie homered and hit a tremendous double, and Ron Guidry allowed the Dodgers only four hits. The Yanks won this fourth game, 4-2.

Don Sutton in the locker room after his fine pitching defeated the Yanks 10-4 in the fifth game of the 1977 World Series at Dodger Stadium.

Dodger catcher Steve Yeager tips his batting helmet to the crowd as they continue to cheer him for his three-run homer in the fifth game of the World Series at Dodger Stadium. The Dodgers went on to defeat the Yankees 10-4 behind fine pitching of Don Sutton. The next day the Yankees won the game 8-4 behind Reggie Jackson's three successive home runs. The Yankees won the World Series, four games to two, in 1977.

Dusty Baker, the Dodgers' great outfield star, goes right into the stands in a attempt to catch this foul ball off the bat of Mickey Rivers in the first inning of the sixth game of the 1977 World Series. Dusty got the ball.

Despite losing the 1977 World Series to the New York Yankees, over 100 Dodger fans greeted catcher Steve Yeager, lower right, and the rest of their "still favorite" team at L.A. airport.

Billy North of the Dodgers is safe on a hurried throw by Cincinnati shortstop Dave Concepcion that pulled Dan Driessen off first base on June 23, 1978, at Dodger Stadium.

Dodger ace Don Sutton fires strike three past San Francisco batter Greg Johnston in sixth inning of Aug. 5, 1979, game (top left); then raises his fist in acknowledgment of his 2,487th career strikeout (top right); he pauses to acknowledge a standing ovation from Dodger Stadium crowd as they pay tribute to the club's all-time strikeout leader (bottom left); then heads for the dugout for a rest after retiring the next batter (bottom right).

In a remarkable series of photographs taken in 1978, Tommy John winds up, rears back, and then . . . another strikeout!

Dodger baserunner Vic Davalillo (33) slides into home plate and jars the ball loose from Mets catcher John Stearns as he scores the tying run in the bottom of the ninth inning at Dodger Stadium. Davalillo scored from second base when teammate Joe Ferguson singled off third baseman Lenny Randle's glove, to tie the score at 3-3. The Dodgers went on to defeat the Mets 4-3 in 12 innings.

Lee Lacy, Dodgers third baseman, is trying to stretch a drive to center field into a triple. In this Sept. 19, 1978, game at Dodger Stadium against the Reds, Lacy starts his slide into third base, but Pete Rose has the ball for an easy out.

Above: Among the celebrities enjoying pre-game festivities at Dodger Stadium prior to Game Three of the National League Playoff between the Los Angeles Dodgers and the Philadelphia Phillies in 1978 are L-R: Frank Sinatra, his wife Barbara, and actor Kirk Douglas.

Obviously a member of the Don Sutton fan club, singer Toni Tennille gets a laugh out of a remark made by Sutton about the tee-shirt she is wearing as she visits him prior to the third game of the National League Playoff between the Dodgers and Phillies at Dodger Stadium. Sutton will be the starting pitcher for the game.

Bill North in 1978.

Philadelphia catcher Bob Boone (8) dives for a foul tip hit by Bill North of the Dodgers in the third inning of the fourth game of the National League Playoff at Dodger Stadium. Boone missed the catch.

Dodgers catcher Steve Yeager literally hangs on the screen of the "Chinese" dugout near the Phillies dugout on a foul ball hit by Mike Schmidt in the sixth inning of the Dodgers-Phillies National League playoff game at Dodger Stadium.

Ron Cey of the Dodgers crosses home plate in victory as he is met by catcher Gerry Grote after Bill Russell hit a two-run single to beat the Phillies and win the National League pennant.

Dejection set in on the Philadelphia bench as the Phillies saw their World Series hopes go down the drain. Bill Russell hit a 3-3 tie-breaking single to win the second consecutive National League Pennant in the tenth inning at Dodger Stadium in 1978. Two players bow their heads and another kneels in grief at the loss of the game.

Phillies infielder Larry Bowa uses a towel to cover up his grief as the Philadelphia Phillies' chances for a National League pennant went down the drain. The Los Angeles Dodgers beat them by a score of 4-3 in the tenth inning of Game Four of the National League Playoff game at Dodger Stadium.

THE 1978 WORLD SERIES DODGERS VS YANKEES (AGAIN . . .)

Above (left and right): New York Yankee catcher Cliff Johnson and Los Angeles Dodgers manager Tommy Lasorda clown as they watch batting practice at Dodger Stadium, prior to the start of the 1978 World Series.

Left: Los Angeles Dodgers outfielder Vic Davalillo poses with his son Jose as the Dodgers work out just prior to the start of the first World Series game against the New York Yankees.

Former Dodger catcher Roy Campanella (in wheelchair), aided by former Dodger pitcher Don Newcombe, throws out the first ball at Dodger Stadium to catcher Steve Yeager to open the 1978 World Series, between the Yankees and Dodgers on Oct. 10.

Los Angeles pitcher Tommy John delivers the first pitch Tuesday night in game one of the World Series in Los Angeles. Batting is the New York Yankees' Mickey Rivers. The umpire is Ed Vargo. Catching for the Dodgers is Steve Yeager. First pitch was a called strike.

Dodger shortstop Bill Russell dives back to first base to beat a pick-off attempt by Yankee pitcher Ed Figueroa to first baseman Chris Chambliss, in the first inning of the first World Series game. Russell was safe.

The Dodgers' designated hitter Lee Lacy (34) is out at second, on the first half of a double play, as New York Yankees shortstop Fred Stanley (11) goes up in the air to avoid him. Stanley fired to first for the second half of the double play to Yeager at first. The action occurred in the second inning of the first World Series game.

In the first game of the World Series at Dodger Stadium, center fielder Rick Monday slides safely into second base after doubling to center. Covering the bag is Yankee shortstop Bucky Dent, and the umpire is John Kibler.

The Los Angeles Dodgers' Davey Lopes (15) reaches out to slap the hand of teammate Rick Monday in Los Angeles after hitting a two-run homer in the second inning of the World Series. At bottom is New York Yankees catcher Thurman Munson.

Dodger Bill North slides safely into second base in the seventh inning after hitting a double to score Steve Garvey and Dusty Baker during the first game of the World Series. Trying for the play for the Yankees is Fred Stanley. Umpire is John Kibler.

Reggie Smith (8) is out at second on a steal attempt as the New York Yankees' Brian Doyle flies through the air on taking the throw from catcher Thurman Munson in the eighth inning of the first game of the 1978 World Series at Dodger Stadium. The Dodgers beat the Yankees 11-5 to take the lead in the first game.

Terry Forster

The Dodgers' designated hitter Lee Lacy (L, 34) shakes hands with a jubilant Terry Forster (51), relief pitcher, after the Dodgers won their Series opener at Dodger Stadium against the New York Yankees, 11-5. Forster relieved Tommy John on the mound in the 7th inning.

Los Angeles Dodgers pitcher Tommy John (L), who started the first game of the 1978 World Series against the New York Yankees, and held them to a 6-0 lead after four innings, and Dodger team captain Dave Lopes, who hit two home runs to lead the team to an 11-5 victory, are all smiles after the game. Lopes had a total of nine hits in the playoffs and first game of the Series.

Dodgers pitcher Tommy John shows his stuff on the mound, during the World Series opener against the New York Yankees. John was credited with the 11-5 win over the Yankees, as he virtually starved the Yankees, feeding them an assortment of sinkerballs. Of the 23 outs John recorded, 17 of them were the result of grounders.

Yankee manager Bob Lemon (left) and Los Angeles Dodgers manager Tommy Lasorda talk things over at Dodger Stadium prior to the start of the second World Series game between the two clubs in 1978.

Dodger pitcher Burt Hooton tosses the first pitch in the second game of the World Series in Los Angeles. At bat for the Yankees is Roy White. The catcher is Dodger Steve Yeager, the umpire is Bill Haller of the American League. The first pitch was a ball.

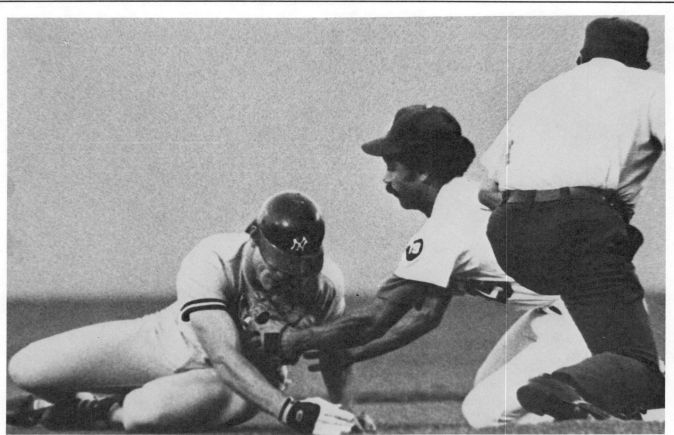

New York Yankees center fielder Gary Thomasson (left, 24) is thrown out stealing, as catcher Steve Yeager threw to second baseman Davey Lopes for the play, in the first inning of the second Series game in Los Angeles. The umpire is Marty Springstead.

New York Yankees centerfielder Gary Thomasson makes a great catch (left) in deep center field on Davey Lopes' long fly ball out towards the wall, then (right) slams into the wall himself, unable to check his momentum in third inning of the second World Series game at Dodger Stadium.

New York Yankees catcher Thurman Munson (right) runs past Los Angeles Dodgers catcher Steve Yeager (background) to score at home plate in the third inning of the second game of World Series. Reggie Jackson had lined a double to right field, to score Roy White and Munson.

Los Angeles Dodger manager Tommy Lasorda (left center) attempts to screen a young fan trying to get Ron Cey to turn around, as the Dodgers whoop it up on the field after handing the N.Y. Yankees their second consecutive defeat in the 1978 World Series: At upper left is Lee Lacy, and behind Cey is relief pitcher Bob Welch, with Bill Russell at right. Cey's three-run homer in the sixth made the Dodgers' win possible.

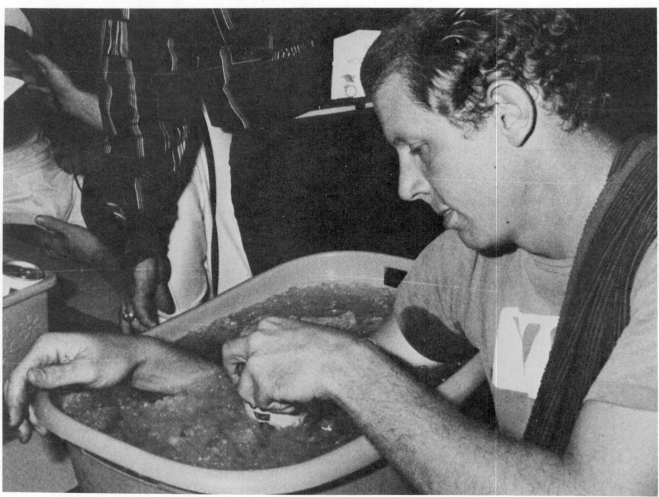

Dodger pitcher Burt Hooten soaks his arm in ice after he led the Dodgers to a 4-3 win over the New York Yankees. It was the Dodgers' 2nd straight win in the 1978 World Series.

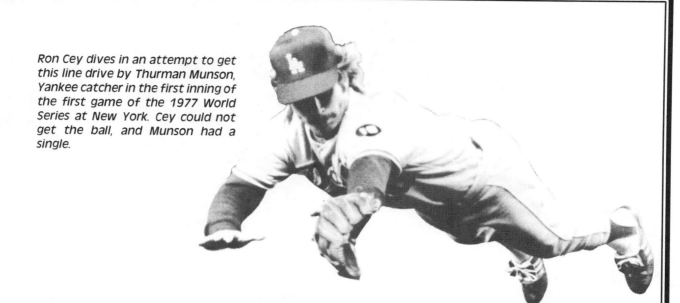

Ron Cey dives in an attempt to get this line drive by Thurman Munson, Yankee catcher in the first inning of the first game of the 1977 World Series at New York. Cey could not get the ball, and Munson had a single.

Steve Garvey is safe at third as the ball sits on the ground next to New York Yankees third baseman Graig Nettles in the seventh inning of World Series Game No. 3 in New York. Garvey doubled and made it to third.

Pedro Guerrero

Brad Gulden

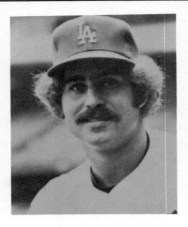

Gerald Hannahs

Rudy Law

Ted Power

Mike Scioscia

Joe Simpson

Kelly Snider

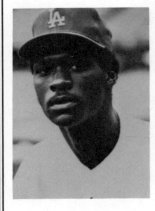

Dave Stewart

Rick Sutcliffe

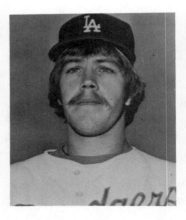

Mike Tennant

Myron White

When these 12 players reported to the Dodgers' spring training camp in February, 1979, they all thought they could and would make the team. Only five were fortunate enough: Rudy Law, Mike Scioscia, Rick Sutcliffe, Dave Stewart and Pedro Guerrero. Guerrero was named one of the outstanding stars of the 1981 World Series.

Six Dodgers stars pose with a new Dodger mascot, "Irving," before a game in 1979 at Dodger Stadium. (left to right) Reggie Smith, Bill Russell, Bob Welch, Jerry Reuss, Steve Garvey and Davey Lopes. . . and Irving.

Jerry Reuss in action.

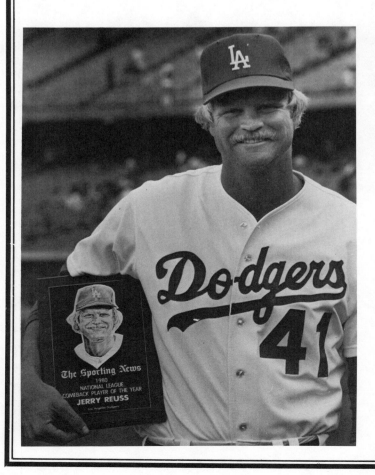

Jerry Reuss was acquired in a deal with the Pittsburgh Pirates on April 8, 1979, and made one of the most impressive comebacks in baseball history. On June, 27, 1980, Reuss pitched the finest game of his career as he no-hit the San Francisco Giants. He went on to win 18 games while losing 6 in 1980. Jerry finished second in the Cy Young Award balloting to Steve Carlton in 1980—but the Sporting News awarded Reuss their "National League Comeback Player of the Year Award" for the year 1980.

Derrel Thomas filled in at every position for the Dodgers except as a pitcher. He caught, played every infield position and hit around .266 since 1979, when he was acquired from San Diego. He wore uniform no. 30 because it was Maury Wills' number, and he idolizes Wills.

Dodger coach Manny Mota goes through his daily ritual, taking the lineup card to home plate (upper left), studying the game from the Dodger dugout (upper right), preparing his bat with pine tar in the on-deck circle (lower left), and making contact at the plate in one of his frequent pinch-hitting assignments (lower left).

Manny Mota is one of the most popular members in the Dodgers organization. A major leaguer for 21 years, 13 of them spent with the Dodgers as a leading player, then a pinch-hitter par excellence from 1974 to 1980, Manny became a Dodger coach in 1980. Manny's best year with the Dodgers was in 1972 when he hit .323.

Danny Ozark had spent 28 years in the Dodger organization before departing to become manager of the Phillies in 1973. Danny won division titles in 1976, '77, '78, and then returned to the Dodgers in 1980 to serve as third base coach. Danny played in the minors from 1942 to 1963 as a first baseman.

Steve Sax—Star of the Future?

Dave Stewart

Joe Beckwith

When he graduated from Auburn University in 1977, Joe Beckwith was considered one of the finest college pitchers in the nation. He had won 31 games during his four years and was drafted by the Dodgers in '77. He spent three years in the minors, came up to the Dodgers in late 1979, and promptly won his first game. Utilized mainly as a relief pitcher, Joe had the best earned run average on the Dodger staff in 1980—an ERA of 1.95. Joe appeared in 38 games that year and won three and lost three.

Dave Stewart made the Dodger squad on the final day of spring practice in 1980. He has a great fast ball and is nicknamed "Smoke." In his first 17 games in 1981, Dave had a 4-1 record. He had five saves for the season. In 1980 Dave won 15 games for Albuquerque of the Pacific Coast League. In 1983, Stewart was traded to the Texas Rangers.

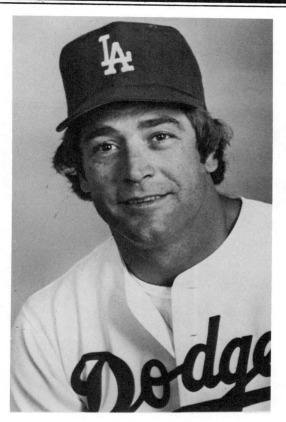

Burt Hooton was acquired from the Cubs and in that first season with the Dodgers won 12 straight games, finishing with 18 games for the season. In 1976 he was 11-15. In 1978 Burt won 19 games. In 1980, he was 14 and 8. In 1981, in the 6th and final game of the 1981 World Series, Burt allowed the Yanks 5 hits and 2 runs as the Dodgers won Game Six, 9-2, and the World Series.

Three days after he graduated from Meadowdale High School, Dayton, Ohio, Steve Yeager signed a contract with the Dodgers and received an $8,000 bonus, and after 4 years in the minor leagues was brought up to the Dodgers in 1972. Steve is considered one of the leading catchers in baseball. Yeager's uncle is Air Force General Chuck Yeager, the first man to break the sound barrier in 1947.

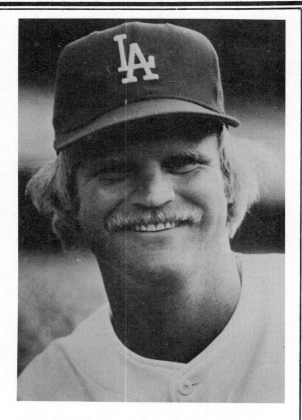

Jerry Reuss (left and above) was acquired from the Pirates in a trade for Rick Rhoden. In his first season with the Dodgers, Reuss won 7 and lost 14 games, but completely reversed himself in 1980 by winning 18 and losing 6. Jerry was the "comeback pitcher of the year" as he came off bullpen duty to replace Dave Goltz in 1980. In Game Five of the 1981 World Series, Reuss beat the Yankees 2-1, allowing them but 5 hits. Reuss won 10 games and lost but 4 during the 1981 season, and was one of the most effective Dodger hurlers.

Ken Landreaux on base in 1980.

In his 15th year as a professional, Dusty Baker had the finest year of his career as he led the Dodgers to victory over the Yankees in the 1981 World Series. Dusty hit .320, to lead all Dodgers for the 1981 season, including 9 homers and 49 RBI. 1981 was also the year that Dusty made the All-Star team.

Dodger pitcher Fernando Valenzuela goes through a variety of moves when not actually pitching the ball, as seen here Thursday, Oct. 2, 1981, against the San Diego Padres at Dodger Stadium in Los Angeles. Fernando's record was held to 13-7 as the Dodgers were defeated by the Padres 1-0. Valenzuela came out of the game in the eighth inning.

Dave Goltz came to the Dodgers as a free agent after the 1979 season. He had spent seven years with the Twins and was in double figures in six of those years. His finest year was 1977, when he won 20 and lost 11. Evidently the pressure of a super six-year contract hampered Dave in 1980. He won 7 and lost 11 and was in the Dodger bullpen much of 1980.

Bill Russell had a somewhat spectacular beginning with the Dodgers in 1969. In his second major league game, he hit a single, a triple and a home run in 4 times at bat. But the pressure of major league ball caught up with Bill and he was sent down to Spokane, where he promptly hit .363 and was brought back to the Dodgers in 1970. Bill broke in as an outfielder, but was converted into a shortstop. He's played there ever since. Bill's best year was in 1978, when he hit .286 and had the 2nd most hits on the club, 179. Troubled by injuries in '81, he was in and out of the lineup for most of the season.

Rudy Law was one of the big hits of the 1980 spring training season, hitting .341, although he slumped to .260 for the year. Rudy had 4 hits in a game against San Diego and stole 4 bases in a game versus Chicago, May 12. In 1980 Rudy set a record for a rookie by stealing 40 bases. Subsequently traded to the White Sox, Law was the starting center fielder on the 1983 AL Division West Champions.

At Edgewood High School in California, Jay Johnstone was MVP in baseball, football and basketball in his senior year. He played with San Jose in 1963 and '64 and was signed by the Angels in 1964 after hitting .340 for Seattle. Johnstone played for the Angels for 5 years, then shuttled to 6 other clubs before being signed by the Dodgers in 1979. He was the team's leading pinch-hitter and paced the team with 11 pinch hits. Jay hit .307 in 109 games in 1980 and played a big part in the club's comeback after Reggie Smith was injured. Jay took over and was outstanding. His zany personality has made him one of the most popular Dodgers.

The date was October 11, 1978, Game No. 2 of the World Series and 22-year-old Bob Welch was in there for the Dodgers in the biggest game of his young life. Brought in as a relief pitcher, Welch faced Reggie Jackson and, with the game on the line, calmly pitched to the Yankee slugger. Reggie fouled off pitch after pitch—it seemed like a duel to the death. Power hitter. Power pitcher. A swinging strike. A high, tight fastball sending Jackson into the dirt. Three straight fastballs, each fouled back. A fastball high and outside for a count of 2 and 2. Another foul. Another high and outside fastball. Full count. Runners moving. Crowd roaring. On his ninth toss to Jackson, Welch steamed a fastball across the plate. . . Reggie swung and missed. Bob Welch had fanned Reggie Jackson in the 9th inning to win the game for the Dodgers, 4-3. It was a classic duel—a young fastball pitcher vs. the crafty slugger—and the 22-year-old pitcher won out.

In 1973 Reggie Otero, a scout for the Cleveland Indians, found young, talented Pedro Guerrero in the Dominican Republic. Guerrero was hitting .438 for a Dominican team and he could play anywhere. He was a slick fielder and was fast on his feet. On April 4, 1974, Al Campanis purchased Guerrero from the Indians and sent Pedro to a Dodger farm team in Orangeburg. Then, during a six-year term in the minors, where he hit better than .300, he was brought up to the Dodgers and utilized as a pinch-hitter in 1979. He hit for a .448 average as a pinch-hitter and also was utilized to fill in for Davey Lopes, Rudy Law and Reggie Smith when they were injured. During the first half of 1981, Pedro hit 10 homers and slugged the ball for a .325 average. He was named to the All-Star team and became a Dodger hero in the World Series in 1981 as he slugged 2 home runs against the Yankees.

In 1981 Reggie Smith started his 19th season as a professional ball player. He came to the Dodgers in a trade with the Cardinals for Joe Ferguson. Reggie's best year with the Dodgers was 1980, when he hit .322 with 15 homers. In 1977 Reggie hit 32 home runs and hit for a .307 average. An All-Star selection 7 times, Reggie has a 15-year major league average of .288.

Rick Sutcliffe was a long shot to make the Dodgers in 1979 and was ready to go back down to Albuquerque, when he suddenly was told that he was going to Los Angeles and work in the bullpen. Rick made his first start, May 3, 1979, and beat the Phils 5-2. He became an instant starter and was a sensation as he came up with 17 wins and 10 losses for the year. He was voted "Rookie of the Year" in 1979.

Alejandro Pena led the Pacific Coast League in saves with 23 and joined the Dodgers in Sept. 1981, when Joe Ferguson was released. Pena had a 1-0 record and 2 saves in his first 12 appearances with the Dodgers. Pena has an outstanding fastball and slider.

Rick Monday was an All-American baseball star at Arizona University, hitting .442 in his final year. He was drafted by the Kansas City A's with a $100,000 bonus and played a season and a half in the minors before joining the A's. In 1971 he was traded to the Cubs. He played with Chicago until 1977 and came to the Dodgers in a trade that was most unpopular — the Dodgers sent Bill Buckner to the Cubs for Monday. In 1981 Monday was used primarily as a pinch-hitter and became a starter in the Dodger lineup when Ron Cey was injured. From Sept. 11 to 23, Monday drove out 6 home runs in 11 games. Monday's home run in the playoff game against the Expos was one of the year's great moments and gave the Dodgers the National League Pennant.

Derrel Thomas played at every position except pitcher in 1980. He was signed as a free agent in 1979 and was to be a utility player, but wound up as the regular center fielder for the second half of the 1980 season. Derrel hit .266 in 1980.

Bobby Castillo would sit up in left field stands at Dodger Stadium as a young boy and dream of someday wearing the uniform of the Los Angeles Dodgers. And one day in 1977 after but 3 years as a minor league pitcher and a 19 and 11 season with Monterrey, Bobby was purchased by the Dodgers. In 1977 he walked out to the mound and won his first major league game. A fine relief pitcher from 1978 to 1981, little did Bobby realize that he would help in creating one of the greatest Dodger heroes. It happened back in 1979, when Al Campanis, the Dodgers' V.P., asked Castillo to tutor a young pitcher. His name: Fernando Valenzuela. Castillo worked with Fernando and taught him to throw Castillo's best pitch, the screwball. The teacher, Castillo, had a great pupil, and Valenzuela proved to be one of the hottest pitching stars of the 1981 season. Castillo is no longer a Dodger. But he will be remembered.

In 1980 Steve Howe came out of nowhere to win "Rookie of the Year" honors, for he saved 17 games with great pitching. It was an extraordinary effort on the part of this 23-year-old with only one-half year of pro experience behind him. In the World Series Steve came into the 4th game with the score tied at 4-4. He pitched outstanding ball against the Yankee sluggers, allowing them but 3 hits and 1 run in the final 3 innings. And the Dodgers came on to score twice to wrap up the game, 8-7. In game 6, Steve relieved Burt Hooton in the 5th inning and held the Yankees to 2 hits, no runs as the Dodgers won 9-2. It was an outstanding effort by the former University of Michigan star.

Mike Scioscia was only 17 years old when he was drafted by the Dodgers in the 1976 draft. A three-sports star at Springfield High, Pa., Mike was already a fine catcher. When he was 17 years old, Mike was sent to the Bellingham club and hit .278. Progressing each year in the Dodgers farm system, Mike was with Clinton in 1977, San Antonio in 1978, and in 1979 hit for a .336 average with Albuquerque and in 1981 Mike won the assignment as the starting catcher for the Dodgers. He played well throughout the year.

On February 8, 1982, Vice President Al Campanis announced that the popular Davey Lopes, the Dodgers' fine second baseman for 9 years, had been dealt to the Oakland A's. Davey's departure opens the way for a new era in Dodger baseball, for Lopes had been a key to the great Dodger infield since 1971. Davey served as Captain of the Dodgers in 1978 and '79, and was one of baseball's great base-stealers. An All-Star selection in 1978, Davey was called "the best clutch hitter," by Manager Tommy Lasorda. Davey's best year at the plate was 1977, when he hit .283 and hit 11 home runs. In 1979 Lopes hit 28 home runs and hit . 265.

Terry Forster was sidelined much of the 1980 and '81 seasons. His best success was late in September, 1981, when, as a reliever, he did not allow a run in his last 4 games. His best season with the Dodgers was in 1977, when he saved 22 games.

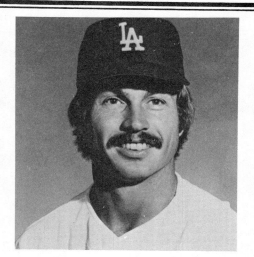

In 1982 Ron Cey celebrated his 10th season as a Dodger. Ron hit 20 or more home runs in six of those ten seasons. He's considered one of the all-time Dodger third baseman. In 1981 Ron earned his 7th consecutive selection to the National League All-Star team. He was one of the most popular members of the team.

Getting ready for his 13th year with the Dodgers, No. 6, Steve Garvey, ranks alongside the greatest Dodgers to ever wear the Royal Blue.

Tommy Lasorda is a bit annoyed by one of Joe Garagiola's gags and says to Joe, "Get up in the TV booth where you belong." Garagiola, a former catcher with the St. Louis Cardinals, knows how to "get on Tommy." "No, Tommy," he says, thumbing him off the field. "You get off the field, and I'll handle the team." Cesar Concepcion of the Reds gets a big kick out of the fun and games between the two old pals as the charade continues.

9

A TEAM OF DESTINY
THE 1981 DODGERS

When great Dodger teams are discussed in the future, certainly the 1981 team will be considered as one of the All-Time Dodger teams.

In the playoff games for the Western Division, the Dodgers came from behind to beat the Houston Astros, 3 games to 2. They were behind the Montreal Expos, and rallied to beat them 3 games to 2.

The Yankees won the first two games of the World Series, and a scrappy, aggressive, not-to-be denied bunch of Dodgers came from behind to defeat a strong New York Yankee team, taking four of the next five games to win the 1981 World Series. It was a remarkable victory for a remarkable team. . . .truly "A Team of Destiny."

"You gotta have a heart, miles and miles and miles of heart" according to the song from the Broadway musical "Damn Yankees." The 1981 edition of the Los Angeles Dodgers had enough heart to extend through a dozen zip codes. It was a team with an experienced infield that had played together for eight-and-a-half years, but seemingly now was self-destructing, a team constantly flirting with disaster, and in the end a team that refused to die.

Going strictly by the records, the Dodgers had no right to be in the World Series, let alone the playoffs. It has been said of the great baseball strike of 1981 that nobody really benefited from the enforced layoff but that wasn't quite true, because the ensuing split season allowed Los Angeles to compete against Houston for the national League West title. Actually, Houston shouldn't have been there either, because the team with the combined (both halves of the season) best record was Cincinnati; it was just another case of doing tricks with meaningless numbers.

In addition to courage, the 1981 Dodgers had added some charismatic mystique in the person of

a gifted, 20-year old pitcher named Fernando Valenzuela, who, in the course of a single season had become an instant folk hero for Dodgers fans. He arrived in Los Angeles at the tail end of 1980, fresh from the Texas League where he struck out everybody in sight. Valenzuela had two things going for him, a beautiful personality and a controlled screwball that danced a cha-cha as it broke over the plate. The Dodgers tried him out as a relief pitcher. He worked something more than 17 innings, struck out 16 batters, walked only five and gave up eight hits. His earned run average was exactly 0.00, and you can't do better than that. Tommy Lasorda decided that the kid might work well as a starting pitcher and managers get rich making such smart decisions.

It was pitching the Dodgers were relying on to get them all the way home. There was Valenzuela to be sure, plus Jerry Reuss, Burt Hooten and Bob Welch, as good a rotation as could be found. Once upon a time Los Angeles used the long ball to blow. away the opposition, like the 1977 Dodgers. That was the year Steve Garvey hit 33 home runs, Reggie

Los Angeles Dodgers' Ken Landreaux (44) dumps Houston Astros' shortstop Kiko Garcia (23) as he was forced in the first inning of the 1981 National League West playoffs at Houston. The Dodgers' Dusty Baker grounded to second to start the double play.

Steve Garvey gloves the ball at first base as Art Howe, the Astros 3rd baseman, dives for first. Both players look to umpire Jim Quick for the call. Howe was called out on this play in the third inning of the National League West playoffs between the Dodgers and Astros in 1981. The Dodgers won the playoffs, 3 games to 2.

In the final inning of the final game, October 19, 1981, in Montreal, the Dodgers won the National League pennant, when Rick Monday slammed a two-out home run off pitcher Steve Rogers to beat the Montreal Expos, 2-1. Lasorda hugs Monday (center) as every member of the squad joins in. The Dodgers won the playoffs, 3 games to 2.

Smith had 32, Ron Cey and Dusty Baker slugged 30 each. It was the first time in baseball history that four men on the same club hit 30 or more home runs. Those days were gone. As second baseman Davey Lopes put it, "This year we had to rely more on intangibles for success, the stolen base, the extra base on a single, the hit and run. But our desire to win was greater in 1981. This team had more character."

Only it didn't seem that character would be enough as the playoffs got under way. According to baseball proverb, in a short series pitching dominates hitting. It's true. But when both teams have good pitching, the series is up for grabs and one timely hit can turn things around. The Houston Astros had some very good pitching, and in the beginning, they had the clutch hits.

Houston started Nolan Ryan in the first game, which gave the Astros a psychological advantage immediately since the million-dollar right hander had tossed a no-hitter against Los Angeles on September 26th. Lasorda countered with Valenzuela, and it was a dandy duel all the way. The game was tied at 1-1 going into the bottom of the ninth when Houston's Alan Ashby socked a two-run homer off reliever Dave Stewart. Ryan limited the Dodgers to two hits.

The second game was even tighter. Neither team dented the plate for 10 innings. Once again the Los Angeles relief corps took the loss. In the bottom of the 11th, with the bases loaded, pinch hitter Denny Waling lined a base hit off young Tom Neidenfuer and that was the ball game.

Before 1981, no team that lost the first two games in a best three-out-of-five series had ever come back to win. Tommy Lasorda knew that, and it was a tribute to his willingness to gamble that kept the Dodgers in contention. The original plan was to pitch Bob Welch in the third game and come back with Burt Hooten, the man with the knuckle curve ball, in the fourth game. Hooten usually did well against Houston and the LA manager had to go with the best he had.

The strategy worked. Los Angeles broke out of the starting blocks fast, scored three runs in the first inning and coasted in to a 6-1 decision. The Dodger bats woke up, perhaps because they were playing in their own back yard and a few friendly faces never hurt a team effort. The early damage was done by Dusty Baker's RBI double and Steve Garvey's two-run homer into the stands, but both batters later confessed that their blows would have been merely loud outs in the Houston Astrodome.

Then came one of those managerial decisions that make a man a genius. The matchup for game four was Valenzuela, pitching with three days' rest, and Vern Ruhle for Houston. It was another beautiful duel. Nobody got on base through four innings, but in the fifth, Pedro Guerrero hit his first home run since September 11th. Both Fernando and

Ruhle gave up just four hits, but the Dodgers scored one more run and won it, 2-1, tying the series.

The showdown game pitted Reuss against Ryan, and now the Dodgers had the psychological edge. It wasn't merely momentum. Ryan, who had humbled the Dodgers the last two times he faced them, had never won a game in Dodger Stadium (he was 0-5 lifetime). Reuss, on the other hand, had allowed Houston only two runs in 26 innings. That was how things worked out. After both clubs had sputtered and left runners on base, Los Angeles broke the game open in the sixth. A walk to Baker, followed by singles by Garvey, veteran outfielder Rick Monday and catcher Mike Scioscia, plus a Houston error, meant three runs and eventually a 4-0 win, featuring a five-hitter by Reuss.

It had been a pitchers' series. The Astros' team batting average for the five games was .179, the Dodgers, .198, which are not the kind of statistics suitable for framing.

With the NL West title tucked away, Los Angeles took on Montreal for the National League Pennant, but a feeling of uneasiness hung over Los Angeles' rooters. The Dodgers were accustomed to sunshine and the kind of weather that permits oranges and grapefruit to flourish. Montreal at the end of October is really polar bear country. Maybe the Expos were distantly related to the Eskimos, but the Dodgers were not. Therefore, it behooved Los Angeles to win the first two games at home, and trust to fate for another victory north of the border.

Montreal never did have much luck at Chavez Ravine. Before game one of the playoffs, the Expos, in 20 attempts, had won one game and lost 18 in the Dodgers' home town. The opener was played under ideal conditions, and Los Angeles fans sat smugly satisfied, especially in the home eighth when Petro Guerrero and Mike Scioscia belted back-to-back home runs. Things were looking up. With one game in hand, the Dodgers were going to send wunderkind Fernando to the mound the following day, to face a journeyman named Ray Burris, who had labored for the Chicago Cubs, New York Yankees and New York Mets before coming to rest in Montreal. The veteran had come on well for the Expos, especially in the second half of the split season. Montreal scored some runs against Fernando. The Dodgers got five hits and no runs against Burris. "It is very nice," said Expo Warren Cromartie politely, "to come here and beat the mayor of Los Angeles."

So Los Angeles had to slink out of town and journey to the neighborly nation of Canada. At game time Expo Andre Dawson came bounding onto the field breathing deeply in the invigorating, 46-degree temperature and remarked, "This is one of our better nights," Yet Jerry Reuss, pitching his heart out, had a 1-0 lead going into the bottom of the seventh. With two out everything fell apart. Dawson singled, Gary Carter walked and Larry Parish got a base hit. There goes the shutout, exulted the fans. Then the unheralded Jerry White

Players of both teams, Dodgers and Expos stand at attention as Gloria Loring sings the National Anthem at Dodger Stadium, Los Angeles for game no. 1 of the 1981 National League playoffs with Montreal.

hit one out and there goes the ballgame, shouted the happy fans. For Steve Rogers it was a well deserved victory. He had been outstanding in the pressure cooker games of October, allowing only two runs in 36 innings.

Once again the Dodgers were teetering on the brink. They were within one game of elimination, and to stave off defeat Tommy Lasorda handed the ball to Burt Hooten. His teammates almost broke Hooten's heart. Time after time they had the Expos on the ropes, only to let them get away. It was 1-1 into the top of the eighth, and Steve Garvey took matters into his own hands. He drilled a Gullickson pitch into the stands with a mate aboard to give Hooten some breathing room. In the ninth Los Angeles added four more and the game ended at 7-1.

The movies couldn't have set up a more dramatic ending for the fifth encounter. Ray Burris, whose off-speed assortment had baffled the Dodgers in game two, was rematched against Fernando, who had lost to Burris. Too add to Dodger miseries, the game had been postponed by rain the previous day, and now, halfway through autumn, the temperature was down to 41 degrees, which is considered ideal weather for football but is dangerous to the welfare of pitching arms.

The Expos got a run in the first on a double by Tim Raines and a Rodney Scott bunt. Valenzuela fielded the ball but his throw to third was too late to catch Raines. The Dodgers had Scott caught off first but failed to run him down, and that proved costly. Andre Dawson shot a grounder to second which was turned into a double play, Raines scoring. Had Scott been tagged out, the grounder might not have scored the run.

Burris blanked the Dodgers until the fifth and the run that knotted the game was his own fault. Rick Monday led off with a single and galloped to third on Guerrero's single to right center. At this point Burris pounced a pitch into the dirt. Catcher Gary Carter alertly blocked the ball toward third base, keeping Monday in check but allowing Guerrero to take second. Mike Scioscia lined out to second, the runners holding. Then Valenzuela bounced one to second base and Monday scored. Had Burris not delivered the wild pitch, Guerrero would still be on first and Valenzuela's RBI grounder would have been a double play.

Burris departed for a pinch hitter in the bottom of the eighth after allowing only five hits, one walk and a somewhat tainted run. He was replaced by Steve Rogers, the ace of the staff, not normally a relief pitcher, but there was no tomorrow for either team and it had to be the best. Rogers got Garvey on an infield popup and Ron Cey on a fly to deep left. Up stepped Rick Monday, a 35-year-old campaigner, who had seriously considered retiring before the 1981 season. The count went to 3-and-1. Rogers threw a sinker that failed to sink, and Monday drove it high and far over the wall in right center, giving the Dodgers the lead.

In the bottom of the ninth, Valenzuela, who had yielded only three hits so far, got the first two batters in routine fashion. Then Gary Carter walked on a 3-and-2-pitch. Larry Parrish walked on a 3-and-2-pitch. Valenzuela walked, too, to the dugout, replaced by young Bob Welch. Welch was the fireballer who had first made a name for himself in the 1978 World Series by striking out Reggie Jackson in a clutch situation. The batter was Jerry White, who had hit that big home run to win the third game of the series. Welch threw exactly one pitch. White hit a bouncer to second and the game was over.

Once again Los Angeles had dodged the bullet, and now they had to face the Yankees, who had defeated the Dodgers in 1978 by taking four in a row after losing the opening pair. The Yanks had been lolling around for four days waiting for the National League pennant winner to come and visit them.

For Lasorda and those Dodgers who had been with the team in '78, it was almost a case of *déjà vu*, starting with leadoff man Davey Lopes. He banged

Bob Welch as he finished game 5 of the 1981 National League pennant playoff.

On October 21, 1981, Dodgers' second baseman Davey Lopes leaps up and over Yankee runner Jerry Mumphrey after tagging the bag for the forceout in the first inning of the first game of the World Series at Yankee Stadium. Yankees' hitter Larry Milbourne was safe at first on the play. Dodger shortstop Bill Russell watches the action. The Yankees won the game, 5-3.

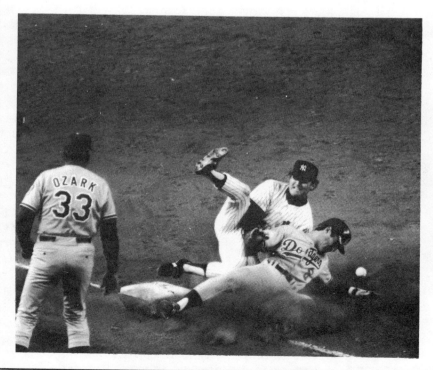

Graig Nettles tumbles over and the ball bounces away as Steve Garvey slams into 3rd base in the 5th inning of game no. 2 of the World Series in 1981. Garvey was safe when Nettles couldn't handle Larry Milbourne's throw. Milbourne at short had fielded a ground ball by Pedro Guerrero.

Red Barber(left)visits with broadcaster Vin Scully in the Dodgers broadcasting booth before the first game of the 1981 World Series at Yankee Stadium. It was a familiar scene for Barber, who was the most famous play-by-play broadcaster ever to sit in front of a microphone. From 1939, when he was hired by Larry MacPhail, until 1953, when he went to work for the Yankees, Barber's colorful, accurate, warm, detailed accounts of Dodger baseball made him a household name, not only in Brooklyn, but all over the nation.

Don Drysdale interviews his former manager over ABC-TV before the 1981 World Series.

Reggie Jackson and Steve Garvey warily eye each other before the start of game no. 1 of the 1981 World Series at Yankee Stadium.

a shot to the left side of the infield. Third baseman Graig "They Shall Not Pass" Nettles made a diving stop and gunned down Lopes at first on a disputed call. In the bottom of the first the Yankees climbed all over Jerry Reuss. Jerry Mumphrey singled, Lou Piniella hit a ground rule double, and first baseman Bob Watson hoisted one over the wall in right center, thus staking Yankee lefty Ron Guidry to a three run lead.

By the bottom of the third Reuss was gone after Mumphrey's second base hit, a stolen base and Piniella's RBI single. In the fourth inning reliever Bobby Castillo walked four batters to force in a run. Steve Yeager got one run back in the fifth with a solo home run, and after seven innings the Yanks led, 5-1. Ron Davis, a tall, lean, bespectacled right hander, came on to close things out, only he didn't. Davis gave his own interpretation of a scatter-arm by walking the first two batters.

Goose Gossage, New York's premier short relief man, entered the fray, but the long layoff had taken the heat out of his blazer. Pinch hitter Jay Johnstone singled home a run and Dusty Baker's sacrifice fly plated another. Up stepped Steve Garvey, who blasted a murderous drive toward the left field corner. But the ball never reached the outfield. Graig Nettles dove to his right and speared the shot in the webbing of his glove. That was it. The Dodgers expired meekly. It was the Yanks, 5-3.

"Nettles is amazing," moaned Lasorda, who had watched helplessly in 1978 as Nettles turned the third base area into a private playground. "I get sick to my stomach seeing him make those plays all the time. He must go to bed hoping and praying he can kill us with his glove."

Said Gossage, "I don't care what the box score shows, that save belongs to Nettles."

Los Angeles faced Tommy John, a former Dodger alumnus in game two, and the man with the "bionic arm" allowed just three hits in the seven innings he worked. Goose Gossage, anxious to get more work, clamped the shackles on the Dodgers in his two innings. Niether pitcher allowed a run. Burt Hooten also pitched a strong game. The Yanks scored an unearned run in the fifth on an error by Davey Lopes and a double by sub shortstop Larry Milbourne. New York got two more in the eighth against the Dodgers' relief corps.

Once again the Dodgers had their backs to the wall. And when a mild earthquake hit southern California the morning of the third game, Los Angeles fans took it as an omen of disaster for the team. Even third baseman Ron Cey's three-run homer in the first inning didn't seem to be enough as the Yankees roughed up Valenzuela in the second with Watson's homer, Cerone's double and Milbourne's single accounting for two runs, and then another pair in the third on Piniella's hit and Cerone's home run. The youngster from Mexico was wild, and when he came in with a pitch near the plate, he was clobbered. The experts in the

A jam-packed crowd of more than 56,000 eager fans greet the Dodgers and the Yankees for the 3rd game of the 1981 World Series in Dodger Stadium, Los Angeles.

"We're Ready"   "2 More 'Dogs"

stands were second guessing Lasorda already. Why was he leaving Fernando in to take the pounding? He just didn't have it.

Lasorda was thinking of giving his rookie flash the hook. In the fifth inning the score was tied at 4-4, and the Dodgers had the bases loaded with nobody out. Mike Scioscia was at bat and if he couldn't knock in the lead run, Lasorda had Reggie Smith in the on deck circle to hit for the pitcher. Scioscia did get the run home by hitting into a double play. Valenzuela hit for himself and stayed in the game. But he wasn't out of the woods yet.

In the eighth Aurelio Rodriguez and Larry Milbourne led off with singles. Bobby Murcer batted for relief pitcher Rudy May with orders to try bunting for a base hit. On the first pitch Murcer did try to bunt, but the ball was hit harder than he intended. It was a kind of soft line drive foul. Ron Cey made a diving catch a-la-Nettles and doubled Milbourne off first. Rodriguez got back to second base. Then Randolph chopped one in Cey's direction. There was no way for Cey to get Randolph at first, but he didn't have to, because Rodriguez ran right into Cey's tag. Valenzuela was out of the inning.

"Terrible base running," fumed Yankee owner George Steinbrenner. And he was right. As Milbourne himself said of his foolish running, "I broke with the bunt. First, I've got to make sure the ball is fair, and it looked fair from my angle. And I've got to make sure the ball is down. I was overly aggressive. I reacted too fast." Rodriguez had a somewhat more valid excuse. With two out, representing the tying run, he had to go on any fair ball regardless of where it was hit. Overall, it was more a case of the Yankees losing the game than the Dodgers winning it.

The Dodgers continued to wage war against adversity in game four, and again it was Yankee ineptness that turned the tide in favor of Los Angeles. Bob Welch started for Los Angeles, and the only man he got out was himself as he gave up three hits and a walk. By the end of three innings the New Yorkers had a 4-2 lead, and going into the bottom of the sixth it was 6-3. However, a walk to Scioscia and Jay Johnstone's pinch hit homer got back two runs. Then came the turn-around play. Davey Lopes looped a high, slicing fly to right. Reggie Jackson said later that he lost the ball in the glare of the sun. The white pill went through his glove and hit his chest as Lopes hustled all the way to second on the error. Relief pitcher Ron Davis seemed dazed. He didn't bother to check Lopes on second, and the runner stole third as Davis was delivering a pitch. Russell singled to left and the score was tied.

In the home seventh, center fielder Bobby Brown misplayed Rick Monday's routine fly into a double, which led to two more Dodger runs. Reggie Jackson's home run halved the Dodger lead, but that was how the game ended, 8-7, Dodgers. Lasorda and his henchmen had tied the series.

Tommy Lasorda shouts some instructions to his Dodger team from the dugout during the 1981 season.

"What the hell do you mean he was safe? You're out of your . . .mind," screams Tommy Lasorda in the 3rd World Series game. Naturally the umpire won the argument.

In game 3 of the World Series, Ron Cey smashes a home run with Davey Lopes and Bill Russell on base to give the Dodgers a 3-0 first inning lead over the Yankees. The Dodgers welcomed Cey as he trotted into the dugout surrounded by Jay Johnstone and Tom Lasorda as the huge Dodger crowd cheered on. The Dodgers went on to win the game, 5-4.

On October 23, 1981, Los Angeles, Fernando Valenzuela wasn't at his best in game 3 of the World Series, but he bore down inning after inning to beat the Yankees, 5-4. "Fernando was like a poker player," said Manager Lasorda, "he was sharp when he had to be and he bluffed the Yankees when he was in a tight spot." Fernando fanned 6 Yanks, walked 7 and allowed the Yankees 9 hits as he pitched the entire game.

Aurelio Rodriguez, Yankee 3rd baseman, leaps high into the air in a vain attempt to catch ball off the bat of Pedro Guererro. The ball fell in for a double and scored Steve Garvey. The play was in the 5th inning of game 4 of the 1981 World Series at Dodger Stadium. Umpire Dick Stello watches the play.

Game 5 in Los Angeles was a thing of beauty, with a pitching duel between Ron Guidry, Yankee ace, and Jerry Reuss of the Dodgers. With the Yankees leading 1-0 Pedro Guerrero and Steve Yeager blasted consecutive home runs to give the Dodgers the 5th game of the Series, 2-1. Yeager doffs his cap to the thousands of Dodger fans, who clamored to see him once more.

In game five Ron Guidry was clinging to a 1-0 lead into the seventh inning when Dodger coach Manny Mota offered a bit of good advice to the Dodger batters. He told them to crouch a bit, wait on the pitch a little and not swing so hard. What a handy tip! Pedro Guerrero and Steve Yeager slugged back-to-back home runs, Jerry Reuss pitched a five-hitter and the Dodgers led in the series. Not even the heart-stopping beaning of Ron Cey by a Gossage fast ball could erase the surge of optimism that enveloped Los Angeles.

The sixth game was anticlimactic. The Yankees were finished and they seemed to know it, even after they got off to a 1-0 lead in the first inning. The Dodgers tied the score in the fourth and got all the runs they needed in the fifth. It was only poetic justice that the bad-pop single that delivered the game-winner should come off the bat of Ron Cey, trying to blot out the horror of having a ball crash into his head. It was 9-2, Dodgers.

To call the Dodgers' comeback incredible would be an understatement. They had been down two games to none against Houston and had swept the next three. They had been behind two games to one against Montreal and had taken the following two to win the National League pennant. Finally, behind two games to zero in the World Series, they had taken the Yanks in four straight, exactly as the Yanks had done it to them in 1978.

According to the running gag in and around Los Angeles, Tommy Lasorda has no red corpuscles in his veins, because when he cuts himself shaving, the blood comes out Dodger blue. He has always been a team man, a Dodger, who waxes emotional about his club for any reason or for no reason. He gave vent to his feelings after the victory:

"This is the greatest thing that ever happened to me in baseball. These guys have given me a lifetime of thrills in one season...I'v always wished that if the good Lord ever let us win the World Series, it would be against the club that beat us twice."

Game no. 1 in New York pitted Yankee ace Ron Guidry and the Dodgers' crafty ace Jerry Reuss, a 10-year veteran of the baseball wars. Reuss failed to last three innings as the Yankees, propelled by Bob Watson's three-run homer off Reuss in the first inning, beat the Dodgers 5-3. Guidry and Reuss had a rematch in the fifth game of the Series, and this time Reuss—and the Dodgers—won. The Dodgers' 2-1 victory was aided by Reuss' 5-hitter and by back-to-back eighth-inning homers by Pedro Guerrero and Steve Yeager off Guidry.

Pedro Guerrero slaps hands with 3rd base coach Danny Ozark on his way to home plate after his home run in the 8th inning of the 6th and final game of the World Series in New York. Guerrero was picked as one of the 3 Most Valuable Players in the 1981 Series.

A SEASON OF TRIUMPHS . . .

Dodger pitcher Steve Howe is hugged off the ground by his catcher Steve Yeager. First baseman Steve Garvey celebrates with them after the Dodgers won the seventh and final World Series' game in New York against the Yankees in 1981.

. . . MOMENTS OF CELEBRATION

Fernando Valenzuela pours champagne over teammates.

Terry Forster makes sure Fernando Valenzuela has enough champagne.

Pitcher Jerry Reuss is ready for more shampoo.

. . . MORE CELEBRATION

Coach Manny Mota (11), Manager Lasorda, Tom Niedenfeuer, Steve Sax and Joe Beckwith.

Three Dodger players named as the Most Valuable Players in the 1981 World Series, celebrate after the Dodgers win over the Yankees in the final game. (Left to right): Outfielder Pedro Guerrero, catcher Steve Yeager and third baseman Ron Cey.

Following their smashing 1981 World Series win over the Yankees, Baseball Commissioner Bowie Kuhn presented the glittering World Championship Trophy to a delighted trio of Dodger Executives: Al Campanis, Vice President, Director of Player Personnel, (left) Dodger President Peter O'Malley and the happy skipper, Tommy Lasorda, in the Dodgers' locker room at Yankee Stadium.

October 30, 1981...Dodger Town. A day to remember. (Above) Los Angeles Dodgers Ron Cey (left) and Steve Garvey greet thousands of Dodger fans along the parade route in downtown Los Angeles during their victory parade as World Champions.

(Right) Manager Tommy Lasorda proudly waves a huge No. 1 sign, which notes: Big Blue Wrecking Crew Always!

(Below) The Dodgers victory parade was led by Los Angeles Mayor Tom Bradley (center) flanked by Dodger Vice President Al Campanis and Manager Tom Lasorda.

CONGRATULATIONS

Los Angeles Dodgers president and owner Peter O'Malley (right) talks with Dodgers manager Tommy Lasorda after it was announced that Lasorda had been selected National League Manager of the Year by the Associated Press. Lasorda lead the Dodgers to the World Championship by coming from behind in postseason play three times to finally take the World Series from the New York Yankees in 1981.

LOOKING AHEAD...

Manager Lasorda registers a mild beef and the umpire lets him know who is boss.

Tommy Lasorda was an outstanding minor league pitcher. He still shows good form as he throws in batting practice.

Wonder what Lasorda is listening to in the dugout???

The 1982 season was not for the faint-hearted fan. It had more reversals and changes of direction than Lombard Street in San Francisco.

10
ROLLER COASTER YEAR: THE 1982 DODGERS

Riding the crest of being the 1981 World Champions, the Los Angeles Dodgers spent the 1981-82 winter on the "banquet circuit." Tommy Lasorda busied himself by testing electronic catcher's gear and batting helmets. Steve Garvey posed for photographs in Lindsay, California, in front of a junior high school named in his honor. Fernando Valenzuela made all the normal appearances that are associated with being named Rookie of the Year. There was even talk of "old" Dodgers returning home. Don Sutton talked to his then general manager Al Rosen, and told him "that if at all possible I would like to finish my career on the West Coast and with the team closest to my new home" (Laguna Hills). With the average player's salary already escalated to $235,000, even rumors of Fernando's request for $1 million per year could not dampen the enthusiasm of everyone associated with the Los Angeles Dodgers organization. So began the 1982 Los Angeles Dodgers' roller coaster to disappointment.

As the February 24 departure date approached, manager Lasorda's main concern was complacency. Davy Lopes was traded to Oakland in early February, but the subsequent insertion of Steve Sax at second base meant that all starting spots were taken. The Dodgers also had their four start-

ing pitchers assigned — Valenzuela, Ruess, Hooton, and Welch. It seemed as if the biggest concern was how to get the players in shape and reinstill that "hungry" attitude that had brought them the 1981 World Championship. By mid February, Lasorda said if you mix veteran players like Garvey, Baker, Cey, Monday, and Russell with the young talent of Howe, Valenzuela, Stewart, and Sax, it spells "winner."

As roller coasters are inclined to do, in late February the fortune of the 1982 Dodgers took a downward turn. As the team boarded the plane for Vero Beach and Dodgertown, Fernando Valenzuela announced his intention to stay behind until his contract negotiations were settled; the two sides were far ($600,000) apart. The negotiations continued, and Burt Hooton replaced Jerry Ruess as player representative. Early in March the Dodgers reported that they intended to renew Fernando's contract at its current offer of $300,000 and that this figure would not be sent to arbitration because of Fernando's status as a second-year player. By March 8 positions had hardened; there were reports that Fernando was in jeopardy of being deported to Mexico because he was a nonresident alien without work. On March 11, Fernando voluntarily left for Mexico to await the outcome of any further negotiations.

Meanwhile in Florida, rookies Greg Brock and Mike Marshall alternated days of hitting home runs. The future for these two players and the Dodgers never looked brighter. But the Dodgers faced a "good news/bad news" dichotomy. As Steve Sax — recovering from a knee injury received in a collision with Atlanta's Brett Butler — got two hits and stole a base in a 10-5 victory over Houston, and as the clubhouse celebrated the victory, a false rumor about Fernando agreeing to terms circulated through Dodgertown. The very next day, Los Angeles newspapers added to the contract negotiations by mentioning that Steve Garvey would be in his option year during the 1982 season. On March 17, Fernando returned to Los Angeles, and the so-called "Koufax compromise" resurfaced. Sandy Koufax had previously suggested that Fernando sign a series of three one-year contracts at $300,000 per year. Under this agreement, if Fernando had a good year in 1982, he could take the remaining two contracts to arbitration; if he had a bad year, he would still be protected for the next two seasons.

As Bob Welch pitched five innings of no-hit baseball, the negotiations approached their lowest point. On March 21 the Dodgers threatened suspension for Valenzuela, but a ray of hope appeared. Mike Brito, the scout who had discovered Fernando, said that the pitcher would be in Dodgertown on the following Tuesday or Wednesday. The Dodgers, buoyed by the news, went out and got their third shutout in the past four games, upping their record to 9-4. Ken Landreaux was hitting a torrid .395. On the following day, as predicted by Brito, Fernando signed to pitch for the Dodgers in 1982 for a reported $350,000. On the final day of March the Dodgers set their roster for the season by sending their three prize rookies (Brock, Marshall, and Maldonado) to Albuquerque. The 1982 roster began with 11 pitchers, three catchers, and 12 fielders.

And so on April 7 the ride began, with the Dodgers beating the Giants 4-3. Four Dodgers (Russell, Yeager, Cey, and Sax) collected two hits, including one home run by Yeager. Terry Forster got the win in relief of Jerry Ruess. On the following day the Big Blue Wrecking Crew kept the train rolling with a crushing 9-2 victory. Ken Landreaux went 4 for 4 and Ron Cey went 3 for 5, including a home run.

Somewhere between this auspicious beginning and the first of May, the Dodger express derailed. After only 21 games they trailed the red-hot Atlanta Braves by six games. For only the second time since 1967 the Los Angeles Dodgers had a losing month. Something was amiss. Changes were needed. On May 24, Jay Johnstone lined a double for his first pinch hit in 21 at bats. When he returned to the dugout, manager Tommy Lasorda informed him he had been released.

By June the Dodgers managed to pull their heads above water with a 25-24 mark, but they still trailed by 4½ games. On June 7 the Braves arrived in Los Angeles for the first head-to-head confrontation of the season. The date also marked Steve Garvey's 1,000th consecutive game. The Braves won Monday's and Tuesday's evening games by identical scores of 4-3. Before the final game of the three-game series, manager Lasorda called a team meeting, the 20-minute kind. Speculation ran high that he may be letting his passions get the best of his reason and that profanity would be the order of the day. "That's the same guy who came out with 163 expletives in a 14-minute meeting," said Rick Monday before the game. "How's he going to get more profane than that?" The game marked the first appearance of Pedro Guerrero at third base. The Braves won the game 11-5, and the roller coaster had hit a valley. The Dodgers were 27-30.

Toward the latter part of June things were beginning to turn around. On June 22, Enrique Romo, Dave Stewart, and Steve Howe combined for a three-hit, 4-1 win in Atlanta. In the rubber game of the series on June 24, Lasorda sent Jerry Ruess to the mound. Up to this point the Braves had only been beaten by two left-handers. Ruess pitched well and the Dodgers beat the Braves 5-3. By July 1 the Dodgers had clawed their way to a respectable 41-37 record. The fortunes of the boys in blue were looking up.

After an uneventful month, Los Angeles and Atlanta played a pivotal game on July 30. The Dodgers, finding themselves down 8-3 and about to drop 11½ games behind the Braves, rallied to a 10-9 win. In the first game of the doubleheader Steve Garvey went 3 for 4, Ron Cey added a home run, and Ken Landreaux added two home runs. The nightcap of the twin bill highlighted the awakening Dodger offense. Baker (3-5), Sax (2-5), Landreaux (2-5), Cey (2-4), and Garvey (2-4) led the attack and contributed heavily to the 8-2 win. Making what could be the largest understatement of all time, Dusty Baker said, "Looked like an emotional night." The following evening the rejuvenated Dodgers took the field behind Fernando Valenzuela. Fernando struck out eight and allowed only six hits in the 3-0 win. Ron Cey and Fernando collected five hits between them to lead the way. On the first of August the Dodger offense unleashed a 17-hit attack with Dusty Baker's 19th and 20th homers and Pedro Guerrero's 20th homer shining through a sparkling display of hitting. The Dodgers were only 6½ back at 55-49, and they were gaining.

After winning five of the past six head-to-head

Dodger Diamond Dandies

Bob Welch became a complete pitcher in 1982 and blossomed into one of the finest hurlers in the league.

Jerry Reuss matched his career high with 18 wins in 1982 and was among league leaders in several pitching categories.

Fernando Valenzuela continued his mastery of National League hitters and was named to the National League's All-Star team for the second time in as many years.

Photo by Daniel J. Murphy.

Burt Hooton was hit by a line drive just shy of his right kneecap in spring training and the 1982 season became one of pain and frustration. After trying to pitch on it the first two months of the season, Hooton underwent arthroscopic surgery on June 21. Returned to the active roster on August 8, Burt recorded a 3-3 season and a 2.83 ERA, including a three-hit 5-0 shutout of San Diego on September 15.

matchings, the Dodgers again took on the Braves on August 5 in a critical four-game series. The now faltering Braves were no match for the fired-up Dodgers. Thanks to Atlanta errors, the long-ball power of Ron Cey and Pedro Guerrero, and a hometown crowd of 51,432 the Dodgers won three consecutive one-run games (3-2, 5-4, and 7-6). Each of the three games went into extra innings — further evidence of their determination. Bob Welch's four-hitter completed the sweep on the following evening as the Dodgers moved to within 1½ games of the division lead. The Dodgers were 62-50.

By September, Los Angeles and Atlanta were as close as horses teamed in tandem, with records of 74-59 and 74-58 respectively. The games of September 8 and 9 could spell the difference.

On September 8, Los Angeles rallied from deficits of 3-1, 8-5, and 10-8 to find itself ahead 11-10 in the seventh inning. Despite home runs by Steve Sax (#3), Steve Garvey (#15), Dusty Baker (#22), and Pedro Guerrero (#28) the Dodgers suffered a heart-breaking 12-11 defeat in 10 innings. Drained, they lost the following night, 10-3. The roller coaster had turned again. Fernando had just won his 19th game and the Big Blue Wrecking Crew left for San Diego with a three-game lead.

As the Dodgers approached the final 10 days of the season, their 85-68 record left them with a two-game lead over Atlanta and a three-game lead over the surging San Francisco Giants. The three-game series with the Giants was critical. Despite Pedro Guerrero's 32nd home run of the season, the Dodgers dropped three consecutive one-run decisions and received little help from the San Diego Padres, who lost two of three to Atlanta. Before the September 27 game with Cincinnati, manager Lasorda called another team meeting: "I told them I still had confidence in them." He then benched Landreaux, Scioscia, and Cey. Lasorda explained: "I wanted to try something different." Something different wasn't the answer. Cincinnati beat the Dodgers 6-1 while Atlanta beat the Giants 7-0. The Dodgers' losing streak continued the following night with a 4-3 loss to the Reds. The Dodgers had lost their last seven games and the resurging Braves were next in line. With a chance to turn the roller coaster one more time, the Dodgers lost a heart-breaker in 12 innings to Atlanta, 4-3. Atlanta now had both Los Angeles and San Francisco by two games with only four left to play.

"Do or die" time was quickly approaching. Playing without their leading home-run hitter, Pedro Guerrero, the Dodger offense unleashed a 14-hit attack and ended their longest losing streak in nine years at eight games. Now, with only three games left, they trailed Atlanta by only one game. The ride had reversed itself one more time. Tied with San Francisco and facing them in the three-game season-ending finale, the Dodgers would need some help with Atlanta. On the first day of October, Rick Monday's grand-slam home run and the three-hit pitching of Jerry Ruess kept the ride at an upbeat pace. The next day home runs by Landreaux, Cey, and Scioscia made a 15-2 laugher out of the game with the Giants.

So it boiled down to the final day — the Dodgers riding a three-game winning streak, but needing help from San Diego. The final game was a classic. Tied 2-2 going into the seventh inning, Lasorda pinch hit for Valenzuela and came up empty. Five batters later, the now infamous Joe Morgan home run ended the Dodgers' 1982 season — one game short of a playoff with the Atlanta Braves. The season ended with the roller coaster going the wrong way. If only . . .

The 1982 season was not for the faint-hearted fan. It had more reversals and changes of direction than Lombard Street in San Francisco. It did have the longest game in Dodgers history (21 innings with the Cubs on August 17 and 18), a new record for attendance (3,608,881), and the rehiring of Tommy Lasorda with his seventh one-year contact. The year illustrated the determination and hard work of both veteran and rookie ballplayer alike, but it ended at the wrong time.

In 1982 Mike Marshall earned the Jim and Dearie Mulvey Award as the top rookie at Dodgertown during spring training.

The Dodgers have two of the finest catchers in baseball—Mike Scioscia (on the left) and Steve Yeager (on the right) shown tagging out Cincinnati's Ken Griffey.

Photo by Daniel J. Murphy.

In 1982 Rick Monday, shown scoring against the San Francisco Giants, continued his substantial contributions to the Dodgers. Whether as a part-time player or a pinch-hitter off the bench, Monday has been a fine player and a steadying influence on the younger Dodger players since he was obtained in a trade from the Chicago Cubs in 1977.

Rick Monday and Dusty Baker "High Five" each other after Monday's home run wins another game for the Dodgers.

Steve Sax stepped into the starting second base role for the Dodgers in 1982 and earned the National League Rookie of the Year Honor, the fourth straight season a Dodger has earned the award. Sax enthused Dodger fans as he hit .282 in his lead-off role and led the Dodgers in at bats (638), runs (88), hits (180), triples (7) and stolen bases (49). For his efforts, he was the only rookie named to the National League All-Star squad.

Photo by Daniel J. Murphy.

Photo by Daniel J. Murphy.

Photo by Daniel J. Murphy.

Pedro Guerrero put together a near MVP season in 1982 for the Dodgers and only the Dodgers' failure to make it to the fall classic kept him from the award. He finished third on the MVP voting behind Atlanta's Dale Murphy and St. Louis' Lonnie Smith. He finished among the National league leaders in almost every offensive category: sixth in hitting at .304; tied for fourth in home runs with 32; second in slugging percentage at .536; seventh in RBIs with 100 and third in game winning RBIs with 18. He was the only National League player to finish in top 10 in each of the Triple Crown categories. Playing right field, center field and third base for the Dodgers, he became the first Dodger ever to collect 30 homers and 20 stolen bases in one seaon. He ended the year with 22 stolen bases. He fell just one home run shy of tying Los Angeles Dodger record for home runs in a season set by Steve Garvey in 1977 at 33. He has a 19-game hitting streak, the longest by a Dodger in 1982 and the longest of his career. A sore wrist plagued him the last two weeks of the season and a hamstring pull forced him to sit out the last four games of the season, only to see the Dodgers lose the title by one game. Despite the late-season injuries, Pedro had a great year.

Greg Brock hit his first major league home run off Montreal's Steve Rogers on April 10 at Dodger Stadium. Despite the stress and attention forced on him as Steve Garvey's replacement at first base, Brock hit 20 home runs in 1983. In the photo above, Mike Marshall congratulates Brock after one of the latter's round-trippers.

11

UNCOMMON VALOR: THE 1983 DODGERS

The Dodgers front office faced some serious questions as it approached February of 1983. The team was missing some familiar names, and the upcoming performance of the replacement players was of foremost concern. Steve Garvey was now a Padre; Ron Cey was now a Cub. Even the famed Dodger airplane, Kay O' II, was sold. The Dodgers now rode United Airlines charters like everyone else in the league. Still, they were considered more talented than anyone else in the National League West, maybe twice as talented as whoever was second.

For the first time since six members of the class of '73 took jobs that they would hold for nearly a decade, there were some fresh faces around. Some of the certainty of spring had been removed, but excitement took its place. Some of the youngsters being asked to fill some very large spikes were:

Greg Brock—Scouting director Ben Wade considered new first baseman Brock to be the best left-handed hitter with power since Duke Snider wore the Dodger blue. The pressure on Brock, being the replacement for Steve Garvey, would be tremendous. The organization did everything it could to alleviate the building of pressure. They even went so far as to note that Garvey didn't hit for big numbers in his rookie season.

Mike Marshall—Marshall was the new right fielder, and he and Brock were thought to be the best new hitting duo of organized baseball. Al Campanis had spent the previous two years touting Marshall's exploits in the Pacific Coast League and then, without any explanation, almost packaged him with Burt Hooton in a deal to acquire Jim Sundberg.

Candy Maldonado—After a so-so year with Albuquerque, Maldonado improved his possibilities by having a good season of winter ball. His base-stealing ability impressed Campanis a great deal. He was also noted for his defensive skills.

Dave Anderson—The "new" shortstop, Anderson was scheduled to replace Bill Russell. The question was: when? Anderson was chosen—ahead of Brock—as the Pacific Coast League's top prospect by the managers after hitting .343 and stealing 43 bases. Other teams made offers for him, but Campanis would not discuss any of them. It seemed the plan was to use Anderson as an insurance policy who would remain just a phone call and a one-hour plane ride away.

Alejandro Pena—Discovered by Manny Mota when he made an emergency start in the Dominican Republic, Pena was cast in the "stay ready" category. Everyone knew he could throw. His arm was complimented by no less than Nolan Ryan.

Joe Beckwith—After a lesson with Sandy Koufax, Beckwith's fortunes began to turn around. However, the biggest boost in his stock came in the Caribbean World Series. In six relief appearances for Manny Mota, he got one win, four saves, and was voted the MVP in both the semifinals and the finals.

The month of February also brought four arbitration cases. Bob Walker, counsel for the Dodgers, had lost only one previous case (Ron Cey), and by winning cases with Mike Scioscia, Pedro Guerrero, and Steve Howe, Walker had already saved the Dodgers $340,000. But the big one was still to come. The Dodgers had offered Fernando Valenzuela $750,000; he wanted $1 million. Fernando's lawyer Dick Moss and Fernando's agent Tony DeMarco assembled a case that included videotape endorsements from Dodgers Executive Vice President Al Campanis and Dodgers manager Tommy Lasorda. In the space of one phone call to the Major League Players Association, Fernando set new standards for the team and the league. Twenty-two-year-old Fernando Valenzuela became the highest-paid third-year player in baseball history, and the first man ever to receive $1 million through the arbitration process.

And so the annual spring training at Vero Beach, Florida, began. Six weeks later the Dodgers boarded their charter flight home with a 10-15 record, wallowed in a five-game losing streak and having committed 48 errors in just 25 games. All these signs failed to dampen the spirits of manager Lasorda, however. "I feel like a fight manager," said Tom Lasorda. "I had a heavyweight champion, but now he's gone by the wayside. Now I'm coming around, and I've got a young guy and I feel like I've got another champion." Optimism springs eternal.

The Dodgers left spring training feeling fine about six fielding positions and their starting pitchers. Greg Brock played first base, Steve Sax was fine at second base, and Bill Russell hit at a .294 clip. In the outfield, Mike Marshall adjusted well to his new position and despite going two for his last 23, finished at .333 with six home runs and 15 RBI. Dusty Baker, recovering from orthoscopic surgery, remained firmly anchored in left field. The four starting pitchers—Burt Hooten, Fernando Valenzuela, Jerry Ruess, and Bob Welch—all had adequate springs and looked good in their last outings.

The remaining fielding positions and the relief corps brought mixed reviews. Steve Yeager (catcher) and Ken Landreaux (center field) were both very pleasant surprises. They finished hitting .333 with three home runs and .338 with two home runs respectively. Although Pedro Guerrero tore up the Grapefruit League (.373, four homers, 11 RBI), his fielding had become one of Lasorda's biggest concerns. (In the language of spring training, "concern" indicates something that wakes you up in a cold sweat. Guerrero had made nine of the team's 48 errors and his sore right shoulder was now placed in the care of Dr. Frank Jobe.)

The relief corps lacked the stability needed to win a pennant. Lasorda summed up the condition of the relievers as plenty of talent, but no consistency. The Dodgers went into the season with Steve Howe as their No. One man in the bullpen; this would become more important as the season progressed.

Nearly as predictably as the swallows returning to Capistrano, the Dodgers made the playoffs. It seemed the natural state for the Dodgers, and the transition was a good one. They finished the season with a 91-71 record and revenged the previous year's second-place finish to the Atlanta Braves. The two teams stayed within striking distance of each other until an injury to Bob Horner provided the Dodgers with new impetus.

However, the 1983 season was one to be remembered for those off-the-field occurrences that affect any human organization. Walter Alston, the long-time ex-manager of the Dodgers, was critically ill in Ohio; Danny Goodman, a name synonymous with Dodgers souvenirs, died after a long illness. Both Bill Russell's and Steve Sax's fathers died during the season. There was also the drug-related problems of Steve Howe that were rumored to extend well beyond the left-handed pitcher. And finally, there were those transitional problems inherent in any youth movement. Real life kept injecting itself into the fun of games.

Nevertheless, the Dodgers were still the concensus favorite among a poll of *Sporting News* correspondents, and the Las Vegas odds-makers favored them. However, the writers traveling with the team picked them to finish somewhere between second and fourth. Had they known, they probably would have picked them much lower. Here's how it went for the Dodgers in the summer of 1983.

Pedro Guerrero—He arrived at Vero Beach still fuming over the loss of his arbitration case. In fact, he said of the arbitrator, "I hope the jerk dies." Part of Guerrero's case was his willingness to change from right field to third base, and now he was clearly unhappy about the switch. The early development of a sore right shoulder did not improve his disposition. Guerrero wound up the season with a total of 30 errors, but would have been the team's MVP regardless of the number. He led the team in batting, homers, and RBI. He was also third in stolen bases. Toward the end of such a productive season one's disposition changes. Laughing one night in Cincinnati, he said "They turned me from one of the best right fielders into a horsefeathers third baseman. But they leave me there another year and I'll be cool."

Jerry Ruess—Being on the last year of his contract and faced with the traditional Dodgers position of barely bargaining during the season, Ruess could have anticipated some extraordinary things to happen. However, no one could have forseen Jerry Ruess going 10 weeks without a victory, having a 6-10 record on August 15. Throughout much of the season Ruess had experienced pain in his left elbow. Not wishing to alert the other general managers (potential employers) he held off getting a shot until early August. The arrival of Rick Honeycutt coincided with the beginning of a five-game winning streak and a return to form for Ruess. Although unsigned at the end of the season, he was still the No. One starter on the staff and he pitched the playoff opener.

Steve Sax—He spent most of the season with a purely mental problem concerning the routine throw to first base. He received cures from strangers on airplanes and was urged to seek out the aid of a hypnotist. In fact, Sax reached the point where a sportswriter in Pittsburgh nicknamed him "R2E4." However, by early August, Sax had "righted the ship" and did not commit an error after August 7.

Greg Brock—Brock entered the season with the unenviable task of replacing Steve Garvey. He started slowly (mild understatement) but by mid-May his 11 homers and 29 RBI placed him among the league leaders. If the early season was not enough, Brock went downhill steadily until he bottomed out at .212 in early August. General manager Campanis thought of sending him down, but kept him up. Brock rallied a little to finish with a .224 average, 20 homers, and 66 RBI.

Fernando Valenzuela—He reported to camp slimmer in stature and fatter in the wallet. With all the distraction of contract negotiations removed, a good season, possibly the best ever, seemed likely. Wrong. Fernando proceeded to have his worst season in his brief but illustrious career. An off season for him included team highs of 15 wins, five shutouts, and nine complete games. During the final seven weeks of the season he pitched well enough to average a strikeout each inning.

Dusty Baker—After the departure of Davey Lopes, Baker looked like the heir apparent to the role of clubhouse leader, but he rejected it. The rejection stemmed from the fear that the front office might have no use for an outspoken player. Coming off orthoscopic knee surgery a month before spring training, Baker decided to concentrate on his personal recovery. By the end of the season he was quoted as saying, "I was tested beyond what I thought I could take."

Mike Marshall—Mike was in and out of the line-up a couple of times early, once by a beaning by Jeff Reardon and again by a lack of hitting. He was only hitting .212 on June 12. Manager Lasorda tried sitting him down and Manny Mota helped him cut down his swing. Something worked because after June 12, Marshall hit .307 and dramatically cut down on his strikeouts.

Derrel Thomas—One of the game's most versatile utility players, Thomas was also in the final year of his contract. Also dismayed by the progress of the negotiations, he started making basket catches at knee level in game situations. Even the normally positive Vin Scully sighed, "Derrel, you march to your own Walkman."

Early in August a turning point of the season occurred. After their second straight loss to Cincinnati, Rick Monday asked Lasorda if he could call a meeting. It only lasted 15 minutes, but the clearing of the air did some good. The next day the Dodgers beat the Reds, and Joe Beckwith and Paul Padilla awarded the first Mr. Potatohead to the Dodgers star of the game. The award was accompanied by the Mr. Potatohead song. The Dodgers moved on to Atlanta and lost a heartbreaker to the Braves on Bob Watson's two-run ninth-inning homer to drop 5½ back. It looked bleak. The next day Valenzuela and Niedenfuer beat the Braves. The following day Bob Horner got hurt, and the day after that the Dodgers started an eight-game winning streak.

Mr. Potatohead and his accompanying song got stronger after each victory until the Friday the Dodgers clinched the NL West and Lasorda won the award for the first time.

The transition might better have been termed a minor miracle. The lessons learned over the long season and the tough playoff loss to Philadelphia will pay untold future benefits for the younger Dodgers. Another step that bodes well for the future of the Dodgers was the signing of Tommy Lasorda to a previously unheard of *three*-year contract. In addition to Lasorda, the Dodgers renewed the contracts of coaches Monty Basgall, Mark Cresse, Joe Amalfitano, Ron Perransoski, and Manny Mota. It would appear that the solid foundation—players and brain-trust—of a dynasty is in place. The Dodgers' commitment to excellence is unquestioned. The Dodgers' future is very bright.

In 1983 Ken Landreaux enjoyed his finest year since coming to the Dodgers in a trade from the Minnesota Twins in March 1981. He hit a career-high 17 home runs and finished with an excellent .990 fielding percentage while playing an aggressive centerfield for the Dodgers.

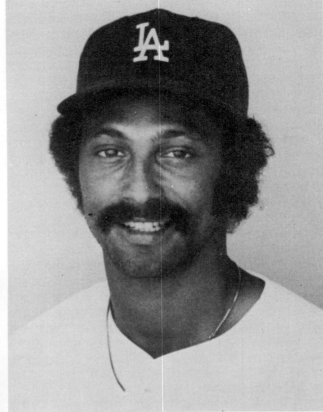

An 11-year major-league veteran, Steve Yeager passed the 1,000-game mark in his career on May 9, 1983, against Chicago. His 96 career home runs places him 17th on the Dodgers' all-time list and eighth on the L.A. Dodgers' all-time list. In 1983, Yeager hit 15 round trippers—the most he has hit since connecting for his career-high 16 in 1977. He is also a superb defensive catcher. In 1983, he threw out 44 of 107 attempted base stealers for a .411 performance.

Photo by Daniel J. Murphy

Photo by Daniel J. Murphy

Photo by Daniel J. Murphy

In 1983, Fernando Valenzuela led the Dodger pitching staff in starts (35), complete games (9), shutouts (4), strikeouts (189) and innings pitched (257). In slightly more than three seasons, Fernando has become one of the most popular Dodger players of all time.

Fernando tags out San Francisco's Johnny Lemaster in a run down between third and home.

Photo by Daniel J. Murphy

Fernando's accomplishments in 1983 earned him a spot on the National League All-Star team for the third time in as many seasons.

Photo by Daniel J. Murphy

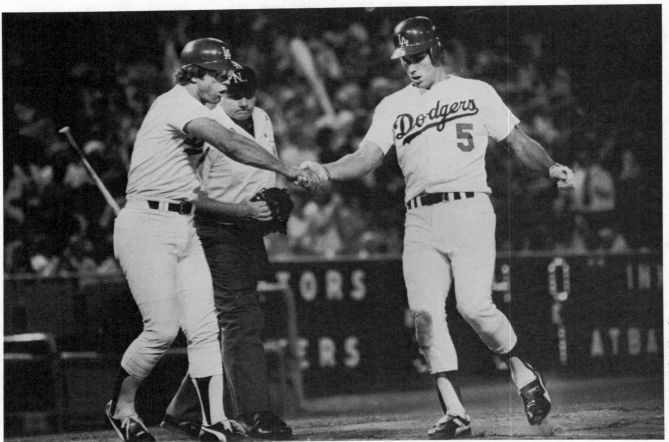

Mike Marshall had a superb season in 1983. He finished the year with the second best average for a regular on the club at .284 and had 17 homes, 65 RBI and 11 game-winning RBI. Above, Steve Yeager congratulates Marshall after another round tripper by Mike.

Tom Niedenfuer emerged as the Dodgers' top right-handed reliever during the 1983 season and was the team's stopper during the absence of Steve Howe who was suspended twice during the season for off-the-field problems.

The Dodgers celebrate another victory—one of 91 in 1983. Pedro Guerrero (#28) had a superstar year—.298 batting average, 32 home runs and 103 RBI. He also duplicated his prodigious feat of '82 when he became the first Dodger in history to hit 30 home runs and steal 20 bases in the same season. He proved to be a valuable addition. He played three infield and all three outfield positions and was also used as a pinch-hitter and a pinch-runner.

Photo by Daniel J. Murphy

PART II
DODGER NOTES

12

BORN TO BE A DODGER

Since 1884 more than 1100 players have had the privilege of wearing "Dodger Blue." Each in his own way was born to be a Dodger. Collectively their efforts have contributed to the commitment of excellence by the entire Dodger organization. This chapter presents a listing of every player who has worn "Dodger Blue" prior to 1984.

Richie Allen and his family.

Doyle Alexander won 6 and lost 6 in 1970, his first year in the majors.

Bill Buckner played eight seasons for the Dodgers. In his best season he hit .319 in 1972.

Peter O'Malley and Al Campanis

Brown, Edward	1924-25
Brown, Elmer	1913-15
Brown, John, J.	1897
Brown, John L. ("Lindsay")	1937
Brown, Lloyd	1925
Brown, Mace	1941
Brown, Tommy	1944-45, 1947-51
Browne, George	1911
Browning, Louis ("Pete")	1894
Brubaker, Bruce	1967
Bucher, Jim	1934-37
Buckner, Bill	1969-76
Buker, Cyril ("Cy")	1945
Bunning, Jim	1969
Burch, Albert	1907-11
Burch, Ernest	1886-87
Burdock, John ("Jack")	1888, 1891
Burk, Charles ("Sandy")	1910-12
Burke, Glenn	1976-78
Burns, Tom ("Oyster")	1888-95
Burrell, Frank ("Buster")	1895-97
Burright, Larry	1962
Bushong, Albert ("Doc")	1888-90
Butcher, Albert ("Max")	1936-38
Butler, John A.	1906-07
Butler, John S. (Johnny")	1926-27

C

Cadore, Leon	1915-23
Caldwell, Bruce	1933
Callahan, Leo	1913
Calmus, Dick	1963
Camilli, Adolph ("Dolph")	1938-43
Camilli, Doug	1960-64
Campanella, Roy	1948-57
Campanis, Alex	1943
Campanis, Jim	1966-68
Campbell, William ("Gilly")	1938
Canavan, Jimmy	1897
Cannizzaro, Chris	1972-73
Cantrell, Dewey ("Guy")	1925, 1927
Cantwell, Ben	1937
Carey, Andy	1962
Carey, Max	1926-29
Carlton, James ("Tex")	1940
Carroll, Owen ("Ownie")	1933-34
Carsey, Wilford ("Kid")	1901
Caruthers, Bob	1888-91
Casey, Hugh	1939-42, 1946-48
Casey, James ("Doc")	1899, 1900, 1906-07
Cassidy, John	1884-85
Cassidy, Pete	1899
Castillo, Robert ("Babo")	1977-81
Catterson, Tom	1908- 09
Cey, Ron	1971-82
Chandler, Edward	1947
Chapman, Glenn ("Pete")	1934
Chapman, William ("Ben"")	1944-45
Cheney, Laurance ("Larry")	1915-19
Chervinko, Paul	1937-38
Chipman, Robert	1941-44
Churn, Clarence ("Chuck")	1959
Cimoli, Gino	1956-58
Cisar, George	1937
Clabaugh, John ("Moose")	1926
Clancy, John ("Bud")	1932
Clark, Robert	1886-90
Clark, William ("Watty")	1927-37
Clement, Wallace	1909

Roy Campanella

*Campy —
catcher extraordinaire.*

Roy was the National League's MVP in 1951, 1953 and 1955. On July 16, 1969, he was inducted into baseball's Hall of Fame. Campy is shown receiving his Hall of Fame plaque with his son (left) and Baseball Commissioner Bowie Kuhn (right) in attendance.

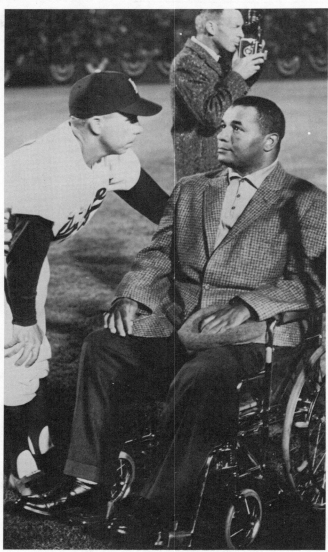

Former teammates Pee Wee Reese and Roy Campanella exchange a few words.

Duke Snider slammed a record 4 home runs in the 1955 World Series. Evidently Jackie Robinson, Pee Wee Reese and Roy figure he deserved a special salute. After the game, they carried the Duke back to the locker room to celebrate homer number 3.

After the Dodgers' 1955 World Series triumph, Walt Alston, Pee Wee Reese, Carl Erskine and Campy (left to right) retreat to the locker room to celebrate.

Second baseman Pete Coscarart played for Brooklyn from 1938-1941. Pete's brother Joe—also an infielder—saw action in the 1930's with the Boston Braves.

In 1955 Roger Craig made his debut with the Dodgers with a sensational three-hit, 6-2 win over the Cincinnati Reds at Ebbets Field. Roger won several important games that year and the Dodgers won the World Championship. He beat the Yankees in the fifth game of the World Series, 5-3 to cap a fabulous rookie year for the youngster from Durham, North Carolina.

Cohen, Albert ("Atla")	1931-32
Colavito, Rocco ("Rocky")	1968
Collins, Bill	1913
Collins, George ("Hub")	1888-92
Collum, Jack ("Jackie")	1957-58
Connors, Kevin ("Chuck")	1949
Conway, Jim	1884
Coombs, John ("Jack")	1915-18
Cooney, Johnny	1935-37, 1943-44
Corbitt, Claude	1945
Corcoran, John	1884
Corcoran, Tommy	1892-96
Corgan, Charles ("Chuck")	1925, 1927
Corkhill, John ("Pop")	1888-90
Corriden, John	1946
Coscarart, Pete	1938-41
Coulson, Bob	1910-11
Covington, John ("Wes")	1966
Cox, Elmer ("Dick")	1925-26
Cox, William ("Billy")	1948-54
Crable, George	1910
Craig, Roger	1955-61
Crane, Edward ("Cannonball")	1893
Crane, Samuel	1922
Crawford, Willie	1964-75
Crocker, Claude	1944-45
Cronin, John	1895
Cross, Lafayette ("Lave")	1900
Crouch, Bill	1939
Crow, Donald	1982
Cruz, Henry	1975-76
Cuccinello, Anthony ("Tony")	1932-35
Cullenbine, Roy	1940
Cullop, Henry ("Nick")	1929
Culver, George	1973
Cunningham, Ellsworth ("Bert")	1887
Curtis, Clifton ("Cliff")	1912-13
Cutshaw, George	1912-17
Cuyler, Hazen ("Kiki")	1938

D

Dahlen, Bill	1899-1903, 1910-11
Dahlgren, Ellsworth ("Babe")	1942
Dailey, Cornelius ("Con")	1891-95
Daley, Judson ("Jud")	1911-12
Dalton, Talbot ("Jack")	1910-1914
Daly, Tom	1890-96, 1898-1901
Daniel, Handley ("Jake")	1937
Dantonio, John ("Fats")	1944-45
Dapper, Clifford	1942
Darnell, Bob	1954, 1956
Darwin, Arthur ("Bobby")	1969, 1971
Daub, Daniel	1893-97
Daubert, Jacob ("Jake")	1910-18
Davalillo, Victor	1977-80
Davidson, Bill	1910-11
Davis, Alfonzo ("Lefty")	1901
Davis, Curtis ("Curt")	1940-46
Davis, Otis	1946
Davis, Herman ("Tommy")	1959-66
Davis, Willie	1960-73
Day, Clyde ("Pea Ridge")	1931
Deal, Lindsay	1939
Dean, Tommy	1967
DeBerry, John ("Hank")	1922-30
Decatur, Arthur	1922-25
Dede, Arthur ("Artie")	1916
Dedeaux, Raoul ("Rod")	1935
Deisel, Edward ("Pat")	1902
De Jesus, Ivan	1974-76

Don Drysdale as a 20-year-old rookie with the Brooklyn Dodgers in 1956.

Jubilant Don Drysdale holds up the ball which tells the story of the third game of the 1963 World Series. Drysdale's 1-0 victory gave the Dodgers a commanding 3-0 lead in games.

For a pitcher, Drysdale was an excellent hitter. In the photo above, Don is hitting fungos to his outfielders.

On the pitching mound Don Drysdale was mean and menacing and his fast ball came in like a cannon shot.

Don Drysdale

Number 53 autographs baseballs for a fan.

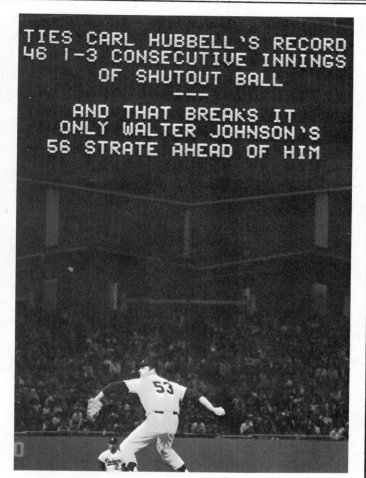

TIES CARL HUBBELL'S RECORD
46 1-3 CONSECUTIVE INNINGS
OF SHUTOUT BALL

AND THAT BREAKS IT
ONLY WALTER JOHNSON'S
56 STRATE AHEAD OF HIM

The scoreboard tells the story ... another chapter in the career of this Hall-of-Famer.

In 1962 Don won 25 and lost 9 games. His efforts earned him the Cy Young Award.

The Dodgers held a "Day" for Don in 1970. Governor Ronald Reagan presented Don with a plaque and called attention to Don's contribution to the Dodgers, to California and to young people everywhere.

Dell, William ("Wheezer")   1915-17
Delmas, Albert ("Bert")   1933
Demeter, Donald   1956-61
DeMontreville, Eugene   1900
Dent, Elliott ("Eddie")   1909,1911-12
Dessau, Frank ("Rube")   1910
Dickerman, Leo   1923-24
Dietz, Dick   1972
Dillon, Frank ("Pop")   1904
Doak, William   1924, 1927-28
Dobbs, John   1903-05
Dockins, George   1947
Dolan, Patrick ("Cozy")   1901-02
Donovan, Patrick ("Patsy")   1890,1906-07
Donovan, William ("Wild Bill")   1899-1902
Doolan, Michael ("Mickey")   1918
Dorgan, Jeremiah ("Jerry")   1884
Doscher, John ("Jack")   1903-06
Douglas, John   1945
Douglas, Philips ("Phil")   1915
Dowd, Raymond ("Snooks")   1926
Downey, Alexander ("Red")   1909
Downing, Alphonso ("Al")   1971-77
Downs, Jerome ("Reds")   1912
Doyle, John ("Jack")   1903-04
Doyle, William ("Carl")   1939-40
Drake, Solomon ("Solly")   1959
Drake, Tom   1941
Dresser, Edward   1898
Drysdale, Donald   1956-69
Dudley, Elzie ("Clise")   1929-30
Duffie, John   1967
Dunn, John ("Jack")   1897-1900
Dunn, Joe   1908-09
Durham, Louis ("Bull")   1904
Durning, Dick   1917-18
Durocher, Leo   1938-41, 1943, 1945
Durrett, Elmer ("Red")   1944-45

E

Earle, William ("Billy")   1894
Earnshaw, George   1935-36
Eason, Malcolm ("Mal")   1905-06

Eayrs Edwin   1921
Eckhardt, Oscar ("Ox")   1936
Edwards, Charles ("Bruce")   1946-51
Edwards, Henry ("Hank")   1951
Egan, Richard J.   1914-15
Egan, Richard W.   1967
Ehrhardt, Welton ("Rube")   1924-28
Eisenstat, Harry   1935-37
Elberfeld, Norman ("Kid")   1914
Elliott, Harold ("Rowdy")   1920
Elliott, James ("Jumbo")   1925, 1927-30
Elston, Don   1957
Ely, Frederick ("Bones")   1891
English, Elwood ("Woody")   1937-38
English, Gilbert   1944
Enzmann, Johnny   1914
Epperly, Albert   1950
Erskine, Carl   1948-59
Erwin, Ross ("Tex")   1910-14
Espy, Cecil   1983
Essegian, Charles ("Chuck")   1959-60
Esterbrook, Tom ("Dude")   1891
Evans, LeRoy   1902-03
Evans, Russell ("Red")   1939

Willie Davis was a mainstay for the Dodgers for more than a decade at bat, in the field and on the basepaths.

Vice President Richard Nixon congratulates Dodger pitcher Carl Erskine after the Dodgers won the 4th game of the 1955 World Series from the Yankees at Ebbets Field by an 8-5 score to even the Series at 2 games each.

Pepe Frias played two seasons for the Dodgers as a utility infielder.

When the Dodgers were in Japan in 1966 for a series of exhibition games, a number of players took the opportunity to visit some of our servicemen in various hospitals in Japan. During a rest and recreation break John Roseboro, Ron Fairly and Tom Davis chat with Major General Lloyd Felienz (2nd from the right) at the Camp Zama golf club.

Steve Garvey

Dodger Vice President Al Campanis watches Steve Garvey sign his Dodger contract.

Steve is an excellent-fielding first baseman.

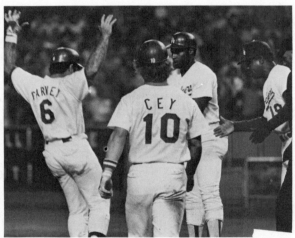

Garvey's clutch hitting won numerous games for the Dodgers.

Garvey's two-run homer on a 3-2 count, with two outs in the bottom of the ninth and the Dodgers trailing Houston 2-1 gives the Dodgers a dramatic 3-2 victory.

In 1976 Steve established a National League fielding record with only three errors in 1,500 chances.

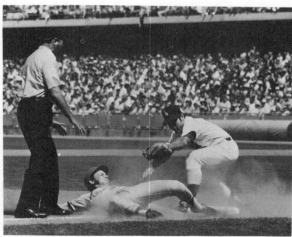

A close play at first base as Garvey stabs at a Cardinal base runner in a 1979 game.

Los Angeles City Councilman Joel Wachs (right) presents City Council resolution to Los Angeles Dodgers baseball star Steve Garvey, honoring him as the National League's Most Valuable Player for 1974. In making the presentation, Councilman Wachs commended Garvey for his dedication, aggressiveness, and generous team contributions to the great American sport of baseball, and his exemplary conduct off the field.

Steve Garvey as a Dodger rookie in 1970.

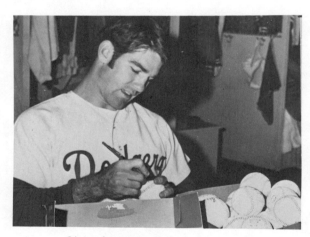

Steve keeps busy before a game.

Garvey's bases-loaded single drives in the winning run against the Philadelphia Phillies in the 8th inning of a game won by the Dodgers 2-1 on May 8, 1981.

A relaxed moment on the bench as the Dodgers are on the way to another win.

A thoughtful Steve Garvey reflects after a workout.

In 1972 Bill Grabarkewitz models one of the Dodgers' new double knit uniforms to recently acquired outfielder Frank Robinson.

Tommy Lasorda talks things over with Jerry Grote—obtained in a trade with the N.Y. Mets as the 1977 pennant race neared its climax.

Jim Bottomly (left) and Babe Herman (right).

Charlie Hough came to the Dodgers as a free agent in 1966 and then spent the next five seasons toiling in the high minor leagues. Brought up to the Dodgers in 1970 and utilized mainly as a reliever, Hough had his best year in 1976, when he appeared in 77 games. Hough claims that Tommy Lasorda saved his baseball career by teaching him to throw a knuckleball.

Hayworth, Ray	1938-39, 1944-45
Head, Edward	1940, 1942-44, 1946
Hearne, Hugh	1901-03
Hechinger, Mike	1913
Hehl, Herman ("Jake")	1918
Heimach, Fred	1930-33
Heitman, Harry	1918
Hemming, George	1890-91
Henderson, James ("Hardie")	1886-87
Hendrick, Harvey	1927-31
Henion, Lafayette	1919
Henley, Weldon	1907
Henline, Walter ("Butch")	1927-29
Henry, Frank ("Dutch")	1923-24
Henshaw, Roy	1937
Herman, Floyd ("Babe")	1926-31,1945
Herman, William ("Billy")	1941-43, 1946
Hermann, "Lefty"	1918
Hermanski, Gene	1943, 1946-51
Hernandez, Enzo	1978
Herring, Arthur	1934,1944-46
Hershiser, Orel	1983
Heydeman, Gregory	1973
Hickman, David	1916-19
Hickman, Jim	1967
Higbe, Walter ("Kirby")	1941-43, 1946-47
Higgins, Robert	1911-12
High, Andrew	1922-25
Hildebrand, George	1902
Hill, William	1899
Hines, Henry, ("Hunkey")	1895
Hines, Micheal	1885
Hoak, Donald	1954-55
Hockett, Oris	1938-39
Hodges, Gilbert ("Gil")	1943,1947-61
Hogg, Wilbert ("Bert")	1934
Holbert, Bill	1888
Hollingsworth, Albert	1939
Hollingsworth, John ("Bonnie")	1924
Holmes, Jim	1908
Holmes, Tommy	1952
Honeycutt, Frederick ("Rick")	1983
Hood, Wallace	1920-22
Hooton, Burt	1975-83
Hopkins, Gail	1974
Hopp, Johnny	1949
Hopper, C.F. ("Lefty")	1898
Horton, Elmer	1898
Hotaling, Pete	1885
Hough, Charles	1970-80
Householder, Charles	1884
Householder, Edward	1903
Howard, Frank	1958-64
Howe, Steve	1980-83
Howell, Harry	1898, 1900
Howell, Homer ("Dixie")	1953, 1955-56
Hoyt, Waite	1932, 1937-38
Hubbell, Wilbert ("Bill")	1925
Hudson, Johnny	1936-40
Hudson, Rex	1974
Hug, Edward	1903
Hughes, James J.	1899, 1901-02
Hughes, James R. ("Jim")	1952-56
Hughes, Michael ("Mickey")	1888-90
Hummel, John	1905-15
Humphrey, Albert	1911
Hungling, Bernard ("Bernie")	1922-23
Hunt, Ronald	1967
Hunter, George	1909

Gil Hodges

At age 35, first baseman Gil Hodges connected in the eighth inning for a home run that gave the Dodgers a 5-4 victory over the White Sox in the 1959 World Series. The victory gave the Dodgers a 3-1 lead in the Series.

AP/World Wide Photos

Gil Hodges scored from second base on a sacrifice fly in the seventh inning of the Dodgers-Pittsburgh Pirates game at Ebbets Field on June 4, 1949. The throw from leftfielder Ralph Kiner to his catcher Eddie Fitzgerald (#9) was too late to nip Hodges. The umpire is Beans Reardon. Watching Hodges slide was the next hitter, Dodger catcher Bruce Edwards.

AP/World Wide Photos

Hunter, Willard	1962
Hurley, Patrick	1907
Hutcheson, Joe	1933
Hutchinson, Ira	1939
Hutson, Roy	1925
Hutton, Tommy	1966, 1969

I

Inks, Albert ("Bert")	1891-92
Irwin, Charles	1901-02

J

Jacklitcsh, Frederick	1903-04
Jackson, Ransom ("Randy")	1956-58
Jacobson, Merwin	1926-27
James, Cleo	1968
Janvrin, Harold ("Hal")	1921-22
Jarvis, LeRoy ("Roy")	1944
Jeffcoat, George	1936-37, 1939
Jenkins, Jack	1969
Jennings, Hugh	1899-1900, 1903
John, Tommy	1972-78
Johnson, Lou	1965-67
Johnston, James ("Jimmy")	1916-25
Johnston, Wilfred ("Fred")	1924
Johnstone, John ("Jay")	1980-82
Jones, Arthur	1932
Jones, Charles	1884
Jones, Fielder	1896-1900
Jones, John ("Binky")	1924
Jones, Oscar	1903-05
Jordan, Adolph ("Dutch")	1903-04
Jordan, James ("Jimmy")	1933-36
Jordan, Timothy	1906-10
Jorgenson, John ("Spider")	1947-50
Joshua, Von	1969-71, 1973-74, 1979
Joyce, Bill	1892
Judge, Joe	1933

K

Kampouris, Alex	1941-43
Karst, John	1915
Keeler, William ("Willie")	1893, 1899-1902
Kehn, Chester ("Chet")	1942
Kekich, Mike	1965, 1968
Kelleher, John	1916
Kellert, Frank	1955
Kelley, Joe	1899-1901
Kelly, George	1932
Kennedy, Bob	1957
Kennedy,, Edward	1886
Kennedy, John	1965-66
Kennedy, William ("Brickyard")	
	1892-1901
Kent, Maurice ("Maury")	1912-13
Kilduff, Pete	1919-21
Kimball, Newell ("Newt")	1940-43
Kimber, Samuel	1884
King, Cldye	1944-45, 1947-48, 1951-52
Kinslow, Tom	1891-94
Kipp, Fred	1957-59
Kirkpatrick, Enos	1912-13
Kitson, Frank	1900-02
Klippstein, Johnny	1958-59
Klugman, Josie ("Joe")	1924
Klumpp, Elmer	1937
Knetzer, Elmer	1909-12
Knolls, Oscar ("Hub")	1906
Knowles, Jim	1884
Koch, Barnett ("Barney")	1944

Tommy Hutton was the leading hitter on the Pacific Coast in 1966. All he did for Albuquerque was hit .340. He was named the Texas League Player of the Year and was brought up to the Dodgers in 1966 and again in 1969.

Lefthander Mike Kekich.

Sandy Koufax

The 1952 basketball team of Lafayette High of Brooklyn, New York, featured a skinny kid named Sandy Koufax (#9).

One of the stars of the 1952 Lafayette High School team, (Brooklyn, N.Y.) was a wiry, shifty, two-handed shooter and passer named Sandy Koufax. (back row center). Sandy was a fine floor man and could outjump any kid in high school play. After graduating from Lafayette High, Sandy received a basketball scholarship at Cincinnati University.

The form that launched 2,396 strikeouts in 12 years.

Koufax was an intense competitor.

Sandy Koufax posed for this World Series photo in 1963. It was the morning before Game One of the Dodger-Yankee World Series. When the game began, Sandy calmly struck out Tony Kubek, Bobby Richardson and Tom Tresh in order. In the second inning, the first batter—Mickey Mantle—struck out and when the next hitter, Roger Maris, also fanned on three pitches, Koufax had set a World Series record of five strikeouts in a row. Sandy went on to strike out 15 Yankees, another Series record. The Dodgers won the first game 5-2 as Sandy gave up but 5 hits.

The message board tells the story as Sandy Koufax walks off the field after blanking Milwaukee 4-0 in a game at Dodger Stadium on September 30, 1965. Dodger coach Lefty Phillips (L) congratualtes Sandy. Third baseman John Kennedy (#11) flanks Sandy.

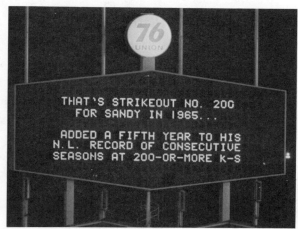

Another record for Hall-of-Famer Sandy Koufax.

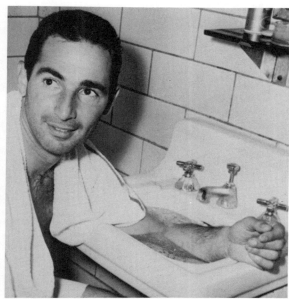

Sandy bathes his arm in ice water after he pitched a seven-hitter and took over the National League strikeout lead by fanning nine batters in the Dodgers 4-1 victory over the Pittsburgh Pirates on May 14, 1966.

In 1938, outfielder Ernie Koy hit .299 for the Dodgers.

Lee Lacy played parts of seven seasons for the Dodgers as a quality journeyman. Fitting in at several positions, Lacy was a valuable player. 1975 was Lee's best year when he hit .314.

Davey Lopes was a key player for the Dodgers for ten seasons. Davey served as captain of the Dodgers in 1978 and 1979 and is considered one of baseball's all-time base-stealers.

In 1974, Mike Marshall appeared in an incredible 106 games as a relief-pitcher. He won 15 games and was named the Cy Young Award winner for 1974. Undoubtedly, the Dodgers' vice-president Al Campanis is discussing Mike's 1975 salary.

M

Name	Years
Macon, Max	1940, 1942-43
Magee, Leo ("Lee")	1919
Maglie, Salvatore ("Sal")	1956-57
Magoon, George	1898
Mails, John ("Duster")	1915-16
Malay, Charles	1905
Maldonado, Candido ("Candy")	1981-83
Malinosky, Anthony ("Tony")	1937
Mallette, Malcolm ("Mal")	1950
Malone, Lewis	1917, 1919
Maloney, William ("Billy")	1906-08
Mamaux, Albert	1918-23
Mancuso, August ("Gus")	1940
Manuel, Charles	1974-75
Manush, Henry ("Heinie")	1937-38
Maranville, Walter ("Rabbit")	1926
Marichal, Juan	1975
Marquard, Richard ("Rube")	1915-20
Marriott, Bill	1925-26
Marrow, Charles ("Buck")	1937-38
Marshall, Michael A. ("Mike")	1981-83
Marshall, Michael G. ("Mike")	1974-76
Marshall, William ("Doc")	1909
Martin, Morris ("Morrie")	1949
Martinez, Teodoro ("Teddy")	1977-79
Mattingly, Laurence ("Earl")	1931
Mauch, Gene	1944
Maul, Albert	1899
Mauriello, Ralph	1958
Mauro, Carmen	1953
Mays, Albert	1888
McBean, Alvin	1969-70
McCabe, Bill	1920
McCann, Henry ("Gene")	1901-02
McCarren, Bill	1923
McCarthy, John A. ("Jack")	1906-07
McCarthy, John J. ("Johnny")	1934-35
McCarthy, Tommy	1896
McCarthy, George ("Lew")	1913-16
McCauley, Jim	1886
McClellan, Bill	1885-88
McCormick, Michael J. ("Mike")	1904
McCormick, Myron ("Mike")	1949
McCredie, Walter ("Judge")	1903
McCreery, Tom	1901-03
McDermott, Terrence ("Terry")	1972
Mc Devitt, Daniel ("Danny")	1957-60
McDougal, John	1895
McElveen, Pryor	1909-11
McFarland, Anderson ("Dan")	1899
McFarland, Charles ("Chappie")	1906
McGamwell, Edward	1905
McGann, Dennis ("Dan")	1899
McGinnity, Joe ("Iron Man")	1900
McGlothin, Ezra ("Pat")	1949-50
McGraw, Bob	1925-27
McGuire, James ("Deacon")	1899-1901
McIntire, John ("Harry")	1905-09
McJames, James ("Doc")	1899, 1901
McKenna, James ("Kit")	1898
McLane, Edward	1907
McLish, Calvin	1944, 1946
McMahon, John ("Sadie")	1897
McMakin, John	1902
McManus, Francis ("Frank")	1903
McMillan, Tommy	1908-10
McMullen, Kenneth	1962-64, 1973-75
McTamany, Jim	1885-87

Andy Messersmith, a hard-throwing righthander, won games four seasons for the Dodgers.

Outfielder Wally Moon receives an award from Long Beach Telegram *editor Hank Hollingsworth.*

Don Newcombe—a giant among men, on and off the field.

Don Newcombe

Don delivers a pitch against the St. Louis Cardinals on September 20, 1956. The Dodgers won the game 17-2 as Don hit a pair of home runs and limited the Cardinals to seven hits. The victory was Don's 25th of the year.

Don fires a fast ball plateward in a spring training game against the Philadelphia Phillies at Clearwater, Florida on March 26, 1957.

Shown covering first base, Claude Osteen won 20 games in 1972 and was one of the most effective Dodger pitchers from 1965 to 1972.

Charlie Neal tears into third base in the 1959 World Series against the White Sox.

In 1963 Ron Perranoski had a 16-3 record for the Dodgers and led the National League's pitchers with a winning percentage of .842. Ron currently serves as the Dodgers' pitching coach and is given much of the credit for the development of what is one of baseball's finest pitching staffs.

Two great lefthanded pitchers, Tom Byrne of the Yankees and Johnny Podres of the Dodgers, shake hands before the final game of the World Series. Podres allowed the Yankees 5 hits and beat them 2-0 as he completely outpitched Byrne.

Pena, Jose	1970-72
Peoples, James ("Jimmy")	1885-88
Perconte, John ("Jack")	1980-81
Perkins, Charles	1934
Perranoski, Ronald	1961-67, 1972
Peterson, Jim	1937
Petty, Jesse	1925-28
Pfeffer, Edward ("Jeff")	1913-21
Pfister, George	1941
Pfund, LeRoy	1945
Phelps, Edward	1912-13
Phelps, Ernest ("Babe")	1935-41
Phelps, Raymond	1930-32
Phillips, Bill	1885-87
Picinich, Valentine ("Val")	1929-33
Pignatano, Joe	1957-60
Pinckney, George	1885-91
Pipgras, Edward	1932
Plitt, Norman	1918, 1927
Podbielan, Clarence ("Bud")	1949-52
Podres, Johnny	1953-55, 1957-66
Poffenberger, Cletus ("Boots")	1939
Polly, Nicholas	1937
Poole, Edward	1904
Popovich, Paul	1968-69
Porter, Henry	1885-87
Posedel, Bill	1938
Post, Samuel	1922
Potter, Maryland ("Dykes")	1938
Pounds, Bill	1903
Powell, John ("Boog")	1977
Powell, Paul	1973, 1975
Power, Ted	1981-82
Pressnell, Forest ("Tot")	1938-40
Purdin, John	1964-65, 1968-69

Q

Quinn, John ("Jack")	1931-32

R

Rachunok, Stephen	1940
Rackley, Marvin	1947-49
Radford, Paul	1888
Radtke, Jack	1936
Ragan, Don ("Pat")	1911-15
Rakow, Edward	1960
Ramazzotti, Bob	1946, 1948-49
Ramsdell, James ("Willie")	1947-48, 1950
Rau, Douglas	1972-80
Rautzhan, Clarence ("Lance")	1977-79
Reardon, Philip	1906
Redmond, Harry	1909
Reed, Howard ("Howie")	1964-66
Reese, Harold ("Pee Wee")	1940-42, 1946-58
Regan, Philip	1966-68
Reidy, Bill	1899, 1903-04
Reis, Robert	1931-32, 1935
Reiser, Harold ("Pete")	1940-42, 1946-48
Reisling, Frank ("Doc")	1904-05
Remsen, John ("Jack")	1884
Repulski, Eldon ("Rip")	1959-60
Reulbach, Edward	1913-14
Reuss, Jerry	1979-83
Reyes, Gilberto	1983
Reynolds, Charles	1889
Reynolds, R.J.	1983
Rhiel, William ("Billy")	1929
Rhoden, Richard ("Rick")	1974-78
Richards, Paul	1932

Harold "Pee Wee" Reese was elected to baseball's Hall of Fame in March, 1984.

Pee Wee Reese

At a big victory party to celebrate the 1955 World Series win over the Yankees, Captain Pee Wee Reese (#1) assists Dodger President Walter O'Malley and manager Walt Alston in cutting a piece of the World Series cake.

The Reese family . . . (L to R) wife Dorothy, son Mark and daughter Barbara.

Two of the greatest Dodger stars meet 25 years after their great careers are over. Pee Wee Reese (L) and Duke Snider talk things over before the Old-Timers game at Dodger Stadium in 1981.

Game Called . . . Dog on Field. The Giants and Dodgers were at each others' throats as usual on May 28, 1953, when the game was halted. A dog ran to second base and dodged all efforts to get him off the field. Finally, Pee Wee Reese (#1), coaxed and wheedled the dog off the field and the game continued. The dog must have been a Dodger fan, for the Giants, who were leading in the game prior to the episode, became rattled and the Dodgers eked out a 7-6 victory.

Jackie Robinson

Jackie slides safely past Andy Seminick with the winning run in a game on July 6, 1948.

Jackie exhibiting the concentration that made him a winner—on and off the field.

Robbie slides safely under Yogi Berra's mitt in the eighth inning of the first game of the 1955 World Series. Umpire Bill Summer is about to call Jackie safe. Frank Kellert, who was at bat when Robinson attempted his theft of home, watches the action.

The Cookie Lavagetto's and the Jackie Robinson's danced the night away at the Dodger World Series party in 1955.

It was a day of days for the incomparable Jackie Robinson. On this day, July 24, 1962, Robinson was inducted into baseball's Hall of Fame. It was also a great day for Branch Rickey (shown with Jackie in the center and right photos) who played an instrumental role in breaking baseball's color line.

In 1966 pitcher Phil Regan (center) won 14 and saved 21 games in relief. In a moment of light-hearted fun, Sandy Koufax (right) nicknamed Regan the "Vulture." Koufax and Don Drysdale (left) are shown holding the wings of Regan's vulture.

Dodgers' catcher John Roseboro makes the putout on the Phillies' Sparky Anderson who was attempting to steal home in the second inning of a game on July 18, 1959. Anderson went on to become a successful major league manager.

Duke Snider

Duke played 16 years for the Dodgers.

Duke was voted into baseball's Hall of Fame in 1980. Duke and Mrs. Snider stand in front of Duke's Hall of Fame plaque at Cooperstown.

The Duke holds 3 of 4 home run balls he hit in the 1955 World Series.

They let Duke Snider blow out the candles on this victory cake at a party celebrating the Dodgers' first World Series Championship in history in 1955. The Duke slugged out 4 home runs as the Dodgers came from behind to defeat the Yankees. The Duke blew out the single candle, while Vin Scully, Carl Erskine, and other friends looked on.

The Duke Sniders in 1960.

Three of the Dodgers' greatest stars—Duke Snider, Don Newcombe and Don Drysdale—pose together for the first time in 1977.

Dodger stars Reggie Smith (8) and Davey Lopes (15) stretch their muscles at a workout on February 13, 1978, at Dodger Stadium.

Two great home run stars—Micky Mantle (left) and Duke Snider (right)—check their favorite bat before the first game of the 1955 Yankees-Dodgers World Series.

Eddie Stanky came to the Dodgers in the middle of the 1944 season. His fiery play earned him the nickname, "The Brat," and in 1947 with Reese at short, Spider Jorgenson at 3rd, and Jackie Robinson on 1st base, the Dodgers had one of the finest infields in baseball.

Catcher Jeff Torborg (right) and teammate, second baseman Nate Oliver (second from the left) talk with two patients at the 106th General Hospital barracks in Yokohama, Japan, during a Dodgers' tour on November 2, 1966.

Stack, William ("Eddie")	1912-13
Stainback, George ("Tuck")	1938-39
Stallings, George	1890
Standaert, Jerome ("Jerry")	1925-26
Stanhouse, Donald	1980-81
Stanky, Edward ("Eddie")	1944-47
Stark, Monroe ("Dolly")	1910-12
Statz, Arnold ("Jigger")	1927-28
Steele, Bill	1914
Steele, Elmer	1911
Steelman, Morris ("Farmer")	1900-01
Stein, Edward	1892-96, 1898
Stengel, Charles ("Casey")	1912-17
Stephenson, Jerry	1970
Stevens, Edward	1945-47
Stewart, David	1978, 1981-83
Stewart, John ("Stuffy")	1923
Stinson, Gorrell ("Bob")	1969-70
Stock, Milton ("Milt")	1924-26
Stovey, Harry	1893
Strahler, Michael	1970-72
Strang, Samuel ("Sammy")	1903-04
Strauss, Joe	1886
Stricklett, Elmer	1905-07
Stripp, Joe	1932-37
Stryker, Sterling ("Dutch")	1926
Stuart, Dick	1966
Sudakis, Bill	1968-71
Sukeforth, Clyde	1932-34, 1945
Sullivan, William, Jr. ("Billy")	1942
Sunkel, Tom	1944
Sutcliffe, Richard ("Rick")	1942
Sutton, Donald	1966-80
Swartwood, Cyrus ("Ed")	1885-87
Swift Bill	1941

T

Tamulis, Vitautis ("Vito")	1938-41
Taveras, Alex	1982-83
Tatum, V.T. ("Tommy")	1941, 1947
Taylor, Daniel ("Danny")	1932-36
Taylor, James H. ("Harry")	1946-48
Taylor, James W. ("Zach")	1920-25, 1935
Teed, Dick	1953
Templeton, Charles ("Chuck")	1955-56
Tepsic, Joe	1946
Terry, Bill ("Adonis")	1884-91
Terwilliger, Willard ("Wayne")	1951
Thatcher, Ulysses ("Grant")	1903-04
Thielman, Henry	1903
Thomas, Derrel	1979-83
Thomas, Fay	1932
Thomas, Raymond	1938
Thomasson, Gary	1979-80
Thompson, Charles ("Tim")	1954
Thompson, Donald	1951, 1953-54
Thompson, Lafayette ("Fresco")	1931-32
Thormahlen, Herbert ("Hank")	1925
Thurston, Hollis ("Sloppy")	1930-33
Tierney, James ("Cotton")	1925
Todd, Alfred	1939
Toole, Stephen	1886-87
Tooley, Albert ("Bert")	1911-12
Torborg, Jeffrey ("Jeff")	1964-70
Tracewski, Dick	1962-65
Treadway, George	1894-95
Tremark, Nicholas ("Nick")	1934-36
Tremper, Carlton ("Overton")	1927-28
Tucker, Tommy	1898
Tyson, Albert ("Ty")	1928

Poppa and Momma Valenzuela are very proud of their son.

Fernando Valenzuela

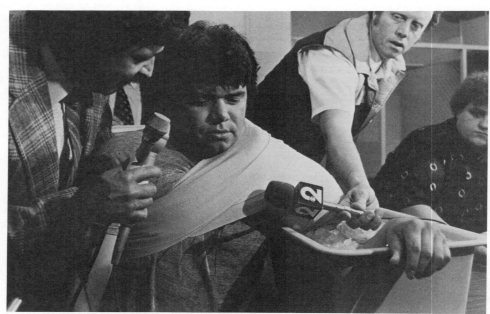

Fernando is besieged by reporters as he soaks his arm after a game.

King of the Hill.

After a base hit, an acknowledgment to the fans.

Hall-of-Famer Dazzy Vance (left) shown at the 1970 Baseball Writers dinner at the Waldorf Astoria Hotel in New York with Joe DiMaggio (center) and Gabby Hartnett (right).

Hoyt Wilhelm came to the Dodgers in 1971 at age 38 and pitched very well for two years.

Accompanied by Baseball Commissioner Bowie Kuhn, former Dodger All-Star shortstops Maury Wills (left) and Pee Wee Reese (right) throw out the first ball before a Dodger game on August 13, 1974.

Each year, baseball's greatest stars are inducted into the Baseball Hall of Fame at Cooperstown, New York, in one of the most stirring, most impressive ceremonies in all of baseball. The old and the young are moved to tears by the sentiments displayed. Here in July, 1972, some of baseball's immortal stars pose for this impressive Hall of Fame photograph.
Back Row: Frank Frisch, Buck Leonard, Sandy Koufax, Chub Feeney (President, National League), Joe Cronin (President, American League), Warren Giles, Stan Musial, Luke Appling, Bob Feller.
Middle Row: Casey Stengel, Joe DiMaggio, Bill Dickey, Stan Coveleski, Harry Hooper, Charley Gehringer, Sam Rice, Lefty Gomez, Bowie Kuhn (Baseball Commissioner)
Front Row: Lefty Grove, Paul Waner, Earl Combs, Jess Haines, George Kelly, Joe Medwick, Waite Hoyt, Ford Frick, Chick Hafey, Rube Marquard, Roy Campanella.

13

BORN TO BE GREAT: DODGERS IN THE HALL OF FAME

The plaques of the Hall of Famers are presented in the order in which they entered organized baseball. All of the following members of the Hall of Fame were players or managers of the Dodgers at some point in the great history of the team. We honor them by presenting a photograph of the plaque which has been placed in the Baseball Hall of Fame in Cooperstown, New York.

John Montgomery Ward

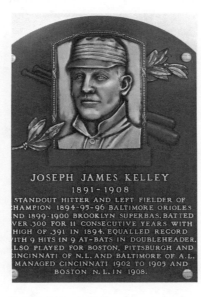

James Joseph Kelly

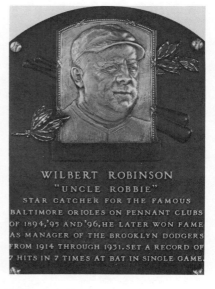

Wilbert Robinson

DAN BROUTHERS

HARD-HITTING FIRST BASEMAN OF EIGHT MAJOR LEAGUE CLUBS, HE WAS PART OF ORIGINAL "BIG FOUR" OF BUFFALO TRADED WITH OTHER MEMBERS OF THAT COMBINATION TO DETROIT, HE HIT .419 AS CITY WON ITS ONLY NATIONAL LEAGUE CHAMPIONSHIP IN 1887.

Dan Brouthers
Played for Brooklyn 1892-93

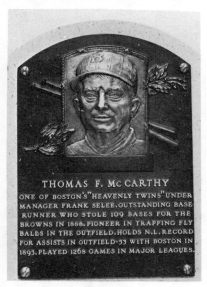

THOMAS F. McCARTHY

ONE OF BOSTON'S "HEAVENLY TWINS" UNDER MANAGER FRANK SELEE. OUTSTANDING BASE RUNNER WHO STOLE 109 BASES FOR THE BROWNS IN 1888. PIONEER IN TRAPPING FLY BALLS IN THE OUTFIELD. HOLDS N.L. RECORD FOR ASSISTS IN OUTFIELD-53 WITH BOSTON IN 1893. PLAYED 1268 GAMES IN MAJOR LEAGUES.

Thomas F. McCarthy
Played for Brooklyn 1896

HUGHIE JENNINGS

OF BALTIMORE'S FAMOUS OLD ORIOLES, HE WAS ONE OF THE GAME'S MIGHTY MITES. A STAR SHORTSTOP HE WAS A CONSTANT THREAT AT THE PLATE. ONCE HIT .397. PILOTED DETROIT TO THREE CHAMPIONSHIPS.

Hughie Jennings
Played for Brooklyn 1899-1900

WILLIE KEELER

"HIT 'EM WHERE THEY AIN'T!" BASEBALL'S GREATEST PLACE-HITTER; BEST BUNTER. BIG LEAGUE CAREER 1892 TO 1910 WITH N.Y. GIANTS, BALTIMORE ORIOLES, BROOKLYN SUPERBAS, N.Y. HIGHLANDERS. NATIONAL LEAGUE BATTING CHAMPION '97-'98.

Willie Keeler

WESLEY BRANCH RICKEY

ST. LOUIS A.L. 1905-1906-1914
NEW YORK A.L. 1907

FOUNDER OF FARM SYSTEM WHICH HE DEVELOPED FOR ST. LOUIS CARDINALS AND BROOKLYN DODGERS. COPIED BY ALL OTHER MAJOR LEAGUE TEAMS. SERVED AS EXECUTIVE FOR BROWNS, CARDINALS, DODGERS AND PIRATES. BROUGHT JACKIE ROBINSON TO BROOKLYN IN 1947.

Wesley Branch Rickey

RICHARD WILLIAM MARQUARD
"RUBE"

NEW YORK N.L.,   BROOKLYN N.L.,
CINCINNATI N.L.,   BOSTON N.L.,
1908 - 1925

THREE-TIME 20-GAME WINNER WITH GIANT CHAMPIONS OF 1911-12-13. TIED ALL-TIME RECORD WITH 19 VICTORIES IN A ROW WHILE WINNING 26 AND LOSING 11 IN 1912. LED N.L. IN WINNING PERCENTAGE AND STRIKEOUTS IN 1911. TIED FOR MOST VICTORIES, 1912. HURLED NO-HIT GAME AGAINST DODGERS IN 1915.

Richard William Marquard

ZACHARIAH (ZACK) DAVIS WHEAT

BROOKLYN N.L. 1909-1926
PHILADELPHIA A.L. 1927

BROOKLYN OUTFIELDER FOR 18 YEARS. HOLDS BROOKLYN RECORDS FOR GAMES PLAYED 2,318, AT BAT 8,859, HITS 2,804, SINGLES 2,038, DOUBLES 464, TRIPLES 171, TOTAL BASES 4,003, EXTRA BASE HITS 766. BATTED .375 (1923) .375 (1924) .359 (1925) LEAGUE BATTING LEADER .335 (1918) LIFETIME BATTING AVERAGE .317 WITH 2,884 HITS. PLAYED 2,406 GAMES.

Zachariah Davis Wheat

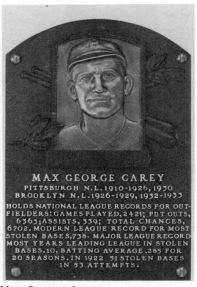

MAX GEORGE CAREY

PITTSBURGH N.L. 1910-1926, 1930
BROOKLYN N.L. 1926-1929, 1932-1933

HOLDS NATIONAL LEAGUE RECORDS FOR OUTFIELDERS: GAMES PLAYED, 2421; PUT OUTS, 6363; ASSISTS, 339; TOTAL CHANCES, 6702. MODERN LEAGUE RECORD FOR MOST STOLEN BASES, 738. MAJOR LEAGUE RECORD MOST YEARS LEADING LEAGUE IN STOLEN BASES, 10. BATTING AVERAGE .285 FOR 20 SEASONS. IN 1922 51 STOLEN BASES IN 53 ATTEMPTS.

Max George Carey

WALTER J. V. MARANVILLE
"RABBIT"

BOSTON, PITTSBURGH, CHICAGO, BROOKLYN AND ST. LOUIS, NATIONAL LEAGUE, 1912-1935

PLAYED MORE GAMES, 2153, AT SHORTSTOP THAN ANY OTHER NATIONAL LEAGUE PLAYER. AT BAT TOTAL, 10078, SURPASSED BY ONLY ONE NATIONAL LEAGUER, HONUS WAGNER. MADE 2605 HITS IN 23 SEASONS. MEMBER OF 1914 BOSTON BRAVES "MIRACLE TEAM" THAT WON PENNANT, THEN WORLD SERIES FROM ATHLETICS IN 4 GAMES.

Walter J. V. Maranville

CHARLES DILLON STENGEL
"CASEY"

MANAGED NEW YORK YANKEES 1949-1960.
WON 10 PENNANTS AND 7 WORLD SERIES WITH
NEW YORK YANKEES, ONLY MANAGER TO WIN
5 CONSECUTIVE WORLD SERIES 1949-1953.
PLAYED OUTFIELD 1912-1925 WITH BROOKLYN,
PITTSBURGH, PHILADELPHIA, NEW YORK AND
BOSTON N.L. TEAMS. MANAGED BROOKLYN
1934-1936, BOSTON BRAVES 1938-1943,
NEW YORK METS 1962-1965.

Charles Dillon Stengel

DAVID JAMES BANCROFT
"BEAUTY"
PHILADELPHIA N.L.,   NEW YORK N.L.,
BOSTON N.L.,   BROOKLYN N.L.
1915-1930
SET MAJOR LEAGUE RECORD FOR CHANCES
HANDLED BY A SHORTSTOP IN A SEASON--984
IN 1922. LED LEAGUE IN PUTOUTS FOR SHORT-
STOPS IN 1918-1920-1921-1922. HIT .319 IN 1921,
.321 IN 1922 AND .304 IN 1923 WITH
NEW YORK GIANTS. HIT .319 IN 1925 AND
.311 IN 1926 WITH BOSTON.
PLAYER-MANAGER OF BRAVES, 1924-1927.

David James Bancroft

BURLEIGH ARLAND GRIMES
1916—1934
ONE OF THE GREAT SPITBALL PITCHERS.
WON 270 GAMES, LOST 212 FOR 7 MAJOR
LEAGUE CLUBS. FIVE 20 VICTORY SEASONS.
WON 13 IN ROW FOR GIANTS IN 1927.
MANAGED DODGERS IN 1937 AND 1938.
LIFETIME E.R.A. 3.52.

Burleigh Arland Grimes

JOSEPH JEROME McGINNITY
"IRONMAN"
DISTINGUISHED AS THE PITCHER WHO HURLED
TWO GAMES ON ONE DAY THE MOST TIMES. DID
THIS ON FIVE OCCASIONS. WON BOTH GAMES
THREE TIMES. PLAYED WITH BALTIMORE,
BROOKLYN AND NEW YORK TEAMS IN N.L.
AND BALTIMORE IN A.L. GAINED MORE THAN
200 VICTORIES DURING CAREER. RECORDED
20 OR MORE VICTORIES SEVEN TIMES. IN TWO
SUCCESSIVE SEASONS WON AT LEAST 30 GAMES.

Joseph Jerome McGinnity

HAZEN SHIRLEY CUYLER
"KIKI"
PITTSBURGH N.L. 1921 TO 1927
CHICAGO N.L. 1928 TO 1935
CINCINNATI N.L. 1935 TO 1937
BROOKLYN N.L. 1938

LED N.L. IN STOLEN BASES 1926, 1928,
1929, 1930. BATTED .354 IN 1924,
.357 IN 1925, .360 IN 1929, .355 IN 1930.
LIFETIME TOTAL 2299 HITS,
BATTING AVERAGE .321.
NAMED TO ALL STAR TEAM IN 1925.

Hazen Shirley Cuyler

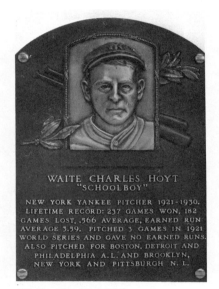

WAITE CHARLES HOYT
"SCHOOLBOY"

NEW YORK YANKEE PITCHER 1921-1930.
LIFETIME RECORD: 237 GAMES WON, 182
GAMES LOST, .566 AVERAGE, EARNED RUN
AVERAGE 3.59. PITCHED 3 GAMES IN 1921
WORLD SERIES AND GAVE NO EARNED RUNS.
ALSO PITCHED FOR BOSTON, DETROIT AND
PHILADELPHIA A.L. AND BROOKLYN,
NEW YORK AND PITTSBURGH N.L.

Waite Charles Hoyt

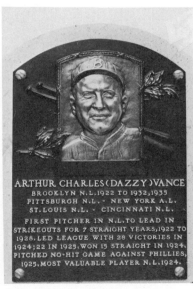

ARTHUR CHARLES (DAZZY) VANCE
BROOKLYN N.L. 1922 TO 1932, 1935
PITTSBURGH N.L. - NEW YORK A.L.
ST. LOUIS N.L. - CINCINNATI N.L.
FIRST PITCHER IN N.L. TO LEAD IN
STRIKEOUTS FOR 7 STRAIGHT YEARS, 1922 TO
1928. LED LEAGUE WITH 28 VICTORIES IN
1924; 22 IN 1925. WON 15 STRAIGHT IN 1924.
PITCHED NO-HIT GAME AGAINST PHILLIES,
1925, MOST VALUABLE PLAYER N.L. 1924.

Arthur Charles Vance

HENRY EMMET MANUSH
1923—1939
SLUGGING OUTFIELDER
FOR 6 MAJOR LEAGUE CLUBS. BATTING
CHAMPION OF A.L. AT .378 WITH 1926 TIGERS.
LIFETIME AVERAGE OF .330 IN 2,009
MAJOR LEAGUE GAMES. HAD 2,524 HITS.

Henry Emmet Manush

PAUL GLEE WANER
(BIG POISON)
PITTSBURGH-BROOKLYN-BOSTON, N.L.
NEW YORK, A.L.
1926-1945
LEFT HANDED HITTING OUTFIELDER BATTED
.300 OR BETTER 14 TIMES IN NATIONAL
LEAGUE. ONE OF SEVEN PLAYERS EVER TO
COMPILE 3,000 OR MORE HITS. SET MODERN
N.L. RECORD BY COLLECTING 200 OR MORE
HITS EIGHT SEASONS. MOST VALUABLE PLAYER
IN 1927 AND FOUR TIMES SELECTED FOR
ALL STAR GAME.

Paul Glee Waner

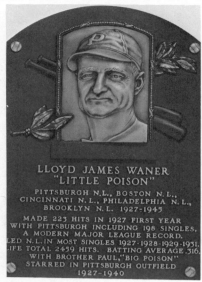

Lloyd James Waner

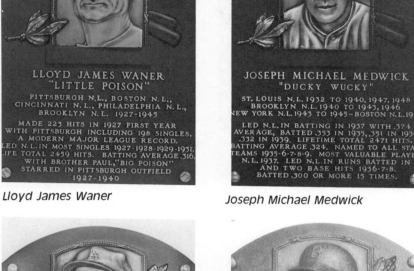

Joseph Michael Medwick

Roy Campanella

Sanford Koufax

Edwin Donald Snider

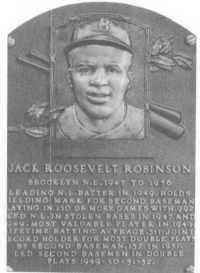

Jack Roosevelt Robinson

Walter Emmons Alston

Don Drysdale pitched for the Brooklyn Dodgers 1956-1957 and the Los Angeles Dodgers 1958-1969. The great right-hander won 209 games for the Dodgers. He was elected to the Baseball Hall of Fame in 1984*. (*His Hall-of-Fame plaque is not yet available.)

Donald Scott Drysdale

Harold "Pee Wee" Reese played for the Brooklyn Dodgers 1940-1957 and the Los Angeles Dodgers in 1958. The multi-talented infielder was elected to the Baseball Hall of Fame in 1984*. (*His Hall-of-Fame plaque is not yet available.)

Harold Henry Reese

Sandy Koufax was inducted into the Baseball Hall of Fame on August 7, 1972.

14
THE DAFFY DODGERS:
ALL WORK
AND NO PLAY MAKES . . .

Perhaps you have wondered how the Brooklyn Dodgers ever picked up their nickname of "Dem Bums." The antics of the Brooklyn players through the years 1915 to 1940 have been responsible. The fans have learned to expect just about anything at Ebbets Field and they are seldom disappointed.

One incident, which probably has never been equalled in major league baseball, took place one hot summer afternoon shortly after the Chicago Cubs great slugger, Hack Wilson, had been traded to the Dodgers. Casey Stengel was the manager of the Dodgers and he had a pitcher who answered to the name of Boom Boom Beck. Those three fellows participated in the incident which had the fans screaming with laughter.

It seems that Boom Boom was well named, for nearly every time he threw the ball that afternoon, an opposing hitter promptly drove the ball out of the park. Naturally, a lopsided score resulted and finally Stengel decided that it was time to send in a relief pitcher. He walked out to talk to Beck and told him that he had pitched enough for the afternoon. However, Boom Boom had other ideas. He was determined to stay in there until he struck out a hitter if it took all day.

Boom Boom had quite a temper and flatly informed Casey that he had no intention of giving way to a reliefer. That made Stengel unhappy, and he began to speak with gestures. The fans could tell that he was telling Beck to either get out of the game or else. But Beck held his ground. All this time, Hack Wilson had been out in his position in center field. He was idly loafing out there, kicking at a piece of sod and probably his mind was a thousand miles from the ball park. He didn't care if Stengel and Beck stood there and argued all afternoon.

Meanwhile, the debate was growing more heated by the second. Boom Boom was pointing as he talked and had his finger under Casey's nose. The manager then issued an ultimatum to the effect that Beck would either leave the game or he was through with the Dodgers. That ended the argument but Boom Boom followed through with a display of temper. He threw his glove on the ground and looked angry enough to eat it. All the time, he had been holding the ball and now as angry as he was, he whirled and threw it towards center field just as hard as he could. Wilson's daydreaming was interrupted when the ball slammed against the center field fence. Years of practice and experience determined his reaction at the moment. When a ball lands near you, there is only one thing to do with it and Hack did just that.

He scooped up the ball, took a short step, and sent the ball sailing towards the plate. He thought the ball had been hit and now thrown to center field. No doubt he figured he would be bawled out for being asleep on the play although he wouldn't have had a chance to make the catch.

The fans were strangly silent for a moment. They weren't sure whether they should boo or cheer. Finally, they decided to do neither. They just laughed and the laughter was so loud that it could be heard for blocks. Tears ran down the faces of the fans as they roared over one of the funniest incidents ever to take place on a baseball diamond.

Casey Stengel laughed, too, for he really enjoyed a good joke. It also had the effect of quelling Beck's temper. He was laughing as he picked up his glove and slowly walked to the dugout. Hack was red as a beet when he realized what had happened but he was still laughing when the inning was over and the fans gave him a good natured round of applause as he came in to bat.

This was only one of the stunts that led to the Brooklyn Dodgers picking up the nickname of "Dem Bums."

A Nazi spy, trained for a lifetime to impersonate an American, was exposed when he failed to name the current shortstop of the Dodgers. A crackpot Hollywood director who dared to produce a war picture without a Brooklyn sergeant wondering how "dem Bums was makin' out against de Giants" was crated off to New Mexico to be used as a fuse for the atom bomb experiment.

Ebbets Field itself was one of the smallest parks in the major leagues. Its absolute capacity was under 35,000. The fact that one Brooklyn fan can make more noise than six fans anywhere else convinced many radio addicts that the figures were the other way round. When 150,000 determined citizens tried to get into 30,000-odd seats, tempers flared high and so did prices. They even endured a character named Hilda Chester (nicknamed Cowbell Hilda), who would have been murdered long ago in a less tolerant community. Hilda supplemented her original cowbell with a variety of other eardrum-shattering devices, and nobody would have been particularly surprised if one day she turned up with a steam calliope. Near her sat another inveterate fan who spent most of his time inflating colored balloons and releasing them at the most inopportune moments. Another group, the Dodger Sym-phony, organized itself into a jazz band, and marched hither and yon in the stands playing something that barely resembled music.

As a matter of fact, when Ebbets Field was completed, in time for the 1913 campaign, it seemed plenty big enough for any contingency. Charlie Ebbets, owner of the club, had had a tough time making ends meet. Even Brooklyn fans had tired of supporting chronic tail-enders. Their nickname was based on the popular idea that everybody in Brooklyn spends his time dodging trolley cars. Ebbets, however, was dodging the sheriff. When he announced his intention to build a new ball park in a section of Flatbush decorated principally at the moment by unpainted shacks, pig sties, and flophouses, his friends hooted and his bankers fled. But Mr. Ebbets had a way with him, and the new home of the Brooklyn ball team gradually arose on the site of an inelegant garbage dump.

The era of the Daffy Dodgers really began in 1914, when Ebbets installed as manager that rotund and genial Wilbert Robinson, erstwhile catcher on the famous Baltimore Oriole squad, which also included John McGraw, Hughie Jennings, and Wee Willie Keeler. Only when Robbie quit eighteen years later was the name "Dodgers" restored—officially, that

is. By that time, Brooklyn ball players were "The Bums" to real fans, "beloved Bums" when they won, plain, unadulterated Bums when they frittered games away.

Robbie was neither a stern task-master nor too astute a technician. Gradually his teams acquired a reputation for all-around wackiness that enraged supporters at first, but actually became a drawing card as the tradition mellowed. Every busher with the naturally screwy instincts of a bird-dog drifted into the Dodger fold as surely as a salmon fights its way upstream to spawn. Undisputed kingpin of the era was the fabulous outfielder Floyd "Babe" Herman, but the stage was all set long before his advent in 1926.

For instance, the Dodgers had men on first and second one day, when the man on first suddenly lit out for the keystone sack, forcing the runner ahead of him. "Yeah, I knew he was there," admitted the offender to the outraged Robbie, "but I had such a big lead, I couldn't resist." Another time, with men on first and second and none out, the batter hit a towering fly to right center. The runners hovered close to their bases for fear that the ball would be caught, but the batter lowered his head and went charging around the sacks like a stampeding bull. While the crowd howled, and Robbie tore his hair, the batter galloped past both runners in high gear. The ball fell safe, and all three Dodgers arrived at third in a neck-and-neck finish, the batter first. In the confusion, all three runners stepped uncertainly off the bag, and the rival third baseman had only to tag them to complete a triple play that certainly could never have happened outside of Brooklyn. Robbie consoled himself by reminding the three runners, "That's the first time you guys have gotten together all season."

A rookie was on the mound for the Dodgers one day when Rogers Hornsby, a murderous hitter, came to bat for the Cardinals. The rookie asked Jack Fournier, Dodger first baseman, "How should I pitch to this guy?" "Inside pitches only," advised Fournier. Hornsby promptly drilled one down the left field line that almost tore off the third baseman's glove. "I thought you said inside pitches were Hornsby's weakness," complained the rookie in the dugout later. "I didn't say that at all," corrected Fournier. "I've got a wife and family to support. I didn't want you pitching on the outside so he'd be lining those drives at me." Robbie added, "There's only one way to pitch to Hornsby: low—and behind him."

Another Brooklyn first baseman earned the jeers of the bleacherites by being picked off base, after singling, on a variation of the hoary hidden-ball trick. The rival first-sacker tucked the ball under a corner of the bag, and simulated a return throw to the pitcher. When the runner took his lead, the

Hack Wilson, (left), great Chicago Cubs home run slugger, and the Dodgers' beloved Babe Herman exchange pleasantries in 1930. That year Wilson had the greatest year in his career as he hit .356 and drove out 56 home runs. Herman, not to be denied, hit .393 with 35 home runs.

The arrival of Babe Herman reduced all previous exploits of the Dodgers' Daffiness Demons to child's play. Herman was a wonderful batter. He was a Dodger from 1926 to 1932 and his feats as a great hitter have been unmatched. The Babe hit .319 in his first year, .340 in 1928, .381 in 1929, and then followed with a .393 average and 35 homers in 1930. In 1931 the Babe slipped to .313 and was then traded to the Reds. But the Babe's fielding lapses were spectacular, and when he got to the base paths, nobody, including himself, had the faintest idea what was going to happen next. He would have had to play in five thousand games, however, to perpetrate all the boners that have been attributed to him since his heyday.

Herman indignantly denies, for example, the story that a fly ball hit him on the head one day and bounced into the grandstand for an automatic home run. "If I ever let a fly hit me on the head," he insisted, "I'd have walked off the field and quit the game for good." "How about the shoulder, Babe?" asked sports-writer Tom Meany. "Oh, no," said Herman, "the shoulder don't count." Another episode generally attributed to Herman casts him in the role of pinch-hitter, with the Dodgers two runs down in the ninth inning, and men on second and third. An inside pitch caught the handle of his bat and trickled into the dirt around home plate. "Fair ball," decreed the umpire. "Foul ball," decreed Herman. The opposing catcher whipped off his mask and threw the pellet neatly into right field. The right fielder fell on his ear. The two runners scored the tying runs. Babe Herman, however, refused to enter into the spirit of the occasion. "I say it's a foul ball, you blank-blank robber," he insisted, poking the umpire in the ribs. The ball was relayed finally into the plate, the catcher tagged Herman, and the umpire remarked quietly, "You're out!" The runs, of course, didn't count, and the Dodgers had dropped another contest.

Casey Stengel was congratulated one night for hitting two home runs in a single game. "Why don't you talk about the real miracle of the day?" he inquired. "Babe Herman threw a ball to the right base!" Another time Stengel sought to loosen up a young recruit. "You're too tense," said Stengel, "you take life too seriously. It's affecting your play. Why don't you be like Babe Herman—relaxed, carefree, happy?" The recruit retorted contemptuously, "That bum Herman isn't really happy. He only thinks he is!"

In the clubhouse one day, Herman pulled a cigar out of his pocket and asked for a match. Before anybody could oblige him, he took a couple of puffs on the cigar. A flame glowed on the end, and a thin line of blue smoke rose in the air. "Never mind the match," said the Babe with no apparent surprise. "I guess it was lit already."

fielder reached down, pulled out the ball, and plastered it on him. The runner thought enough of this trick to try it on himself when another team—the Boston Braves—visited Ebbets Field. After a Boston player singled, our hero hid the ball under the first bag, and essayed an attitude of unconcern that would have put a Barrymore to shame. Sure enough, the Boston runner strayed off base, and the triumphant mastermind reached down for the ball. Unfortunately, however, he had tucked it so far under the base that by the time he managed to pry it loose, the runner was perching contentedly on third. On his way back to the bench, he was called names by grandstand critics that even Dodger players never had heard before. About that time, wives were forbidden to travel with the club on the road. A pitcher protested, "My wife can play first base better than that clunk out there. If he can make trips with us, why can't she?"

In due course, Herman disappeared from the Dodger dugout, and so did Manager Robinson, to be followed in turn by Max Carey and Casey Stengel. Herman was traded, Manager Robinson retired. Stengel made his debut as pilot in 1934, the year when Bill Terry, leader of the Giants, made a crack in spring training that bounced back to hit him between the eyes. Somebody asked him, "How do you think Brooklyn will make out this season?" "Brooklyn," laughed Terry. "Is Brooklyn still in the league?" The Dodgers didn't forget. They licked the Giants in the last two games of the season, and cost them the league championship. The Dodger fans didn't forget either. To this day even without the Brooklyn Dodgers, Bill Terry is Brooklyn's Public Enemy Number One.

The Flatbush Follies continued to pack them in during the regime of Stengel and his merry men. One day an umpire ordered Stengel from the field. Stengel doffed his cap in mock deference, and a sparrow flew out. Another time the team traveled to the wrong town for an exhibition game. The Dodgers were the visiting team on an occasion when a local hero was being given a "day." He received an automobile, a set of dishes, a traveling bag, and various other gifts from grateful local fans—and then proceeded to strike out four times in the game that followed. "The only time I ever got a 'day'," commented the Dodger pitcher thoughtfully, "was when the sheriff gave me a day to get out of town."

Stengel was coaching at third one afternoon in a ding-dong contest at the Polo Grounds when a Dodger batter named Tony Cuccinello hammered a hit to the bull pen in right field. Mel Ott fielded the ball brilliantly, and threw to third base. "Slide! Slide!" screamed Stengel, but Cuccinello came in standing up, and was tagged out. "I told you to slide," roared Stengel. "You'd have been safe a mile! Why didn't you do what I told you?" "Slide?" repeated Cuccinello with some dignity, "and bust my cigars?"

Casey Stengel gave way to Burleigh Grimes as manager, and then came the golden era of Larry MacPhail and Leo Durocher, with Burt Shotton on deck. Frank Graham gave the details in his sparkling "Informal History of the Brooklyn Dodgers." Pennants were won, the crowds grew even larger, the days of the Daffiness Boys became a nostalgic memory. No longer could anybody refer to the Dodgers as "The Marx Brothers with bleachers." But even with the ascendancy of so sober and canny a president as Branch Rickey, an indefinable quality kept Dodger players and supporters in a world somewhat apart.

Only a Brooklyn pitcher could have reacted as Kirby Higbe did when Ted Williams pickled one of his curves for a terrific home run in an All-Star game. "A windblown pop," snorted Higbe. "I thought the first baseman was going to grab it. Then the wind caught hold of the darn blooper and hoisted it over the top of the right field bleachers!" And only a Brooklyn crowd could have achieved the ecstasy that attended the Dodgers' winning of the 1947 pennant. Arch Murray, in the **New York Post**, described the scene perfectly when he reported, "There's no use going across the East River today to look for Brooklyn. It isn't there. It's floating dreamily on a fluffy, pink cloud, somewhere just this side of Paradise. Flatbush is reeling in mass delirium. Canarsie is acting like an opium jag. The Gowanus is flowing with milk and honey. Because 'Next Year' finally came. Our Bums are in! Pinch me, Moitle, and hold me tight. We're living with the Champions of the National League..."

What if the Yankees had won the seventh, and deciding game of the World Series? What if there had been moments (in the second game, for instance) when Dodger outfielders seemed bent on eclipsing the antics of Babe Herman himself? The artful Dodgers were aristocrats of the diamond —and, what's more, gave every promise of continuing so for the many years to come. The Dodger jazz band (swollen to record size) tooted proudly while the inevitable Lucy Munroe warbled "The Star-Spangled Banner." For above Lucy's sweet notes sounded the protests of Hilda Chester, so outraged by her failure to receive a complimentary strip of Series tickets that she threatened to bring only three cowbells to home games the next season. High up in the press box, a reporter draped his coat carelessly on the outside rail. In the middle of the game, the coat slipped off and descended upon the head of a gent in the grandstand below. It took more than that to startle a typical Dodger rooter. He looked up at the pressbox and inquired mildly, "Where's de pants?"

It was thought that the Daffy Dodgers were part of the Wilbert Robinson era in 1920, but here, on June 22, 1950, the Brooklyn Dodgers have two men on third base. Jackie Robinson, on second base, tried to score in the eighth inning, when Furillo beat out a hit to short. Jack was caught in a rundown, went to third and found Carl Furillo also there. Kluszewski took no chances and tagged everybody. Umpire Dascoli surveyed the play, then called Furillo out.

"Hear no evil, see no evil, speak no evil." That's what Steve Yeager (left) Rick Monday and Don Sutton seem to be saying after the Dodgers clinched the 1977 Western Division Championship.

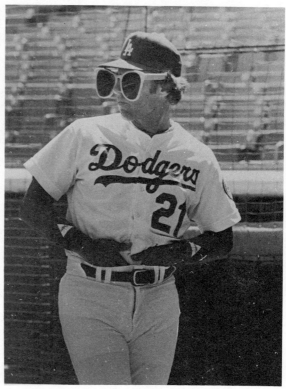

Here Jay Johnstone, the team flake, is incognito.

Looks like Bill Buckner's bubble is about to burst.

A playful teammate has just nailed Von Joshua's spikes to the floor. Here's his reaction when he tried to move.

Dodgers (left to right) Jerry Reuss, Jay Johnstone, Rick Monday and Steve Yeager appeared in costume for ABC-TV's program "Fridays," taped in Los Angeles. The sketch that the players appeared in takes place during the reign of King Ferdinand and Queen Isabella of Spain. The four Dodgers played heroes who bring back to the monarchs the spoils of their conquests, including a ball, bat, glove and "George Steinbrenner's good hand."

"Fellow workers," says Jay Johnstone, "we are here," etc. etc.

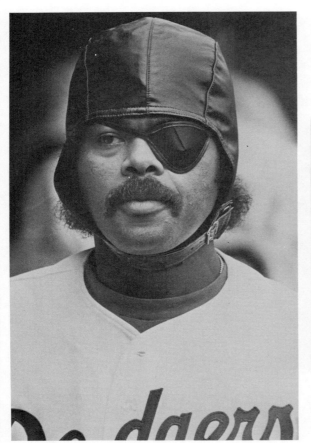

Reggie Smith looks more like a Pirate than a Dodger.

With leather jackets, combs, and slicked-down hair, Dodgers and former Dodgers rehearse a dance step for a November 29, 1978, charity benefit for multiple sclerosis. Left to right are: Steve Garvey, Burt Hooton, Jim Campanis, and Joe Moeller with their dance instructor Devra Korwin.

Dusty Baker and a friend.

Tommy Lasorda makes a guest appearance on the TV show, "Hee Haw." George Lindsay, a regular on the show, gives Tommy some tips on how to gag up a joke.

It was Manny Mota Day, September 2, 1976, and his Dodger teammates honor him by wearing these Manny Mota faces.

Robin Williams presents Tom Lasorda with new headgear (above). Ron Cey is shown with his favorite penguin (left). A couple of Daffy Dodgers (below).

Fernando (left) shows Don Drysdale (bottom left)
and Jay Johnstone (bottom right) how to blow a
"grande" bubble.

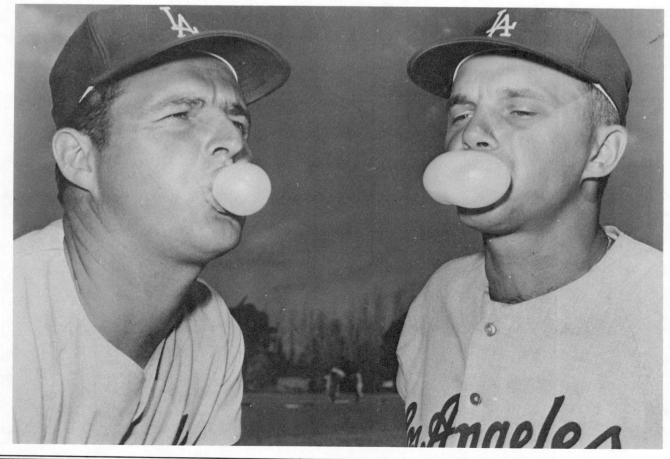

15
SPECIAL MOMENTS IN DODGER-LAND A GOOD TIME FOR ALL

For over 100 years, the Dodgers have been an organization committed to total excellence on on the field and wholesome entertainment for the entire family. This chapter presents a visual chronicle of several of the most popular events in Dodger-land. As the years pass by, the faces on the field and in the stands sometimes change, but one constant remains forever — the Dodgers provide a good time for all in Dodger-land.

Photo by Daniel J. Murphy

Photo by Daniel J. Murphy

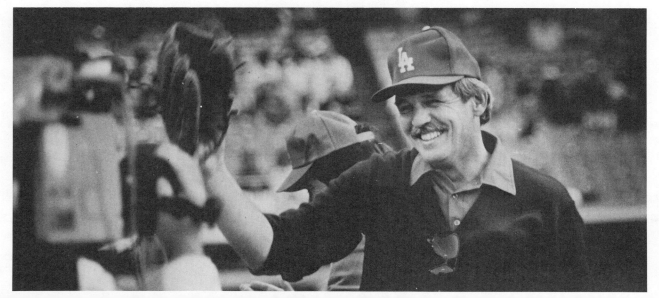

Photo by Daniel J. Murphy

SPECIAL EVENTS

"I finally got one!"

"Mr. Honeycutt, may I have your autograph?"

In 1951 the Dodgers ran afoul of the musicians' union, so Walter O'Malley decided that every Dodger fan who had or could get hold of a musical instrument would be able to see the Dodgers play free of charge. The ball park had never seen the likes of it, for the fans came in by the thousands with musical instruments of every kind and shape. And the music was unbelievable. They called it Music Depreciation Night at Ebbets Field—August 14, 1951.

Manager Chuck Dressen (left) and President Walter O'Mally (right) with City Council President Sharkey, Brooklyn Borough President Cashmore, New York City Mayor Vincent Impellitiere and Bronx President Lyons.

In 1964 the Dodgers took a day off their spring training program to go through a NASA missile launching site in Florida. Here at Launch Complex 37, for the Saturn Missile SA-6, the team listens to a briefing from an information officer.

Ron Fairly at the Zama Hospital visits with Sgt. Derril Howe of California.

Catcher John Roseboro autographs a ball for Sgt. Joe Pettis at Zama Hospital.

Brooklyn became the fashion center of the baseball world as manager Leo Durocher (L) and coach Charley Dressen modeled the Dodgers' dazzling baby-blue, piped-satin uniforms for 25,585 ga-ga eyed Ebbets Field fans on May 24, 1944.

On July, 1943, the Dodgers were in Cooperstown, New York, for a Hall of Fame Game. Here they are shown taking a wild ride through town.

On the Hollywood set of the motion picture "Pride of the Yankees, The Lou Gehrig Story," Dodgers greats Babe Herman (center) and Lefty O'Doul (right) are teaching actor Gary Cooper how to swing a bat. The film was one of the few baseball pictures to be a big box office hit.

The Dodgers are ready to board Kay O' II, the plane designed especially for the ball club.

It's "Ball Night" at Dodger Stadium, and pitcher Tommy John and catcher Steve Yeager "roll out a barrel" of balls for the kids on April 29, 1975. Kids under 14 got an autographed ball free.

Usherettes at Dodger Stadium model Dodger T-Shirts. Usherettes, from left to right, are: Kathy Taylor, Liz Munoz, Janice Tschudin, Kim Lewis, Mary Williams, and Maria Gutierrez.

Two Dodger fans at cap night.

(Left) Bill Russell, outstanding young outfielder with the Dodgers, gives a group of fans a preview of cap night.

Above, Chris Cannizzaro (left), and Claude Osteen of the Dodgers fit their sons—Chris, Jr., and David—with Dodger caps.

Dodger pitcher Joe Moeller tries a cap on his son, Gary.

Once each year Dodger fans are encouraged to bring their cameras to the ball park to photograph their favorite player. And hundreds of old and young fans bring their photo equipment and shoot hundreds of pictures.

Tommy Lasorda and Sutton.

Don Sutton and friends.

Jay Johnstone.

"Now if I can only figure out how this thing works."

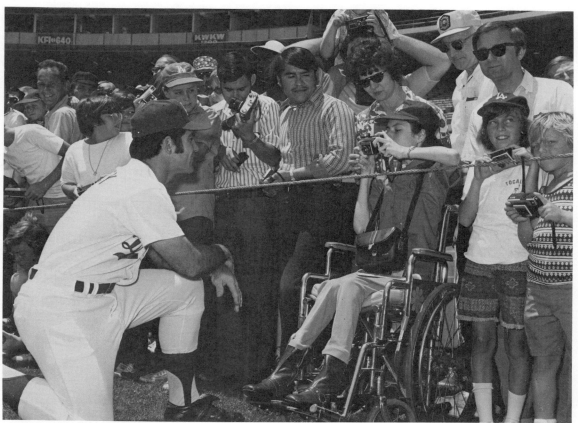

Camera Day is one of the most exciting days for the fans at Dodger Stadium, for then they have an opportunity to photograph and talk with their favorite players. Here Steve Garvey is the choice of kids and adults.

School bands are bussed to Dodger Stadium to compete in a "Battle of the Bands" contest. Prizes are awarded, and the fans appreciate the good music. Lawrence Welk is shown conducting the bands before a ball game in 1981.

Don Sutton (left) shows his stuff, assisted by an attractive duo. Davey Lopes (right) is thrilled by the fashions displayed.

A Dodger fashion show for charity in 1977.

Can you pick the real Jerry Reuss?

Which one is the real Bill Russell?

Dodger pitcher Jerry Reuss displays the Dodger batting gloves which will be given away on Batting Glove Night at Dodger Stadium.

In 1981 the Tokyo Giants visited the Dodgers at Vero Beach, Florida, to train alongside them and to watch them prepare for their upcoming season. Here Dodger coach Ron Perranoski checks on the Giants' pitchers and offers some advice.

Celebrating National Little League Baseball Week on June 15, 1966, meant a visit with Sandy Koufax in the Dodger dugout.

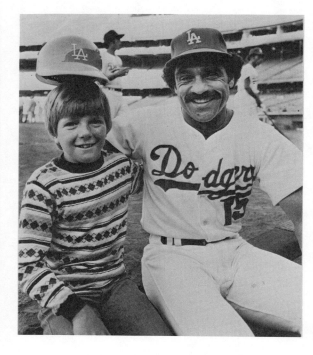

Davey Lopes with a young fan.

The Dodgers gave Maury Wills a "Day" on September 20, 1970. The entire team participated in the ceremonies honoring the popular Wills.

When Don Drysdale retired, he was given a "Day" by the Dodgers. Willie Mays is shown presenting Don this huge portrait.

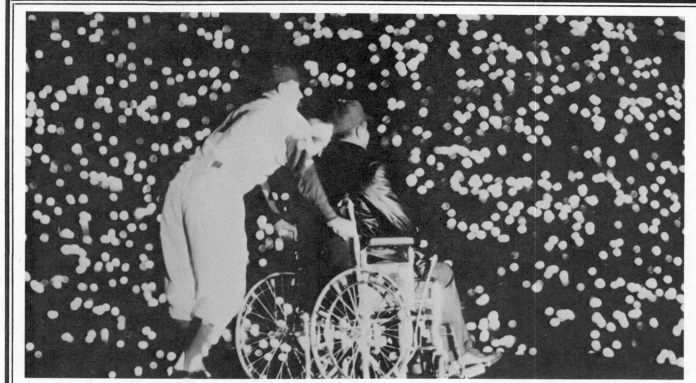

Pee Wee Reese wheels Campanella to 2nd base as 86,000 candles light up for Campy.

A Tribute to Roy Campanella

Organized baseball has had numerous historic games. Many carried more statistical importance and perhaps more involved League impact...but it is doubtful if any was more dramatic and memorable than the game between the Los Angeles Dodgers and the Yankees at the Los Angeles Coliseum, May 7, 1959.

The drama, color and excitement provided a unique stamp of its own. Several of them in fact. As far as emotional impact is concerned, the inter-league exhibition was surely as dramatic and emotional as any single game ever played.

The game was an exhibition to honor the Dodgers' great Roy Campanella, whose courage and fighting spirit had won the salutes of sports-men and women everywhere.

Campy was on hand for the stirring tribute, witnessed by a record crowd of 93,103, and more than 25,000 fans were turned away. It was one of the few times in history that the Coliseum was completely sold out.

Campanella was pushed out onto the field, just before game-time, by Dodger coach Pee Wee Reese, who played with Roy in Brooklyn. The huge crowd stood and cheered Campy for fully five minutes and there wasn't a dry eye in the huge stadium when Roy spoke. The words came slowly and emotionally. "I thank God," said Campy, "that

I'm here. I thank each and every one of you from the bottom of my heart. It is something I'll never, ever forget. I want to thank my friends, those great New York Yankees, for taking the time to play this game, and also my old, my wonderful Dodger teammates." The former Dodger was now in tears and the voice came more slowly, "I want to thank my family, my wife and children and all of you marvelous people here tonight for this great game."

As Pee Wee Reese pushed Roy onto the green carpet at second base, the incredible crowd rose and each person lit a small candle, passed out to the crowd. Suddenly the lights dimmed and the sight of 86,000 candles in the shimmering black night, was a sight to raise the drama of the evening to its height.

Celebrities by the dozens were at the Campy celebration, including Cary Grant, Frank Sinatra, Edward G. Robinson, John Wayne, George Jessel, Jimmy Cagney, Pat O'Brien, Ginger Rogers, Barbara Stanwyck, Gene Kelly and others too numerous to mention.

After the game, won by the Yankees 6 to 2, Campanella disclosed that he will work with the Dodger organization in the Community Relations Department and would move his family to Los Angeles.

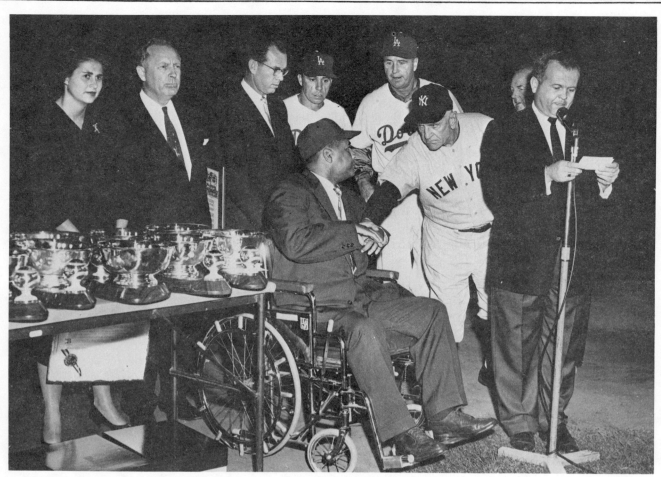

Popular TV host, Johnny Grant of KTLA, Los Angeles, emceed the program and presented numerous celebrities to the huge crowd. Casey Stengel shakes Campy's hand. Behind Stengel is manager Walt Alston, and Pee Wee Reese.

Warren Giles, President of the National League (left) and Actor George Jessel (right).

Alston, Roy, and Stengel.

Old-Timers games bring together very special people.

First Old-Timers game at Dodger Stadium, June 6, 1971.

Participants in the first Old-Timers game at Dodger Stadium—held June 6th, 1971. Front row, from left: Carl Furillo, Sandy Koufax, Andy Pafko, Jim Gilliam, Charlie Neal, Carl Erskine, Andy Carey and Babe Herman. Second row, from left: Roy Campanella, Art Pasarella, Jocko Conlan, Beans Reardon, George Shuba, Maury Wills, Norm Larker, Dick Tracewski, John Roseboro, Casey Stengel, Wally Moon, Roger Craig, Don Demeter, Bill Skowron, Dixie Walker and Ed Roebuck. Back row, from left: Joe Pignatano, Gil Hodges, Pat Orr, Cookie Lavagetto, Sal Maglie, Johnny Podres, Don Newcombe, Gene Hermanski, Larry Sherry, Pee Wee Reese, Don Drysdale, Larry Burright, Chuck Essegian, Clem Labine, Joe Black, Duke Snider and Ralph Branca.

The Dodgers have always been noted for their outstanding pitchers. Here four of the great ones (left to right) Don Drysdale, relief pitcher Mike Marshall, Sandy Koufax and Don Newcombe, get together before a Dodger Old-Timers game at Dodger Stadium, August 24, 1975.

Three of the greatest—Joe DiMaggio, Duke Snider and Willie Mays are introduced at the 1980 Old-Timers game held at Dodger Stadium, Los Angeles.

The 1980 Old-Timers game at Dodger Stadium featured some of the greatest players to ever wear the Old Dodger Blue uniform, and some of their greatest rivals. As the two teams line up along the sidelines, the crowd of 55,000 sends up cheer after cheer as Number 24, Number 4, and Number 5 are introduced (24: Willie Mays, 4: Duke Snider, and 5: Joe DiMaggio). Here they are shown walking into the plate from center field.

At the Old-Timers game in 1980 at Dodger Stadium, (left) Don Drysdale, Pee Wee Reese, Walter Alston, and Sandy Koufax.

July, 1973. The great Hall of Fame pitching star of the Cleveland Indians, Bobby Feller, chats with Dodger ace Andy Messersmith. "This is how I hold the ball for my best curve," says Feller.

Once they were bitter rivals on the field, but here in this candid photo at Dodger Stadium before the 1980 Old-Timers game, Early Wynn, Bob Lemon (standing), Whitey Ford and Bob Feller reminisce and joke with each other.

The Record Setters: 1973 Old Timers Day Teams: The Dodger Oldtimers staged a last-inning comeback to edge the All-Star Oldtimers, 4-3, at Dodger Stadium, Sunday, June 3rd. The oldtimers: (front row, kneeling left to right) Pat Orr, Art Passarella, Babe Pinelli, Ed Runge, Beans Reardon, Walt Dropo, Don Newcombe, Pee Wee Reese, Bob Nieman, Carl Erskine. (Standing from left to right) Casey Stengel, Whitey Ford, Maury Wills, Don Larsen, Rocky Colavito, Stan Musial, Dixie Walker, Johnny Mize, Johnny Podres, Johnny Vander Meer, Larry Sherry, Mickey Mantle, Duke Snider, Bob Feller, Wally Moon, Don Drysdale, Elroy Face, Carl Furillo; (in back) Ralph Branca, Al Gionfriddo, Dale Long, Lou Johnson, Walt Alston, Lefty Gomez, Joe Medwick, Dizzy Dean, Jim Gilliam, and Monte Irvin. Missing from picture: Satchel Paige, Carl Hubbell, George Kelly, Lefty Grove, Ron Hunt, and Babe Herman.

(Left to right), Dodger pitcher Kirby Higbe, Dolph Camilli and Dixie Walker.

Ollie O'Meara was the regular shortstop on the 1916 championship Brooklyn Dodger team. Ollie is shown with Steve Garvey in 1981.

Mrs. Tom Bradley, Danny Kay and Pee Wee Reese with Roy Campanella at the 1980 All Star Game in Dodger Stadium.

Hollywood Stars Night

One of the most unique nights in the season-long schedule of the Los Angeles Dodgers is the annual Hollyood Stars Night, wherein a team of motion picture stars and TV stars play a three-inning game against a team of sports-writers or sports broadcasters.

The game is played prior to the regularly scheduled Dodger game and it is so full of fun and mirth that the annual Hollywood Stars Night is usually a sellout.

The Hollywood Stars night was initiated back in 1958 by the Dodgers' outstanding advertising and promotion director, Danny Goodman, who has been with the Dodger organization since the team's first game in Los Angeles.

Originally, the celebrity format consisted of a team of stars headed by the late great Nat "King" Cole. Nat's team usually played a game against a team of Hollywood's leading men. The game was an immediate hit and provided the fans with so many hilarious moments that Goodman and Walter O'Malley made it an annual event.

Since the first game in 1958, the game has involved many of Hollywood's greatest stars. Such personalities as Cary Grant, Frank Sinatra, Jack Benny, Walter Matthau, Jack Lemmon, Jerry Lewis, Jackie Gleason, Milon Berle, John Wayne, Danny Kaye, Bill Cosby, Dean Martin, Redd Foxx, Peter Falk, Sugar Ray Robinson, Joe Louis, and Archie Moore are but a few who have participated in this unusual event.

It's Jackie Gleason in 1977 all suited up and ready to take his position at first base in the annual Hollywood Stars game at Dodger Stadium.

In 1962 the Hollywood Stars fielded such guests as Dean Martin, Chuck Connors, Joe Louis, Phil Silvers, Archie Moore, and Nat "King" Cole among others as they battled a team of Los Angeles sportswriters in the annual game at Dodger Stadium.

Danny Goodman of the Dodgers and then-Governor of California Ronald Reagan at the 1975 game.

One of the smallest and most popular stars, Billy Barty, exchanges words with umpire Emmett Ashford in 1976 game.

The stars who really stole the show in 1963 were two American heroes, astronauts Virgil Grissom and Alan Shepherd. Wally Moon gives them an autographed baseball.

Robin Williams as a "Star."

Duke Snider and Buddy Hackett relive the 1979 game.

The 1976 game is over. Cary Grant and Dodger president Peter O'Malley attend the victory banquet to forgive and forget.

Jack Lemmon seldom misses a Stars Night at Dodger Stadium. Here he rounds third base in 1979.

Walter Matthau is a study as he masterminds his all-star Hollywood team in the annual charity game in 1979.

Comedian Marty Feldman and Steve Garvey at the game.

(Above) Chuck Connors was a Dodger first baseman in 1949. The big 6ft-5in Connors became a leading TV star. Here are Chuck and manager Walter Alston before the 1975 game.

(Right) Milton Berle has been a Dodger fan for as long as he can remember. Here are "Mr. Television" and a friend before the 1977 game.

Here's a group of Hollywood's leading personalities who appeared in 1974 for the annual charity game at Dodger Stadium. Milton Berle (left), Vin Scully, Danny Goodman (chairman of the game), Cary Grant, and Dodger pitcher Tommy John.

Bing Crosby at a Hollywood Stars game with the Dodgers' Frank Howard in 1964. Bing was one of the owners of the Pittsburgh Pirates and played baseball at Gonzaga University.

Producer-director Francis Ford Coppola points out some basic mechanics about the operation of a motion picture camera to Tom Lasorda, Tom Paciorek and Bill Buckner, who are in costume for a scene in "The Godfather, Part II." The film's assistant director, Newt Arnold, listens in.

Al Pacino, star of "The Godfather, Part II" poses with fellow "actors," L.A. Dodger coach Tom Lasorda, Steve Yeager, Tom Paciorek, and Bill Buckner. In a scene from the picture, set in a Havana night club in the 1950s, Lasorda, Paciorek and Buckner play American tourists "on the town," the last being a soldier on leave from Guantanamo Base. Steve Yeager pitched in behind the scenes as a welcome member of the film's technical crew.

Steve Garvey and Steve Martin shake hands before the 1978 game.

Heavyweight champion Joe Louis was a great baseball fan. Here is the Brown Bomber with another great former lightheavyweight champion, Archie Moore, before an annual Hollywood Stars game at Dodger Stadium in 1962.

Here are Dodger coach Leo Durocher and Nat "King" Cole before the contest in 1962.

"Kojak" gets his baseball cap as he suits up for the annual Hollywood Stars game at Dodger Stadium in 1979. (Left to right) Dodgers Mickey Hatcher, Rick Sutcliffe (center) Gary Thomasson (right) and Telly Savalas.

Bob Newhart and Dick Martin

Redd Foxx

Manager Tom Lasorda stands in front of a wall in his office that he has dubbed the "Sinatra Wall."

Manager Tommy Lasorda has a couple of important guests in his Dodger office after a game at Dodger Stadium.

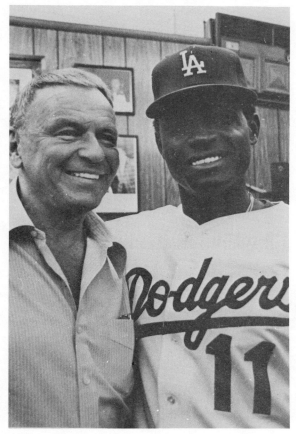

Dodger coach Manny Mota, the greatest pinch-hitter in Dodger history and a 19-year major leaguer, poses with his good friend, ardent Dodger rooter Frank Sinatra, before game number 3 of the 1981 World Series.

Frank Sinatra doesn't miss a play in the sixth and final game of the 1981 World Series.

SPRING TRAINING

Vero Beach, Florida, is the home of the Dodgers from February to April.

. . . **Exercise**

Fernando stretches it out at spring training.

In spring training in 1953, Carl Furillo told sports writer Howard Liss that he would hit 100 points better than his .247 batting average in 1952. Carl was wrong. He hit 97 points higher in '53, posting a gaudy .344 average, slugging out 21 home runs for his finest year as a Dodger.

"Pumping iron"—Tommy John-style.

Doug Rau attempts to get ready for the 1980 season.

Don Stanhouse, Jay Johnstone, Jerry Reuss and Derrel Thomas enjoy a February work-out at Dodger Stadium.

Bill Russell toughens up his legs prior to the season.

. . . Work

When Ted Williams talks about hitting at Vero Beach, everyone stops to listen.

Ralph Branca tunes up for the start of the season.

Charlie Neal shown working out in spring training in 1957.

Spring training in Florida 1942. (L to R) Dodger catcher Don Padgett, Johnny Rizzo, Jack Graham, Augie Galan and Tom Tatum appear ready to make 1942 a "hit."

The 1943 Dodgers at the U.S. Military Academy's field house (West Point, N.Y.) for spring training.

It was springtime at Bear Mountain, New York, for these Dodger players reporting for their first workout of the 1944 season. Because of travel restrictions during World War II, the Dodgers trained at West Point, N.Y. Several players spent their time throwing snowballs. (Left to Right) Tom Warren, Howie Schultz, Lou Olmo, Frank Drews and Hal Gregg. March 22, 1944.

. . . **Play**

Bob Miller and Don Drysdale stand in front of the dormitory after a hard day's work in spring training.

In spring training, 1942, pitchers Ed Head (L) and Chet Kehn sample some ice cream.

Sliding practice on the wet grounds.

Manager Walt Alston regales his audience with another spring training story.

Don Drysdale (L) and Clem Labine check the rain that caused the spring exhibition game on March 19, 1960, to be postponed.

"Now all you have to do is to swing the bat this way."

Catcher Steve Yeager and a friend in the dugout, 1980.

Sandy and a friend.

Pee Wee Reese with wife Dorothy, Barbara Lee, and Mark Allen.

Bettye, Zola, Wally Joe and Wally Moon.

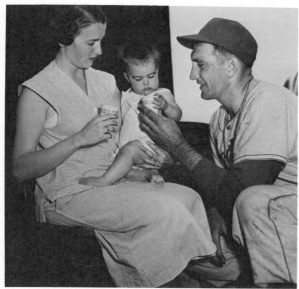

The Branca family—Ralph, Ann, and Patty.

The Carl Erskine family.

Patti, Daron and Don Sutton.

Tommy and Sally John, 1972.

Wally Moon and his son Wally Joe.

Manny Mota and his family.

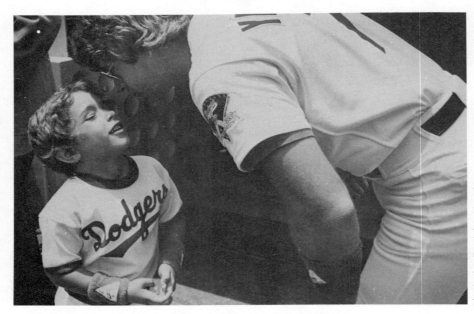

Steve Yeager and his son in 1983.

Photo by Daniel J. Murphy

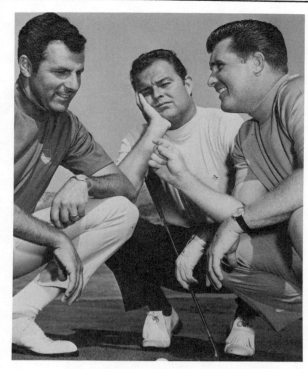

Los Angeles Dodger Ron Fairly (right) seems to be rubbing it in a bit as he points out to PGA professional Mike Dowaliby how close Dodger pitcher Don Drysdale (center) came to making a successful putt. The event was the first annual "Dodger Day" held at the Calabasas Park Golf and Country Club.

Next to his family and his love for baseball, Don loves working his farm, pitching hay and taking care of his fine horses.

Los Angeles Dodgers pitcher Don Sutton (left) presents a Dodger cap to a Dodger fan, Nancy Kissinger, wife of Secretary of State Henry Kissinger, prior to the 1975 All-Star game in Milwaukee. Sutton was one of six Dodgers selected to the National League squad. Kissinger and Baseball Commissioner Bowie Kuhn look on.

Maury Wills, shown with Tommy Lasorda, was originally signed by the Dodgers in 1951 and reached the Dodgers in 1959. He appeared in 83 games for the Dodgers that year, hit .260 and helped the Dodgers win their first World Series in California in 1959, when they defeated the White Sox. Maury was the starting shortstop for the Dodgers pennant-winning teams of 1963, 1965 and 1966, and the Dodger World Championship teams of 1963 and 1965.

Dodgers stars Richie Allen and Wes Parker entertain a group of youngsters and oldsters at a Los Angeles dinner. Parker and Allen are part of a group of stars who are taking an active role in talking to youth groups about the devastating effects of drugs. Their group is called "Athletes in Action".

Vin Scully, the great Dodger broadcaster, interviews Walt Alston and some happy Dodgers in the locker room after the Dodgers defeated the Yankees in the final game of the 1955 World Series. The Scully broadcast was heard coast-to-coast.

(Left) Manager Tommy Lasorda gets the full champagne treatment in the Dodgers' locker room following their 3-1 win over the Giants. The game played at Candlestick Park, Sept. 21, 1977, clinched the National League West title for the Dodgers.

Photo by Daniel J. Murphy

The word *Dodgers* is synonymous with baseball.